The Lexicon of Labor

The Lexicon of Labor

More Than 500 Key Terms, Biographical Sketches,
and Historical Insights
Concerning Labor in America

REVISED AND UPDATED

R. Emmett Murray

THE NEW PRESS

NEW YORK
LONDON

First published in the United States by The New Press, New York, 1998
This revised edition published in the United States by The New Press, 2010
Distributed by Perseus Distribution

Photographs courtesy of Archive Photos

LIBRARY OF CONGRESS CATALOGING-IN-PUBLICATION DATA

Murray, R. Emmett.
    The lexicon of labor : more than 500 key terms, biographical sketches, and historical insights concerning labor in America / R. Emmett Murray. — Rev. and updated ed.
        p. cm.
    Includes bibliographical references.
    ISBN 978-1-59558-226-3 (pbk. : alk. paper) 1. Labor—United States—Dictionaries. 2. Industrial relations—United States—Dictionaries. 3. Labor laws and legislation—United States--Dictionaries. 4. Labor leaders—United States—Biography—Dictionaries. I. Title.
    HD8066.M87 2010
    331.0973'03--dc22
                                    2010008276

The New Press was established in 1990 as a not-for-profit alternative to the large, commercial publishing houses currently dominating the book publishing industry. The New Press operates in the public interest rather than for private gain, and is committed to publishing, in innovative ways, works of educational, cultural, and community value that are often deemed insufficiently profitable.

Printed in the United States of America

Book design by BAD

9 8 7 6 5 4 3 2 1

Contents

Introduction to the Revised Edition

ELAINE BERNARD

Have you ever felt like you wish you had a secret labor decoder so that you could figure out the meaning of all those references, names, and organizations with odd initials that sound like a random spill of letters from a bowl of alphabet soup? Since the overwhelming majority of us work for a living, why is there so little information about the world of labor? In particular, how about a reference that you can turn to quickly to get the basic information you need in a hurry? Well, here it is—*The Lexicon of Labor*, an indispensable and entertaining cheat-sheet on the labor movement.

Distinguished journalist R. Emmett Murray first published a lexicon of labor two decades ago because friends were constantly asking him about labor terms, issues, and events. Word spread quickly about his fascinating collection of biographical sketches, historic events, famous disputes, and legislative landmarks. And naturally, everyone who saw it wanted a copy. Eventually, the lexicon grew beyond the scope of what could comfortably be printed and stapled at home. The New Press understood the value of this compilation and published the first book edition of *The Lexicon of Labor* in 1998. In short order it became a standard reference for journalists, students, researchers, unionists, and even managers. And, more than ten years later, it's still going strong.

Emmett's career in journalism stretched back to the time when most reputable newspapers had labor journalists who reported on issues involving unions, working people, and labor struggles. These writers not only knew the labor movement, they knew its history and personalities and understood the "web of rules" and confusing cross-road of organizations, institutions, and agencies that characterize the North American workplace. With the declining fortunes of both the labor movement and newspapers we've seen the near disappearance of the labor beat at newspapers across the country. But the world of work and labor has not become any easier to decrypt, and while people may change employers and careers more times during a working life than they have in the past, the underlying character of the employment relationship, with its unequal power relation between capital and labor, remains unchanged.

Of course, unions have for some time been in decline, not because they are no longer needed but as a result of weak labor laws and employer resistance to union organizing. Today, only one in eight workers in the United States is a union member, compared to fifty years ago, when one in three workers carried a union card. Although these figures tell the story of a long decline, there are over 15 million union members in the Unites States, and the labor movement remains the largest multiracial, multi-issue, democratic membership organization in the country. Unions still matter, and they remain the premier vehicle for improving all aspects of people's working lives. With *The Lexicon of Labor* in hand, one can get a complete education about the language and history of labor and the vital world of work and workers.

Cambridge, Massachusetts
November 2007

Foreword

THOMAS GEOGHEGAN

Lately people who know I am a labor lawyer often ask: "What about this guy John Sweeney? Can he bring labor back?"

Yes, I say. But also, no. Sure, it is crucial to have the best people. But what if the rules are drawn up so that even the best people cannot win? What if we do not even know what the rules are? It is possible to organize under existing law, sure. It happens all the time. But it is impossible, under existing law, to bring labor "back" in any meaningful sense. That is why it helps to start with a book like this. If you start with a little "vocabulary"—the words—you can learn the grammar, go on to the rules. You can see that the words and stories that follow are like a "lost language" in America today.

Take the Wagner Act, as modified by Taft-Hartley in 1947. If business breaks the law, there are virtually no penalties; if labor breaks the law, there are. It is as if the referee in a game cannot call any fouls on the "business side." What happens to the game after thirty or forty years? The players on one side learn they can go up and slug the opponents in the head, and nothing happens. They can pick out the pro-union workers and fire them—deliberately break the law—and nothing happens. They can turn every organizing drive into three or four years of litigation. Meanwhile the players on the other side, and their fans in the stands, shake their heads and wonder what is going on. It is true that sometimes labor wins, but labor cannot win enough times; it lacks the money, the lawyers, to win enough to "come back."

What is so galling is that even people who are pro-labor and should know better talk as if, with the right people, with the right intent, labor can "come back." Wishing well will make it so, they seem to think. "Wishing well" is, of course, very important. Indeed, it is important we all struggle to keep labor from disappearing. But "wishing well" alone cannot bring labor back.

It is equally mistaken to think there is a state of mind in our culture that keeps labor from "coming back." If you read the lexicon, the words, the stories, you can see how false this is. You can almost begin to think that Americans invented labor unions. After all, even Tocqueville saw it in our nature to form associations. These are the same sort of people who crow endlessly about organized labor in Europe, how much stronger it is than here. But I am skeptical that the French, the Dutch, the Germans would have formed as many unions, had as many strikes, as people in this country, if they had faced the resistance and violence that American workers did. Indeed, at various times labor has disappeared in those countries. Poof. Gone out of existence. Remember fascist Europe? It never has done so here.

In the 1930s, people in Europe looked to America, to the New Deal, to have a model of the social democracy they wanted. Because there was a New Deal, it was easier for them to create social democracy after the war. If we want America to have more of the social justice and equality of Europe, we should look back to our New Deal, too. After all, to imitate Europe is, in this way at least, to imitate us. Much of what is best in labor's heritage is the heritage of that time, the time of labor's flowering. The New Deal was really a time when the Progressives were united in thinking there was one public policy that really mattered most: to strengthen labor.

Even in the Gingrich era, some of the New Deal laws that still exist, like overtime, should amaze us. Imagine if it did not exist, as indeed it does not in many European countries. No time and a half. Once you can imagine this, it seems incredible that the law on time and a half ever came to be at all. It would be unthinkable today.

The other day a management lawyer and friend (yes, I have management lawyer friends) told me of a meeting with a Swedish multinational that had just bought a plant in Dixie. "I told them about the overtime law, and they kept saying, 'Well of course we are not going to do that.' I said, 'No, y'all look, I mean, you *have* to do it.' And I knew these Swedish guys were thinking, 'Well now this is America, what is this? How we have to pay this thing, time and a half?'"

I am sure in Sweden they think we all run around here in the New World without any clothes and pay people with trinkets. But once, when labor was a living language, when you did not need a labor lexicon like this, when people knew their rights and could stand up at union halls and give speeches like Cicero's, this was not merely a "paradise for labor." It was a republic for us all.

If we take time with books like this, we can speak with the tongues of angels for this kind of republic again.

Chicago, Illinois
November 1998

Prefatory Note

For more than two centuries, we in the American labor movement have spoken our own language. It is a rich idiom, laden with humor and barbs, heady with history. In its purest form, it gets right down to calling a spade a spade, without gobbledygook. Problem is, fewer and fewer of us speak it, and even fewer on the outside understand it or know how it came about. Labor history is not taught—or even mentioned—in U.S. elementary and high schools.

This *Lexicon* aims at reacquainting our own members with both the language and the history (what, you don't know what a zipper clause is or who the Workies were?) and with key acts of legislation and high-court decisions through the years that brought labor, for better or for worse, to where it is today.

I am grateful, first of all, for the assistance of my wife, Nancy L. Rising, staunch union member, member of the Martin Luther King County Labor Council Executive Committee, and public relations consultant with American Income Life (AIL), the only all-union insurance company in North America. It's no exaggeration to say that without Nancy's gentle but firm browbeating this revised edition, as well as its predecessor, never would have been written. Also thanks to AIL's monthly labor newsletter, which keeps me abreast of the latest union developments. Another thank-you goes to the Pacific Northwest Labor History Association, whose fellow members and president, Ross Rieder, always keep me on my toes with suggestions and contributions.

Special appreciation goes to Elaine Bernard, executive director of the Labor and Worklife Program at Harvard Law School, whose faith and foresight were instrumental in getting the *Lexicon* published in the first place. Lastly, posthumous thanks must go to the late Richard H. Nolan, cousin and a former vice president of the International Union of Operating Engineers, whose influence in placing a raw, naive, just-out-of-high-school teenager on heavy-construction jobs in the late 1950s introduced that kid to the world—and benefits—of unions.

R. Emmett Murray
Summer 2007

The Lexicon of Labor

*Note: Terms that are in **boldface** type appear elsewhere in the* Lexicon *as separate items.*
<u>*Underscored*</u> *entries refer to court cases.*

A

across-the-board increases—A negotiated raise in which all members of a **bargaining unit**, regardless of classification, receive the same wage increase (e.g., 50 cents an hour, $20 a week). See **contractual raise.**

Adamson Act—Law enacted by Congress in September 1916 establishing the **eight-hour day** for railway workers. It marked the first time a group of private workers had its working hours regulated by the federal government. See **eight-hour day** and **Fair Labor Standards Act.**

affiliated—With individual members, those of the bargaining unit who belong to the union, as opposed to **excluded** or **exempt** employees. With unions, those that belong to the **AFL-CIO** or a regional centralized body such as a state or county labor council.

affirmative action—In its labor context, a policy of state or federal government to effect "set-asides" in which construction contracts financed with public money must allow for a certain percentage of bids by minority and women subcontractors. In recent years, support for this concept in Congress and individual state legislatures has eroded and is in danger of being eliminated altogether. See **Philadelphia Plan.**

AFL-CIO—American Federation of Labor–Congress of Industrial Organizations, a voluntary federation of labor unions—*not a union itself, despite continual references as such in the media*— currently composed of 56 unions representing 12 million members in the United States and Canada. Created in 1886 by cigar-maker **Samuel Gompers** and others as an alliance of **trade** or **craft unions**, the AFL was an outgrowth of the Federation of Organized Trades and Labor Unions of the United States and Canada, founded in 1881. With its 1906 enunciation of "Labor's List of Grievances," in which it laid down the challenge to the major political parties and championing of the slogan, "a fair day's wage for a fair day's work," the AFL became the most important force in the American **labor movement**. Eerily prescient of the 1980s and 1990s, the new federation at the turn of the century made concentration of wealth a central theme and advocated "compulsory (public) education laws . . . prohibition of labor of children under 14 years . . . sanitation and safety provisions for factories . . . repeal of all conspiracy laws . . . a National Bureau of Labor Statistics . . . [and] protection of American industry against cheap foreign labor." Unfortunately, while the AFL leadership preached—and might have believed in—an end to racial segregation, the federation remained highly exclusionary at the local craft union level.

The AFL's power waned with the onset of mass-production technology, and the CIO (originally the Committee for Industrial Organization) was founded in mid-Depression 1935 by mineworker chief **John L. Lewis**, **Philip Murray**, and others in response to the AFL's failure—or refusal—to organize unskilled workers on the assembly line. The CIO would organize "vertically"; that is, include all workers in a given industry, as opposed to merely the **journeyman-apprentice** level of a particular skilled craft. Originally formed within the AFL, the CIO, with its ten member unions, was expelled from the parent body in 1937 because, while all too successful, it was considered too militant and confrontational. The CIO was formally established as an independent federation in 1938 and remained so until both groups merged in 1955 under the presidency of **George Meany**.

With a combination of a strong postwar economy and forceful leadership, Meany presided over the heyday of the AFL-CIO, when union membership reached a high-water mark of 37 percent of the U.S. workforce. Meany's 1979 successor, **Lane Kirkland**, however, unwittingly became the symbol of decline in the American labor movement. Handicapped by his own less-than-fiery leadership, Kirkland also had to contend, unsuccessfully for the most part, with a falloff in **organizing**, increasing corporate multinationalism and **outsourcing**, official and open Reagan-era hostility toward unions and, as a by-product of the latter, the expansion of a **union-busting** industry: **management**

THE LEXICON OF LABOR

consultants. By the time Kirkland was virtually forced into retirement, in August 1995, union membership had dropped to around 14 percent. Kirkland's successor, **John Sweeney**, has tried to turn the tide with new bodies in the top ranks of the federation, aggressive organizing drives, a massive funneling of money to pro-union political causes and advertising, recruitment of youth into the labor movement, and a high-profile public-relations effort to get unions' side of the story into the media during disputes. At first, Sweeney's presidency seemed to result in a slight rise in union membership. But that was illusory. It had dropped to 12 percent of the overall workforce and 8 percent in the private sector shortly after the turn of the 21st century—a major reason behind the formation of the breakaway **Change to Win** federation in 2005. See **Knights of Labor, sit-down strike, no-raiding agreements, Code of Ethical Practices**. Also, **Appendix I** for the list of AFL-CIO unions.

African Americans—See **blacks in the labor movement**.

agency fee payer/agency shop—Formerly a contract provision, now a federal requirement, allowing individuals within a **bargaining unit** to opt out of joining the **union** provided they pay a regular "fee"—roughly equivalent to prevailing union dues—for the benefits of union representation. Agency fee payers are found throughout unions; agency shops are usually found in public-employee jurisdictions. The agency shop was a compromise between the union's desire to eliminate the **free rider** by means of compulsory membership and management's desire to make membership voluntary. Agency fee payers are *not* **exempt** or **excluded** employees.

Air Transport Act—Law enacted by Congress in early 1936 that extended provisions of the **Walsh-Healy Act** to cover employees of airlines receiving government subsidies; that is, it directed the secretary of labor to determine **minimum-wage rates** and forbade the employment of minors at such airlines.

Alliance for Labor Action—A late 1960s tie-up between the Teamsters and United Auto Workers, both of whom the **AFL-CIO** accorded "outcast union" status at the time. A brainchild of the

UAW's **Walter Reuther**, with the willing cooperation of the Teamsters' Frank Fitzsimmons, the ALA sought to revitalize the American **labor movement** by combining the "vision" of the progressive UAW with the organizing drive of **Jimmy Hoffa**'s old union. Incurring the immediate hostility—some said envy—of the AFL-CIO's **George Meany**, the ALA met with only modest success and fell apart after Reuther's 1970 death in a plane crash.

Alliance for Retired Americans—Advocacy organization created and funded by executive action of the **AFL-CIO** in May 2000. Its membership of roughly 5 million is composed mainly of retired union workers and their spouses, although other labor-force retirees "who share [the federation's] values and agenda" can join.

Allis-Chalmers strike (1941)—Begun in January by United Auto Workers CIO Local 248 as a protest against the Wisconsin-based tractor manufacturer's systematic moves to weaken and/or break the union. The 75-day strike was notable principally for the supposedly labor-sympathetic Roosevelt administration's role in breaking it via back-to-work edicts from the **U.S. Department of Labor**. Another first was an armored car, manned by police, firing tear gas and smashing through a **picket line** of 3,000 workers, injuring and sickening an untold number. The company eventually agreed to accept terms the union would have settled for at the beginning. See **North American Aviation strike**.

Altgeld, John Peter (1847–1902)—German-born lawyer, judge, and  chief justice of Illinois. As Democratic governor of Illinois (1893–97), he gained fame— and notoriety—by pardoning three **Haymarket affair** anarchists. A staunch friend of labor, he advocated **child labor laws** and opposed use of federal troops to crush the 1894 **Pullman Strike**. Memorable quote (in pardoning the Haymarket prisoners): *"It is an axiom of the law that mere talk, no matter how abusive, does not constitute a crime."*

ambushing—A longshoremen's **union** term for zeroing in on a particular problem—a safety hazard, for example—on the docks and pursuing it strategically so it can be grieved as a "good beef" or constitute grounds for a legal **work stoppage**. Reasons for an ambush are often found while "patrolling," another longshore business-agent term, meaning a routine check of work conditions. International Longshore and Warehouse Union officials maintain patrolling and ambushes are "the first moves the union makes to use the contract self-interestedly but without subverting it . . . ambushes keep management honest. The threat of work stoppages is incentive for most employers to keep contractual promises, at least minimally." (Quoted from David Wellman's *The Union Makes Us Strong*.)

American Institute for Free Labor Development (AIFLD)— Controversial foreign-policy arm of the **AFL-CIO** in Latin America, created as an adjunct of the Alliance for Progress in 1962. AIFLD's supporters say it has been a needed catalyst for the development of **trade unionism**, fair **wages**, and the raising of living standards in impoverished countries. Opponents claim it has been nothing but a tool of U.S. big business (early directors were Nelson Rockefeller and J. Peter Grace), Latin American strongmen and military dictatorships; moreover, that it has, in close cooperation with the CIA and State Department, helped crush Latin American **labor movements** that were not aligned with U.S. Cold War policies in the region. AIFLD—not coincidentally, critics say—is more or less dormant now that the Cold War has ended. Sister agencies of the AFL-CIO abroad are the African American Labor Center, founded in 1964, and the Asian American Free Labor Institute, founded in 1968.

American Labor Party—A phoenix-like faction that first arose in New York City in 1919 but was subsumed that same year when delegates met in Chicago and created the **National Labor Party**, opening it to all workers, farmers, and Socialists. The latter, however, saw the party as "dualistic" and urged their members to vote a straight Socialist ticket. **Samuel Gompers** of the **AFL**, himself a former Socialist, was against it, too, for different reasons, and threatened **locals** with a loss of their **charter** if they so chose to mix union business with politics. As a result, the NLP died of natural causes in the mid- to late 1920s. But in 1936—again in New York City—a new American Labor Party was born and this time was influential enough to swing an estimated 250,000 votes President Franklin D. Roosevelt's way, contributing to FDR's landslide that year. At that point, the party was an esoteric mix, composed of such conservative unionists as Joseph Ryan, head of the **AFL** International Longshoremen's Association, and **George Meany**, then chief of the New York Federation of Labor and later president of the mainstream **AFL-CIO**, and the right wing of the Socialist Party. At the time, a biographer of labor leader **David Dubinsky** was to note, Stalinists had gained considerable power in this regenerated labor party and "one of the reasons the right-wingers continued to stay in the **ALP** was that the New Deal wanted them there." In 1940, the ALP threw its weight behind the reelection of New York Mayor Fiorello La Guardia, a Republican, albeit an extremely progressive one. The party died out in the World War II years, but a reincarnation has been germinating since the 1980s under the rubric of the Labor Party Advocates and has shown signs of becoming at least a minor contender in future elections.

American Labor Union—A federation of brief duration founded in 1901. Previously the Western Labor Federation, it was composed mainly of **Western Federation of Miners** (about 4,000) and 400 members of other trades. Chief **affiliates** were a small group of Colorado railway workers, some Colorado coal miners' **locals**, and western hotel and restaurant workers.

American plan—Slogan of antilabor employers during the 1920s **Red scare**, equating a nonunion workplace with patriotism and a **union shop** with disloyalty. Its natural by-product was the **open shop**. See **blacklist** and **Rockefeller Plan**.

Americans with Disabilities Act (ADA)—Enacted by Congress in July 1992 and affecting all workplaces with more than 25 employees, the Act prohibits discrimination against qualified employees and applicants with disabilities and requires employers to make "reasonable accommodations" where a disabled employee could perform the "essential functions" of his or her job with such assistance, unless this adjustment would pose "undue hardship" on the employer—to be determined case by case. The Act includes, but does not limit, the definition of disability as: someone who is crippled, partially paralyzed, an amputee, a stroke victim, and anyone who uses crutches, braces, or a wheelchair to get around; anybody suffering from **repetitive strain injury** or **carpal-tunnel syndrome**, epilepsy, alcoholism, past and/or recovering (but not current) drug use/abuse, hearing or sight loss, AIDS, high blood pressure, back injuries, or dyslexia.

annual improvement factor—See **productivity**.

Anthony, Susan B. (1820–1906)—Known mostly for her tireless activity in the abolition and women's suffrage movements, Anthony also fought hard for women's rights in **labor unions** and was a briefly a delegate of the **National Labor Union**.

apprentice/apprenticeship training—Someone learning a trade from experienced workers with both classroom and on-the-job training. The length of training varies from two to six years, the successful completion of which allows admission to **journeyman** or journey-level work and correspondingly higher pay. A term from 1362 that originated with medieval craft guilds in the 14th century, apprentice used to mean someone who was legally bound through indenture to a master craftsman in order to learn a trade. A dirty little secret is that this was generally the case throughout Colonial America, down through the first half of the 19th century. In an age before orphanages, **working-class** orphaned boys who were not taken in by a relative or guardian would wind up as indentured apprentices—a polite term for legalized white slavery—until they reached 21. This was also a common method by which poor young immigrants paid their passage and gained a foothold in the New World. That said, apprenticeship for centuries the world over has been the much-sought-after main level of entry to professionalism for millions of young men—and, in recent times, young women—whereby they learned a valuable skill or trade and secured a niche in an ever-growing middle class.

arbitration—The means by which labor and management settle an unresolved **grievance** by submitting it to a third, outside party (e.g., the American Arbitration Association). The arbitrator, selected from a list of recognized labor law experts and academicians, must be mutually agreed upon by the contending parties. The procedure involves hearings, affidavits, depositions, and oral testimony from both sides, after which the arbitrator prepares a written finding—called an **award**—often months later. This finding, in most **contracts**, is final and binding, meaning it establishes a **precedent** for similar contractual disputes in the future. See **binding arbitration, mediation, fact-finding, Federal Mediation and Conciliation Service**.

assembly line—A key component of the second **Industrial Revolution**, putting into practice the theories of motion-studies guru Frederick Taylor. Until about 1915, factory production was largely a matter of **piecework**; after this time machines, tools, and workers were arranged in a particular sequence to assemble products as they moved along a direct line or route. Antiunion automaker **Henry Ford** was a pioneer in the technique, which enabled his plants to turn out a new car every 93 minutes. Ironically, the drive to unionization began around 1937 in the auto industry, providing impetus to the Congress of Industrial Organizations (CIO) because the American Federation of Labor (AFL) had shunned the unskilled workers of the nation's assembly lines. See **Taylorism** and **AFL-CIO**.

associations, brotherhoods, guilds, & unions—When referring to labor organizations, a difference in semantics rather than substance. Some unions adopted "guild"—a medieval term (from the Norse/Old English *gildi* and *gield* meaning payment or tribute) for craft association—in their title, believing it more acceptable to their members than the more **blue-collar**-sounding "**labor union**." But the Newspaper Guild, the Screen Actors Guild and the Police Guild, to name but three, negotiate for **contracts** just as any other union. A variation is "association," as in

National Education Association, which a number of **collective-bargaining** groups composed of professional employees have adopted. The term "guild" has also been used in England since 1340 as a synonym for "brotherhood," which survives today in the International Brotherhood of Teamsters and the International Brotherhood of Electrical Workers.

Atkins v. Kansas—Established in 1905, via the U.S. Supreme Court, maximum work hours for men—three years before **Muller v. Oregon** sustained a similar precedent for women.

authorization cards—Cards signed by members of a potential **bargaining unit** to show the **union** has majority status in the workplace and should be recognized as a **bargaining agent**, in which case a workplace election supervised by the **National Labor Relations Board** is held. In rare instances, the NLRB has allowed this procedure to substitute for a **certification election**. But American labor critics of the cumbersome and often fatally slow NLRB certifying procedure have long pointed to Canadian labor law, under which authorization cards representing a majority of employees are almost always all that is needed for certification. Ironically, such was the case in the United States during the very early years of the **Wagner Act**, when fully a third of union certifications were granted on the basis of card checks. Even today, **Taft-Hartley** law allows unions to be certified under that relatively quick procedure—provided the employer agrees. Few employers do, for obvious reasons. The **AFL-CIO** attempted to remedy this with the proposed **Employee Free Choice Act** in 2007, but the bill failed to marshal the requisite number of votes.

automation—A word coined in the 1940s at the Ford Motor Co., and a major factor in the workplace since the early 1950s in the substitution or supplementation of machines for workers. It's usually characterized by three principles: (1) mechanization; (2) feedback (i.e., machines that are self-regulated so as to meet predetermined requirements, push-button elevators, thermostatically controlled furnaces, etc.); (3) continuous processes (i.e., separate production facilities are linked together to form a unified whole). There are three basic kinds of automation: (1)

assembly-line, long in use in the automotive industry; (2) computers; (3) complex electronic controls in manufacturing and processing, such as that used in the refining industry. Labor **contracts** have long attempted to address the issue in new-technology and **job-security** clauses.

award—The final decision of an arbitrator. See **arbitration**.

B

back-loaded contract—A multiyear labor agreement in which the greater increases in **wages** or benefits are weighted toward the final year. For instance, a three-year contract that calls for an overall increase of 15 percent might distribute that with 4 percent the first year, 4 percent the second year, and 7 percent the third year. See **front-loaded contract**.

back pay—Wages due an employee because of employer violation of **minimum-wage laws**, layoff or discharge in violation of the contract, or adjustment of piece rate following a grievance. It's often stipulated in an **arbitration** award. Not to be confused with **retroactive pay**.

back-to-the-bench rule—A kind of informal, free-floating "term limits" system in some **unions**, most notably West Coast locals of the International Longshore and Warehouse Union, in which elected officials are turned out of office if it is feared they are getting too "political" or too far removed from the problems and conditions of the **rank and file**. They are, in effect, sent "back to the bench" that is, the workplace, so they can become reacquainted with everyday reality.

back-to-work movement—A return of strikers to their jobs before their **union** has declared the **strike** ended. Some back-to-work movements are induced by employers, others by the strikers themselves, either as a protest against the stand of their union leaders or because economic pressures force them back to work.

bargaining agent—As generally used, a group, agency, or organization (i.e., a **labor union** rather than an individual) authorized to bargain collectively on behalf of its members or employees. The Screen Actors Guild, for instance, is the bargaining agent for movie actors.

bargaining in good/bad faith—Good-faith bargaining, an evolving concept rooted in statute, is defined as **negotiations** in which the two parties meet and confer at reasonable times, with minds open to persuasion and with a view to reaching a mutually acceptable **contract**. It is characterized, among other things, by both sides putting their proposals "on the table" enough in advance to allow consideration or counterproposals, no sudden introduction of a new issue, and no unilateral changing of the rules once negotiations are under way. Bad-faith bargaining is characterized by the reverse of any of these elements, plus, among other things, undue procrastination or failure to meet with the other party, the placing of onerous conditions (by the employer) on the execution of a contract, or introducing frivolous or impossible to meet proposals. Bad-faith bargaining is an **unfair labor practice (ULP)**, subject to sanctions and often a fine, by the **NLRB**. See **Boulwarism**.

bargaining issue—Any issue deemed important enough by either management or the **union** to be placed on the table for **contract** negotiations. The issue does not have to be significant per se— **wages** or hours, for example—it suffices that either side *believes* them to be. For the employer, it might be a perceived need for more **flexibility**; for the union, the perceived need for a greater shift **differential**. A bargaining issue can often become a **strike issue** if either side feels strongly enough about it. See **illegal**, **mandatory**, and **permissive subjects of bargaining**.

bargaining table—Generic term used to mean labor-management **contract** negotiations; over a table is usually where such bargains are struck and a **settlement** reached.

bargaining unit—The **labor union** or other group of workers that negotiates collectively with the employer or employers. As defined by the **National Labor Relations Act (NLRA)**, a bargaining unit is composed of "representatives designated or selected for the purposes of **collective bargaining** by the majority of employees in a unit appropriate for such purposes [who] shall be the exclusive representative of all the employees in such units." The boundaries of the bargaining unit often are a subject of dispute between contending unions and between union and employer, since these can determine whether the union is entitled to representative status. A union that may have organized a sufficient number of employees within a small unit may not be able to establish its majority in a larger unit. Similarly, the union found "appropriate" by the **National Labor Relations Board (NLRB)** may determine which of two contending unions gains representative status. See **jurisdiction**.

Beck, Dave (1894–1993)—Longtime Seattle-based Teamsters organizer and leader and later the union's president, who perfected the fine art of "business unionism" and whose professional trajectory went from rapid rise to rapid fall to slow rise again.

Brought up in Seattle's rough-and-tumble Belltown neighborhood, Beck was a newsboy at the age of 7 and dropped out of high school at 16 to become a full-time laundry-truck driver to supplement his family's meager income. Almost immediately, he joined the Teamsters and quickly took to **organizing**. During the **Seattle General Strike** of 1919; the 25-year-old Beck, though not yet a labor leader, carried enough clout to influence local and international American Federation of Labor **(AFL)** officials to strongly oppose the radical ten-day strike, thus helping bring it to an end. In 1925, he was elected president of his laundry-drivers **local** and the following year was appointed as general organizer for the Teamsters. By 1930, he had organized virtually every truck driver in Seattle. Six years later, he accomplished a "first" for that autonomy-minded **union** by welding the locals of 11 states and British Columbia into the Western Conference of Teamsters. Beck's success in those days was attributed by both friend and foe to a paradoxical mixture of conservative business unionism to win over reluctant employers and physical violence to subdue rival unions. But he had achieved respect. By the end of the 1930s, he had served on the Seattle Boxing Commission and—ironically, as it turned out—on the Washington State Board of Prison Terms and Paroles. He was later made a regent of the University of Washington—the only member of the board to have done so without ever completing high school.

Under the wing of Teamsters president **Dan Tobin**, Beck rose rapidly in the **international** beginning in the 1940s. In 1947, he was made a vice president. In 1952, with sometime ally **Jimmy Hoffa** persuading the aging Tobin to step down, Beck was elected head of the entire union. In 1955, he negotiated the landmark employer-paid but union-controlled Teamsters Central States Pension Fund, later the source of fiduciary scandal in the Hoffa years. In 1957, five scant years after his ascent to the presidency, Beck was before the U.S. Senate's **McClellan Committee** to answer to allegations of corruption and racketeering. Instead of answering, he took the Fifth Amendment—117 times in one May 1957 session. Once was enough for **AFL-CIO** president **George Meany** who, accusing Beck of violating the federation's newly enacted **Code of Ethical Practices** (Beck's had been the sole vote against it on the Executive Council), had him ousted from his AFL-CIO vice presidency and from the Council. Accused in federal court on charges of misappropriating some $370,000 in union finds, Beck was convicted only of misusing $1,900 from the sale of a union-owned Cadillac—and not paying the corresponding income tax.

Beck entered McNeil Island Federal Penitentiary in 1962 but served only half of a five-and-a-half year sentence. Granted a state pardon in 1964 (a federal pardon came in 1975), Beck emerged not only healthier and, some said, happier but with none of the opprobrium usually attached to an ex-con. In fact, in old age he became an engaging, quotable pillar of the Establishment, boasting on the banquet circuit that "For every enemy I made in the ranks of labor, I made two friends in the Chamber of Commerce." **Business unionism** had paid off.

Memorable quote: *"Unions are big business. Why should truck drivers and bottle washers be allowed to make big decisions affecting union policy? Would corporations allow it?"*

Beck rules—A system of **union** financial record-keeping in which a **local** must separate "chargeable" or "representational" activities, such as negotiations, **grievances, arbitrations**, member welfare, **collective-bargaining** lobbying, member training, union publications, internal union administration, etc., from "nonchargeable" activities—political lobbying, **COPE** contributions, **organizing** outside existing bargaining units, and campaigning for a labor-friendly politician, for instance. The rules, a bookkeeping headache for many understaffed locals, came out of a U.S. Supreme Court ruling, <u>Beck v. The Communications Workers of America</u>, in June 1988 stipulating that **agency fee payers** were entitled to a reimbursement of that part of their **dues** equivalency fees spent in nonchargeable activities. In some instances, so-called Beck objectors, encouraged and financed by employers, have further complicated things by legally challenging a local's criteria for segregating the two types of activities.

benefits—See **fringe benefits**.

bid-rigging—A practice in which contracting regions or "turfs" are set up and only one company, or two companies in collusion, bid on a job or service. A growing concern as **privatization** proceeds. See **double-breasted**.

binding arbitration—The method by which public-sector **unions** such as police **guilds** and firefighters associations, legally denied the right to strike because of public-safety considerations, arrive at a **contract** in the event of an **impasse**. In the private sector, binding arbitration is generally an adjunct of the contract and operates outside of labor **negotiations**.

blackleg—Early synonym for **scab**, first used in 1834 to refer to a craftsman who undersold others or a worker who replaced another for lower **wages**. Though this, like the labor use of *scab*, is an Americanism, it is thought to go back to the 18th-century English use of blackleg to mean a gambling swindler.

blacklist—A list circulated among employers of undesirable workers who were not to be hired because of **union** membership or union activity. In labor usage since 1888 (and in use as a noun since 1692, as a verb since 1718), the word acquired widespread notoriety in the antiunion 1920s, just as it did 30 years later during the McCarthy era. Though declared illegal by the **Wagner Act** of 1935, the practice has survived sporadically in various forms. One is to sound out an applicant's attitude toward unions during a job interview and, if pro-union tendencies are perceived, simply not hire that person. This has become more common since the early 1980s and President Reagan's breaking of the air-traffic controllers union. See **PATCO strike**.

blacks in the labor movement—**Labor unions** have been both bane and blessing for African Americans. Long denied entry into most of the **AFL**-dominated **craft unions** (exceptions were the AFL-affiliated United Mine Workers and the International Longshoremen's Association) and relegated to the lower end of the **wage** scale in the larger "vertical" unions for decades, they made their biggest breakthroughs in wage parity—and, as a consequence, civil rights—in the mass **organizing** drives of the CIO in the 1930s and in subsequent wartime production in unionized heavy industries. The third dynamic was the emergence of black leaders such as **A. Philip Randolph** and **Martin Luther King Jr.**, who were able to impart a moral, civil rights spirit into the labor struggle—King, after all, was killed while in Memphis in support of a sanitation workers **strike**.

The plight of the black worker became apparent after the Civil War. No threat as a slave, as a free man he represented, to his white counterpart, a mass infusion of low-**wage** labor on the market. By the end of the 1860s, violent clashes between black and white laborers had become frequent in the northern industrial cities. Attempts around that time by some leaders in the **National Labor Union** and by **Isaac Myers** and his **National Colored Union** to get African Americans integrated into the working world were brief and doomed; many whites felt they'd be "false to unionism" and become **strikebreakers**. Callous coal and rail operators would often not hesitate to bring in lower-paid black and white workers who would be at each other's throats—better that than they organize *together*! (For a dramatic treatment of this aspect, see John Sayles's excellent 1987 movie *Matewan*.)

Though the **Knights of Labor** gave lip service to an integrated workforce, and in some cases acted on it—at one point the Knights had some 60,000 black members—the nearest African Americans came to equal treatment in organized labor between Reconstruction and World War II was in the **IWW** in the early years of this century. But that, too, went awry in the **Red-scare** years immediately following World War I. By the 1920s and 1930s, however, a greater force than discrimination was beginning to shape labor economics: demographics. Between 1900 and 1940, the greatest internal migration in American history was taking place, as some 6 million blacks made their way from the South to the big cities of the North and from Southern rural areas to Southern big cities.

It was just in time for World War II, when the **National War Labor Board**'s efforts to present to the outside world a unified workplace, added to the CIO's campaign to organize a multiracial workforce into plantwide industrial unions, plus the creation of the **Fair Employment Practices Committee** gave black workers enormous leverage to press their **grievances**. By 1944, there were 775,000 black labor-union members—350,000 in the AFL, 425,000 in the CIO. And their earnings went from 40 percent of the average white wage earner's to 60 percent at war's end—far from ideal, but a considerable improvement. Even that was not without great cost and white resentment. In the 1943 Detroit race riots—one of 250 such incidents that year—25 blacks were shot dead. Significantly, only **Walter Reuther**'s United Auto Workers and the Michigan CIO demanded an investigation into Detroit police collusion with white rioters. In 1946, the CIO launched **Operation Dixie** in an effort to fully unionize the still-feudal South, but it met with no more success than Isaac Myers's abortive action three-quarters of a century earlier. Anything approaching wage parity, let alone civil rights for blacks, had to wait until the marches and sit-ins—and violence—of the 1960s.

Even then, the battle was far from won. As the 1960s drew to a close, virtually all-white bastions of unionism could still be seen, mostly in the construction trades. In fact, when in 1969 the Nixon administration presented its so-called **Philadelphia Plan**, which established **affirmative-action** goals for six building trades, the unions resisted fiercely and the following year struck a deal by which the administration backed off on enforcement in exchange for the unions' active support of the president's Vietnam policy. Today, the average black worker, even in union jobs, still earns from 10 to 20 percent less than his white counterpart, most because of skilled versus nonskilled job classifications. The disparity, however, is far greater in nonunion jobs.

blanket injunction—See injunctions.

blue-collar workers—Term originally used to describe factory workers, from the blue workshirts often worn; later extended to maintenance and construction workers and anyone else doing manual work. In 1900, such workers—though they weren't called that until the mid-1940s—accounted for almost 70 percent of the U.S. labor force. Ninety years later they constituted barely 15 percent, though their actual numbers increased, from 22 million to 26 million, between 1950 and 1970. Throughout the American **labor movement**, blue-collar workers have been the greatest source of union membership. See **pink-** and **white-collar workers, hard hat.**

"Bloody Thursday"—See West Coast waterfront strike and **Bridges, Harry A.**

Blue Flash rule—The guidelines a company must follow in polling employees before a **union** election. The polling must be by secret ballot, the purpose must be only to determine a union's claim of majority, this purpose is communicated to employees, and assurances against reprisal must be given. Named after a 1954 case involving Blue Flash Express. See **Employee Free Choice Act.**

blue flu—A tactic at first employed by unionized police officers involved in a labor dispute who, enjoined from striking for public-safety reasons, would call in "sick." It later became a tactic for other public-service employees lacking the weapon of a direct

strike, particularly federal workers prohibited from such by **Taft-Hartley**. See **sick-out**.

bogus type—A practice, since made obsolete by technology, in which members of the International Typographical Union were allowed to set type manually for an advertisement that had already been typeset in a master "mat" or mold. Even though the bogus type was later discarded and never put to productive use, the practice was upheld by the **National Labor Relations Board (NLRB)**—over newspaper publishers' strenuous objections to **featherbedding**—as a lawful way of preserving work that would have been lost otherwise.

boomer—A construction lineman, though the term is used more by utility linemen. More commonly—in railroading, bridge building, oil drilling, and machine shops—it was a worker who changed jobs as he moved around the country, probably because he moved to areas that were "booming." In logging, a boomer was the man in charge of the log boom. The term dates to the late 19th century. In Northern California line work, "boomer" has been replaced by "line tramp."

Boulwarism—In strategic terms, a management concept to convince employees the company is responsive to their needs and no **union** is necessary to force it to grant what it would voluntarily provide. In tactical terms, it's used at the **bargaining table** in asserting that the company's first offer is the "final and best" employees can hope to get. It was ruled an **unfair labor practice** by the **National Labor Relations Board (NLRB)** in 1964 and held illegal by the U.S. Second Circuit Court of Appeals five years later. The name comes from a General Electric vice president, Lemuel Bulware, who formulated the concept following a disastrous GE strike in 1946.

boycott—Concerted refusal by **union** members and supporters to buy a product or service. A good example was the largely successful United Farm Workers–inspired nationwide boycott of domestic wine and table grapes in the 1960s and '70s. A "Do Not Patronize" list is kept by most regional labor councils; a similar list is published regularly by the **AFL-CIO**. Only boycotts sanctioned by action of the AFL-CIO executive are on the national list. Primary boycotts are aimed at a company allegedly engaged in **unfair labor practices** and directly involved in a labor dispute; a **secondary boycott** is directed at a company with whom the union has no dispute but hopes will be pressured into not doing business with the primary boycottee. The term comes from the practice initiated by Irish tenants in the mid-19th century on the island of Achill, County Mayo, to shun, economically and socially, Captain Charles Cunningham Boycott, a land agent representing British interests who was noted for extortionate rents and miserly wages. The tenants succeeded; Boycott eventually left Achill in disgust and bewilderment, never to return. The word was subsequently coined, and the tactic employed, by Charles Stewart Parnell's militant Irish Land League in the 1880s. See **unfair/unfair list.**

Boys Markets Case—A 1969 U.S. Supreme Court ruling that declared open season on **injunctions** to enforce **no-strike clauses** in contracts, hitherto largely ignored; further, that no-strike clauses would be "implied" even if not there. And, the court said, it would enjoin all **strikes** over issues that were "arbitrable"; that is, that could be raised before a neutral arbitrator. Although the specific target was coal-mining **wildcat strikes**, the net effect was to make strikes in general illegal 99 percent of the time, except for certain "window" periods when the **contract** would end.

bracero program—A series of agreements begun in 1942 between Mexico and the United States whereby the latter, hit by a wartime worker shortage, allowed a certain number of Mexicans to work seasonally in the fields of California, Texas, and other states without the usual visa restrictions. In the years following World War II, however, the bracero (from the Spanish *brazo*, or arm; ergo, one who works with his arms) program was seen by many as a growers' tool to undercut U.S. farmworkers' attempts at unionization. The program ended in 1964, a victim of both President Lyndon B. Johnson's antipoverty legislation and congressional concern over the outflow of gold, but was replaced by

Public Law 414—the so-called green card proviso—an outgrowth of the 1952 McCarran-Walter Immigration Act. However, green-carders—Mexicans allowed into the United States under a temporary work visa—soon proved as much an obstacle to **organizing** efforts by the United Farm Workers union of **César Chávez** as the old bracero program, since the vulnerable foreign migrants could undercut any **wages** sought by the UFW. The issue has been largely resolved by Mexican-U.S. labor **solidarity** groups and increased organizing by the UFW. See **farmworkers, excluded positions.**

branch—See local.

Bridges, Harry A. (1901–90)—Australian-born U.S. labor leader who went to sea at age 16 and entered the United States in 1920 by jumping ship. Founder of the International Longshoremen's and Warehousemen's Union in 1933 and leader of a major West Coast dock **strike** the following year, Bridges was a primal force for decades on the Pacific docks, fighting off bitter and often vio-

lent Teamster rivalry for dockworkers' allegiance and a frequent target of Red-baiting because of his radical views. In the 1940s and 1950s, the federal government frequently, and unsuccessfully, tried to have him deported as a communist sympathizer. In 1971, not long before 20-year arch-nemesis FBI Director J. Edgar Hoover died, Bridges had the last laugh: He became commissioner for the Port of San Francisco, a post he held for 11 years. But for all his leftist idealism, Bridges was a pragmatist. Knowing it was useless to slow the containerization of maritime cargo in the 1950s, he agreed to employers' plans to eliminate certain safety rules and install the necessary technology in exchange for fat **pensions** for older stevedores. In 1991, the University of Washington took the unprecedented step of establishing the Harry Bridges Endowed Chair in Labor Studies, believed to be the first at any university to honor a U.S. labor leader and certainly the first to be funded not from a multimillion-dollar endowment trust but from the voluntary contributions of scores of unions and thousands of individual members, to the tune of $1,057,000.

brotherhood—See **associations, brotherhoods, guilds, & labor unions**.

Brotherhood of Sleeping Car Porters—The nation's first fully chartered black **labor union**, founded in 1925 by **A. Philip Randolph**. The first significant step for African American workers since the days of the **National Colored Labor Union** more than half a century earlier, the Brotherhood was opposed at first not only by its natural foes, George Pullman and the Pullman Co., but also by supporters of late black educator Booker T. Washington and craft unionists. In addition, the Hotel & Restaurant Employees International claimed **jurisdiction** over the porters. As a result, Randolph's union did not receive an international **charter** until 1936. The following year, the Brotherhood wrested from a highly reluctant Pullman Co. a contract that won its members a reduction in hours, **job security**, a **wage** increase, and the right to union representation. Ultimately, under Randolph's forceful leadership, the union became more prominent for its work in civil rights than in labor negotiations. Randolph resigned its presidency in 1968, and the Brotherhood, hit hard by the steady decline in luxury rail travel, merged with the Brotherhood of Railway & Airline Clerks in 1978. This in turn eventually merged into the Transportation Communications International Union.

Broun, Heywood C. (1888–1939)—Brooklyn-born journalist, remembered best as a 1930s Algonquin Round Table wit, reporter, and highly acclaimed columnist for a number of New

York newspapers, and as a short-story writer. But, once described by a fellow columnist as "an unmade bed," the hulking, Harvard-educated Broun is even more remembered among **union** news workers as founder and first president of the American Newspaper Guild (later the Newspaper Guild), which he launched in mid-Depression 1933 with his popular Scripps Howard–chain column, "It Seems to Me." "After years of holding down the easiest job in the world," he wrote, "I hate to see other newspapermen working too hard. It embarrasses me even more to think of newspapermen who are not working at all. . . . The men and women of the newsroom need a union, a labor organization, rooted in history, to lead them toward a better way of life." Within four months, the ANG was **chartered** and within months after that Broun was walking the **picket lines**, even getting himself arrested on occasion to make test cases. He held the presidency of the Guild until his death in 1939.

Memorable quote: *"It is better to be Guilded than gelded."*

Brown & Sharpe strike (1981–82)—What started out as a **boycott** initiated by the International Association of Machinists (IAM) over what the union saw as a refusal to **bargain** in good faith by Brown & Sharpe (B&S), a Providence, Rhode Island, machine-tool manufacturer, turned into a bitter **strike** during which police sprayed pepper gas on some 800 **picketers** and violence escalated as B&S brought in **permanent replacement workers**, or **scabs**. The strike pitted a management that insisted on **flexibility** against a union that had hired labor **organizer** Ray Rogers, head of the consulting firm Corporate Campaign, Inc., who had forced the giant textile firm J.P. Stevens to recognize the textile workers' union in 1980 after a 17-year struggle. The **National Labor Relations Board (NLRB)** subsequently charged B&S with regressive and bad-faith bargaining. See **bargaining in good/bad faith, corporate campaign**.

bug (as in union bug)—That little logo, about the size of a shrew's eye, at the bottom of a letterhead, campaign brochure, or any other printing that indicates the material was printed in a **union shop**. By the same token, its omission—particularly in the literature of Democratic aspirants to office—indicates to many labor leaders and activists that the candidate is not sufficiently attuned to labor issues and may have a ways to go before securing labor support.

bull gang—In International Brotherhood of Electrical Workers outside line work, a large crew consisting largely, if not exclusively, of groundmen. Oil workers use the expression in a similar way to mean a crew of unskilled laborers. Loggers would refer to a crew, or gang, "bulling" their way through a job by brute strength.

bumping—The right of a **union** member with **seniority**, in the case of a company **reduction in force (RIF)** to "bump down" or over to a previous job classification he or she once held. In such cases, the less-senior employee occupying that position gets bumped or "riffed." This right is normally defined in the **contract**.

Bureau of Labor Statistics—Massachusetts had the first one as early as 1871; a similar agency was established in the mid-1880s as part of New York City's Tammany Hall political machine. Their methods of data-gathering and analysis were later incorporated—under new "management"—into the U.S. **Department of Labor**, where it today collects and publishes information on the cost of living, the rate of employment and unemployment, labor turnover, industrial disputes, etc. The bureau also publishes an annual "market basket" list of essential goods and services and their price, compared with buying power for the same items in previous years, thus indexing increases and decreases in **real wages**. See **COLA**.

business agent—A salaried **union** representative who operates out of a **local** and handles day-to-day local union affairs, such as collecting individual members' **dues**, resolving minor disputes at the job site, and filing **grievances** when needed. So named because he'd be the one who would "take care of business" at the local level. In some unions, such as the Newspaper Guild, a business agent's title may be administrative officer or administrative secretary. See **pie card**.

Business Roundtable—An antilabor activist organization founded in 1972 with a clear economic, educational, and legislative agenda to combat unionization in the face of declining profit rates. At its core are representatives of 125 major corporations, many of them big contractors such as Fluor and Bechtel, though 1,000 other smaller firms are involved. Its stated purpose is "labor-law reform" (i.e., the blocking of it) and deregulation. The Roundtable's aims of the 1970s formed the basis of the Reagan agenda of the 1980s. It has scored major successes in Congress, *even when that body has had a Democratic majority*, in stemming or rolling back labor's advances. The Roundtable's rise coincided with that of the corporate political-action committee, or PAC, thanks to a post-Watergate reform that made it legal for corporations to contribute to candidates and parties. Ironically, the PAC was an invention of the **labor movement**. In the 1982 elections, for example, labor, through **COPE**, contributed $35 million; business $84.9 million. The Roundtable's greatest achievement, however, has been to devise educational programs through the schools and local chambers of commerce designed to show, through omission, that labor has no place on the American economic scene—a view successfully reflected in the media. See **Davis-Bacon Act**.

business unionism—To quote from the book *Taking Care of Business* by Paul Buhle, the practice of "running unions like a business or corporation, with **dues** payments as the bottom line and assorted perks normal to executives of the business world." One of its hallmarks was a fixed social order of racial, ethnic, and gender hierarchies—one reason the American Federation of Labor (**AFL**) craft unions excluded women and minorities for so long— and hostility to **industrial unionism** with its **wall-to-wall**, industrywide approach to **organizing**. The term has a faintly derogatory connotation, though proponents say business unionism merely reflects the realistic side of labor relations, as opposed to the pie-in-the-sky idealism of class-struggle purists. Past practitioners include AFL founder **Samuel Gompers** and his successors **George Meany, Lane Kirkland**, and a host of others. The irony is that many of these labor-side advocates of capitalism began their careers as socialists or something like it. See **Change to Win; Wal-Mart Watch; blacks in the labor movement; working women's movement; Beck, Dave; Tobin, Daniel J.**

C

CAFTA—Central America Free Trade Agreement—Now commonly called DR-CAFTA to include the Dominican Republic. Formed along the same lines as its predecessor, **NAFTA**, and equally repudiated by **organized labor** in the United States and other countries, which contend it is only "free" for the corporations involved. Public advocacy, environmental, and Central American community groups in the United States also oppose the agreement, contending that it is part of the "race to the bottom," promotes privatization and deregulation of key public services, increases poverty, forces agricultural economies to import basic commodities they used to produce, and tends to wipe out independent family farms—all of which has happened with NAFTA. Four of the five Central American nations have ratified the pact, and Costa Rica planned a referendum in September 2007. The U.S. Congress approved it—barely—in midsummer 2005, and President George W. Bush signed it into law that August.

call-back pay—Compensation, often at higher rates, for employees called back on the job after their regular **shift** is over. **Contract** provisions usually specify the minimum number of hours' pay, regardless of the number actually worked.

call-back premium—A wage **differential** attached to notifying an employee, after a regular shift has ended, that he or she is to report to work earlier or later than the next regular **shift**. Common in newspaper publishing, with its erratic deadlines and sudden, breaking news stories.

call-in pay—Guaranteed hours of pay (ranging from two to eight) to a worker who reports in on the job and finds there is little work to do, or because bad weather makes it impossible or risky to carry out. Provisions for call-in pay are usually spelled out in the **contract**. Common in the maritime and construction trades.

Canadian Labour Congress—Canada's equivalent of the **AFL-CIO**, formed in 1956 as a result of a merger of the Trades & Labour

Congress of Canada and the Canadian Congress of Labour. It had an initial membership of more than 1 million.

captive-audience meeting—A **union** term for meetings of workers called by management, on company time and company property, to "instruct" about unions or to warn of the dangers of unionism. The usual, immediate purpose of such meetings is to try to persuade employees to vote against union representation.

cards (certification)—Sign-ups of potential new union members during an **organizing** drive, by which organizers have an indication—*not* a certainty—that employees at a company are interested in sufficient numbers to warrant filing a petition to the **National Labor Relations Board** for a **representation election**. See **authorization cards**, **Employee Free Choice Act**.

Carey, Ron (1936–)—International Brotherhood of Teamsters president from 1991, when elected in the first secret ballot in the union's 88-year history, to late 1997, when he stepped down—technically, took a leave of absence. His departure followed federal rulings that, first, invalidated the 1996 Teamster election in which Carey narrowly bested rival **James P. Hoffa** and, second, declared Carey ineligible to take part in a rerun against Hoffa because of financial "irregularities" in the 1996 Carey campaign. Carey left vowing to clear his name. During his relatively brief term, however, reformer Carey was credited with a number of major accomplishments:

- He was the first Teamster head since 1952 not to have been indicted or tainted with Mob corruption.
- He threw out more than 400 corrupt or inept local leaders in the 1.4 million-member union and put 189 **locals** under **trusteeship** (though opponents maintain that criteria for the latter relied more on Carey loyalty than proven corruption or ineptitude).
- In his first few weeks in office, Carey sold the union's limousine and two private jets, slashed his own salary from $225,000 to $150,000, and ordered his executive council to meet in Washington rather than Hawaii.
- On Carey's watch, the union stopped losing 40,000 members a year and began to increase its membership.

- A former United Parcel Service driver, Carey led the Teamsters to resounding victory—and public sympathy—in a 16-day nationwide **strike** against UPS in the summer of 1997, ending years of labor impotence that began with President Reagan's quashing of the **PATCO** strike in 1981. See **United Parcel Service Strike.**

carpal tunnel syndrome—The more serious of the many manifestations of **repetitive strain**—or stress—**injury (RSI)**, often requiring corrective surgery and a wrist splint and, if not diagnosed soon enough, possibly resulting in irreversible nerve abnormalities. Like tendinitis and other RSI-associated maladies, it is occasioned by repetitive motion, and in the past was most often found in meat cutting, rock drilling, and assembly-line work. But the incidences of carpal tunnel exploded with the advent of computer technology in the workplace in the 1980s, and it now commonly afflicts supermarket checkers, office workers, newspaper employees, and anyone else occupied in constant keyboarding. The affliction has prompted a whole new appreciation of **ergonomics**, and employers, who once dismissed complaints of RSI as imaginary, self-induced, or the result of too much tennis, now tend to take corrective measures in the workplace. Part of this inducement comes from fear of litigation via the **Americans with Disabilities Act.** See **kangaroo paw.**

"cat in the hat"—Symbol adopted in the mid-1990s by the labor rights organization **Jobs with Justice**, of a silhouette of a black cat on a baseball cap, to remind demonstrators of the **Sabo-Tabby** of the **Industrial Workers of the World** at the turn of the century.

Center for Union Facts—Just the opposite of its name; it exists to discredit unions and the **labor movement** as a whole. Begun in February 2006 by Washington, D.C., tobacco and alcohol lobbyist Richard Berman, who once pilloried Mothers Against Drunk Driving (MADD), the center is funded by corporate interests—Tyson Foods, Host Marriott, Philip Morris, and Coca-Cola among them—and had a budget estimated at $5 million in 2006. An **AFL-CIO** brief that year offered proof that Berman's "facts" distorted and misrepresented the truth repeatedly.

central labor council (CLC)—A voluntary association of local unions in a geographical area, usually—but not necessarily—affiliated with the **AFL-CIO**. Such bodies, generally county labor councils, are autonomous, though they coordinate actions and activities with a larger entity—in most states, a state labor council—which in turn answers to the labor federation.

Central Labor Union—A powerful New York City–based coalition of the 1880s, allied with the **Knights of Labor** and responsible for holding the nation's first **Labor Day** parade (in 1882) as well as for organizing the so-called United Front labor/political movement to offset widespread antilabor harassment brought on by the **Haymarket affair**. The Central also gained a nationwide reputation with its vigorous support of **boycott** campaigns. Central labor unions—trades and labor assemblies representing a number of individual unions in a given geographical area—have been in existence in the United States since 1828 and flourished considerably in the latter years of the century. See **central labor council**.

Centralia Massacre—Name given to an incident that began November 11, 1918, in which an armed contingent of an American Legion–sponsored Armistice Day parade stopped in front of the union hall of the **Industrial Workers of the World (IWW)** in Centralia, Washington, and attacked it—or threatened to; accounts vary. The defenders, forewarned of the assault by previous threats and events, shot and killed three of the attackers; the latter broke through and beat and arrested the IWW men. One, newly returned veteran Wesley Everest, escaped and held off the pursuing mob long enough to kill one of them, the son of the town's leading banker, before he was captured. He was jailed and taken out in the middle of the night and lynched, his body riddled with bullets and his genitals cut off. An inquest jury later rendered the verdict of "suicide." The remaining Wobblies, including their lawyer Elmer Smith, were tried on charges of second-degree murder and conspiracy. Smith and two others were acquitted; the rest were given long prison sentences. None of the attackers was ever indicted, let alone jailed.

certification—Official designation of a **union**, by the **National Labor Relations Board (NLRB)**, as the exclusive bargaining representative for employees in a specific **bargaining unit.** A unit is generally certified by a secret-ballot majority vote of the employees in an election supervised by the NLRB. If close, the outcome can be challenged by either side, usually on grounds that certain voters were ineligible either because they were **exempt employees** or weren't there long enough to qualify for employee status. In the long history of such elections, employers have been known to dismiss beforehand employees showing pro-union affections—a practice that triggered the **Blue Flash rule.**

Change to Win Federation (CTW)—Coalition of breakaway U.S. **labor unions** formed in 2005 as an alternative to **AFL-CIO** in hopes of putting new emphasis on **bargaining** and **organizing** the unorganized over what the group saw as politics-as-usual **business unionism** and internal bureaucracy that contributed to the big decline in unionism over the past several decades in the United States. Initial CTW affiliates were Service Employees International Union, UNITE (hotel, restaurant, needle-trades, and textile workers), United Food and Commercial Workers, the International Brotherhood of Teamsters, Laborers International Union, United Brotherhood of Carpenters and Joiners, and the United Farm Workers. Opponents of the move contend it ignores larger issues and weakens **organized labor** at a time when labor is experiencing an unprecedented hostile political (Republican) environment. In response, the labor federation initiated a solidarity charter program whereby disaffiliated CTW unions would continue to participate in state, local, and regional AFL-CIO elections.

chapel—Among printers, an association of **journeymen**—compositers, Linotype operators, etc.—usually within a **union** unit, who meet periodically to discuss matters of common interest and take decisions affecting conditions of employment, a meeting presided over by a "father of the chapel," or chairman. This use of the word seems to derive from the earliest days of English printing when presses were set up in chapels attached to abbeys or cathedrals, as printer-illustrator-publisher William

Caxton (1422–91), considered the father of English printing, did in 1476 in the shadow of Westminster Abbey.

charter—In labor usage, the official recognition granted a **local** by its **international union**, or parent organization, to act as its representative in **collective bargaining**, **organizing**, collection of **dues**, and all other activities and functions incumbent on a **labor union**. With the charter comes a number designating, in most cases, the chronological order in which it was founded. Local 82, for instance, would indicate it was the 82nd local to be chartered in that particular union. Charters can also be revoked for a number of reasons ranging from gross malfeasance to continued defiance of the international in basic rules and regulations, including the deliberate withholding of **per capita dues**.

Chávez, César (1927–93)—Charismatic Latino leader, founder and first president of the United Farm Workers union. Born in Yuma, Arizona, to Mexican immigrant—and migrant—parents, Chávez had attended 65 elementary schools by the time  he finished seventh grade, the highest point in his formal education. Involved in farm-labor unionism since 1946, he joined radical organizer Saul Alinsky's Community Service Organization in 1953 and the following year was put in charge of its San Joaquin Valley operations. He quit CSO in 1962 to form the National Farm Workers Association, which became the United Farm Workers (UFW) in 1966 upon formal **affiliation** with the **AFL-CIO**.

In 1965, Chávez's Delano, California–headquartered union launched what was to be a five-year-long, ultimately successful nationwide **boycott** of grapes, securing in the meantime an agreement with Schenley Industries in 1966, hailed as the first contract outside Hawaii in the history of U.S. farm labor and raising farmworkers' hourly **wage** from $1.40 to $1.75. A **jurisdictional** dispute with the Teamsters union, largely over the latter's **sweetheart contracts** with Salinas Valley growers and occasional **strikebreaking** tactics, generated often bloody strife between the two unions in the early 1970s, although today they work amicably in organizing agricultural workers throughout the West. To counteract what he felt was a growing tendency toward violence in the farmworker movement, Chávez went on a 25-day fast in 1968. That and subsequent fasts—25 days in 1972, 36 days in 1984—were thought to have brought on weaknesses that hastened his death at age 64. Although Chávez was instrumental in passage of the landmark California Labor Relations Act in the mid-1970s, he became disillusioned after grower opposition and successive hostile governors undercut it, reducing it to a law that existed on paper only. In 1976, Chávez led the UFW through a major reorganization, and in 1984, in response to the grape industry's refusal to control the use of pesticides in the fields, began an international boycott of table grapes, an action that continued intermittently through his death seven years later. Chávez's greatest legacy, aside from bettering wages and benefits for UFW members and introducing *huelga* (strike) and *La Causa* (The Cause) into the national vocabulary, is that he instilled a sense of dignity, respect, and purpose in Chicanos and Mexican Americans in general and farmworkers in particular. See **farmworkers, bracero program**.

checkoff—Usually called automatic checkoff: the deduction of union **dues**, assessments, or agency fees via company payroll. This is a negotiated provision, and members must give their authorization in writing for a checkoff. In large workplaces, the checkoff has supplanted the old practice of **shop stewards** collecting dues from individual members, though in smaller jurisdictions some **locals** and their members prefer this personal contact. See **Rand formula**.

Chicagorillas—Name given to labor racketeers—**union** counterparts to company **goon squads**—operating in the Windy City during the bitter labor wars of the 1920s and 1930s. In one notorious incident in May 1930, Chicagorillas shot and killed contractor William Healy, with whom the Chicago Marble Setters Union had been having difficulties.

child labor laws—Statutes at both state and federal level that have sought for the past century and a half to restrict or abolish the gainful employment of children. Minimum age and allowable time has varied. In 1840s New England, the **Female Labor Reform Association** of Lowell was able to pressure state legislatures into banning the labor of minors under 15 for more than ten hours a day without written consent of their parents. Only seven states had enacted child labor laws before 1880, meaning a 10-hour day, 60-hour week was the *limit* for children. The number of states grew to 26 by 1900, though by then most states prohibited children from working in hazardous industries—a stricture that went unheeded in the anthracite mines of Pennsylvania and Appalachia. Beginning in 1914, a 10 percent federal excise tax was levied on firms employing 14-year-olds, and in 1916 President Wilson signed a Child Labor Act forbidding some industries from hiring those under 16. But both laws were struck down by the U.S. Supreme Court within a few years, and in 1925 a congressional amendment to empower the federal government to regulate and prohibit the labor of minors under 18 went nowhere in the face of a well-orchestrated business campaign that painted the move as "socialism." The labor-law reforms of the 1930s—plus the mechanization of jobs once done by children, growing popular support for children's education, and a strong desire in Depression times to replace youngsters with adult breadwinners—alleviated many of the child-labor abuses. It remains a problem today, however, in the fast-food industry, with migrant agricultural workers, and with the children of immigrants in clandestine garment-industry **sweatshops**.

CIO—Congress of Industrial Organizations. See **AFL-CIO**.

classified employees—Employees of the federal government who occupy positions established by the Classification Act of 1949, which classifies positions that range in responsibility—and pay—and specifies the duties each job entails.

Clayton Act—A federal law passed in 1914 hailed by the **AFL** as the "Magna Carta for [American] labor" because it at long last established that **labor unions** were not **conspiracies** and that labor itself was not a commodity or article of commerce. Its antecedent had been a Massachusetts Supreme Court ruling almost 75 years before. In effect, the Act recognized the legality of unions and *appeared* to free labor from the antitrust laws and the application of "judicial ukases" (edicts) in the form of **injunctions**. The optimism, however, lasted only as long as World War I, with its great demand for labor, and a sympathetic Wilson administration. With the 1920s came endless volleys of injunctions from the states, always to "prevent irreparable injury to a property or a property right"—a threat that virtually any union action can be construed to pose. And labor found its supposed immunity against antitrust laws nearly useless against decision after negative decision from a decidedly antilabor U.S. Supreme Court. Relief was not to come until the labor-law reforms of the 1930s. The British equivalent of the Clayton Act came four decades earlier, in 1871, with parliamentary passage of the Trade-Union Act. See **Commonwealth v. Hunt**, **unions as conspiracies**, **Sherman Antitrust Act**, **Danbury Hatters' Case**.

closed shop—A contract provision, now illegal under 1947 **Taft-Hartley** revisions to the **National Labor Relations Act**, that requires all employees to be **union** members *before* being hired. The earliest recorded instance in the United States of the closed shop is 1799, when organized Philadelphia cordwainers prevailed upon master shoemakers to hire none but association men. In 1867, boot and shoe workers had contracts specifying that factories could only hire union shoemakers. The term itself, however, didn't make its first appearance until 1904, at a time when laborers' unions felt that only by regulating the flow of casual laborers onto the job could they hope to raise **wages** above the level fixed by grim competition among immigrant job seekers. **Hiring halls**, the last vestige of closed-shop practice, have been allowed to continue in the maritime and construction industries provided they don't operate exclusively for union members. The closed shop is, in effect, the obverse of the **blacklist** coin. See **union shop**, **open shop**, **right-to-work laws**.

closed union—A union that makes it difficult if not impossible to gain entry to it by setting inordinately high **initiation fees**, limiting admission to **apprenticeship** training, setting racial and ethnic barriers, or using other methods to protect the job opportunities of union members. The closed union, once quite common in the crafts and trades, was largely prohibited by **Taft-Hartley Act** law and subsequent civil rights legislation—thanks to the efforts of black labor leader **A. Philip Randolph**—and is all but nonexistent today. Not to be confused with **closed shop**.

coalition bargaining—See **pattern bargaining**.

Coalition of Labor Union Women (CLUW)—Organization founded in 1974 composed largely of women union officials whose goals were day care, **affirmative action**, **comparable worth**, and advancement of women in the **trade-union** bureaucracy. "We have a message for [**AFL-CIO** head] **George Meany**, for [Teamsters head]" announced delegate Myra Wolfgang of the Hotel & Restaurant Employees Union in a speech at the founding convention. "We did not come here to swap recipes." The challenge became a catchphrase and later the title of a documentary film as CLUW sought to remedy a situation in which women workers on average made only two-thirds the pay of men. But the message got through to Meany, who addressed the organization's 1976 convention with: "If supporting a living wage for all workers makes me a feminist, move over, sisters." In 1980 CLUW launched an 18-month project called the Empowerment of Union Women. However, its one foray into organizing the unorganized, the 1982 Baltimore/Washington Women's Organizing Campaign, organized jointly with the AFL-CIO's **Industrial Union Department**, was abandoned as a failure in 1984. But CLUW has never been easily discouraged. As early as 1975, only a year after the organization's founding, other women were writing about "the death of CLUW"; almost a quarter-century later, the coalition is still going strong, even flourishing. See **working women's movement**.

Code of Ethical Practices—A code drawn up a year or two after the **AFL-CIO** merger in 1955 setting standards of **trade-union** morality. Suspected breaches of these standards by **affiliated** unions

may be investigated internally and recommendations for reme-
dial action—up to and including outright expulsion—made to
the federation's Executive Council.

COLA (cost-of-living adjustment)—An escalator clause in **union**
contracts that provides automatic **wage** increases to cover the
rising cost of living due to inflation, usually pegged to the
national Consumer Price Index and usually calibrated to kick
in only if the inflation rate rises beyond a certain percentage.
Popular in the inflation-ridden 1970s, it has since lost its appeal
at the **bargaining table** now that inflation has held to a relatively low rate.

collective bargaining—In the dry but precise language of labor
law: The negotiation of employment matters between employers
and employees through the use of a **bargaining agent** (viz., a
union) designated by an uncoerced majority of employees within a **bargaining unit**. In short, it is the heart and soul of **organized labor**. The **American Federation of Labor's (AFL) Samuel
Gompers** put the goal more bluntly: collective bargaining, he
said, was all about securing *higher wages, shorter hours, and better
working conditions*. It is no accident that the term collective bargaining was coined in 1891, when the AFL was in its formative
stages. It goes without saying (almost) that it's an **unfair labor
practice** of the first magnitude for employers to interfere with
their employees' right to bargain collectively.

collective negotiations—Often called professional negotiations;
used in the public sector as an alternative to **collective bargaining**, which it resembles in most respects except for the restrictions it places on public employees' right to **strike** or even use
the leverage of a **strike threat**.

collusion—A conspiracy between an employer and a **union** or **bargaining agent** to defraud the employees represented while providing the appearance of genuine negotiations. Such an arrangement is taboo under the **AFL-CIO's Code of Ethical Practices**, as
is the similar **sweetheart contract**.

Colored National Labor Union—See **National Colored Labor Union**.

common-situs picketing—A form of **picketing**, most commonly used in the building and construction trades, when "neutral" employers share the same site as struck employers. A neutral gate is set up, and picketing is restricted to the entrance of the struck employer. A variation of this is ambulatory-situs picketing, where the primary target is inaccessible and pickets must choose the next-best site, or the struck employer has no fixed place of business locally (e.g., a trucking company headquartered in another state). See **informational picketing**.

Commonwealth v. Hunt—A Massachusetts Supreme Court ruling of 1842 establishing, for the first time in U.S. judicial history, that it was not inherently criminal for workers to organize a **union** or try compelling recognition of that union by a **strike**. Three years before, the Boston **Journeymen** Bootmakers' Society had called a strike against all employers who insisted on hiring nonunion bootmakers. Although the strikers were not charged with violence or with intending to destroy businesses, seven union leaders were indicted for criminal conspiracy. The high court reversed the municipal ruling on the ground that seeking to induce one's fellow workers to join a union was not illegal unless the methods used to accomplish that aim were unlawful. The court held that since no contracts were broken, the bootmakers' refusal to work for particular employers was *simply the legal exercise of their "acknowledged right to contract with others for their labor,"* even though it might have the indirect effect of impoverishing those employers. It took 72 years for this ruling to bear fruit as labor law via the **Clayton Act** of 1914. See **unions as conspiracies**.

company spotter—A term coined in 1907 to mean an employee hired to spy out union organizers or **union** activists. See **labor spies, blackleg, blacklist, scab, yellow-dog contract**.

company store—A retail store owned and operated by the company or chief employer in a mill town or mining community, ostensibly for the "convenience" of employees but in reality most often a means of retaining employees by getting them deeper in debt. Established in the 1870s and lasting well into the 1970s and beyond, such stores usually charged inflated prices, payable in

scrip. A turn-of-the-century United Mine Workers chronicle records that one company store made $1,000 a month just by selling blasting powder to its workers at $3.25 a keg, more than $1.25 over the going rate. The American public became most acquainted with the practice, and the lament, with singer Tennessee Ernie Ford's 1950s popularization of the Merle Travis hit "Sixteen Tons," whose refrain went:

> *St. Peter, don't you call me 'cause I can't go;*
> *I owe my soul to the company store.*

company town—A settlement or community owned and operated by a corporation to house employees who work at the company's nearby factory or mine. Instituted in the United States in the 1830s to accompany the huge, sprawling mills that sprang up in the Northeast in the wake of the **Industrial Revolution**, such towns, though paternalistic, often represented the best deal for low-**wage** workers: easy access to job sites, reasonable rents, and low-cost necessities at the **company store**. Later in the century, however, they turned increasingly exploitive as employers resorted to rent and price gouging to enhance earnings. A classic example of a company town gone sour was Pullman, Illinois, where conditions became abusive enough to spawn the great **Pullman Strike** of 1894.

company union—Sometimes called an "employee representation plan," it is a union in name only because it's fostered, financed, and dominated by management to discourage a bona fide union from being organized. In effect, the company "negotiates" with itself. The **National Labor Relations Act (NLRB)** of 1935 declared such employer domination an **unfair labor practice**, but understandably few employees under these circumstances will risk their jobs by filing a complaint to the **NLRB**. The *Wall Street Journal* has a "union" of this type. See **TEAM Act**.

comparable worth—A concept, originating with the **working women's movement** and now part of labor's overall goals, that takes **equal pay for equal work** one step further: It equates levels of skill required for one job with comparable (but different) skills on another job and requires equal or similar pay. A real-life example: Two notices on a bulletin board in the Seattle area, one for legal secretary, requiring five years' experience, types 120 wpm; the other for park custodian, no experience—but it pays $150 a month more. Organizations such as the **Coalition for Labor Union Women (CLUW)** for years have targeted departments or sections of government or private-sector business that have a high percentage of usually underpaid woman employees as ripe for an infusion of comparable worth.

compensation—Something given or received as an equivalent for services, loss, or injury. Much in the news—at least *some* news— today are the whopping compensations granted to working, retiring, or dismissed corporate CEOs, compared to that of their employees. In 1982 the ratio was 42 to 1; it stood at 411 to 1 by 2006. See **Executive PayWatch**.

compensatory or "comp" time—Time taken off in lieu of **overtime** pay for extra time worked. **Union contracts** that mention it usually stipulate that comp time be taken only by mutual consent between employer and employee, that is, it cannot be offered as the *only* alternative to overtime compensation. Employers as a rule prefer comp time to overtime pay because it looks better on the books and is usually taken as **straight time** rather than **time and a half**. Many unions, however, are demanding—and achieving—the latter rate in contractual comp-time provisions. Some states' labor statutes insist that comp time be taken in the same week the overtime is worked. In 1997, congressional Republicans, under the banners of **"flexibility"** and "free choice in the workplace," began pushing for a universal comp-time law. Labor's response was that unless there were stringent guidelines, this would be another abuse of low-paid, low-skilled, nonunion workers who more likely would find themselves working the overtime and getting neither paid nor comped for it. See **FLECS**.

conciliation—See **mediation/conciliation**.

confidential employees—Employees such as private secretaries who, because they are closely related to managerial and supervisory personnel and participate in determining general company policy, are implicitly **excluded** from **collective bargaining** agreements.

conspiracy doctrine—See **unions as conspiracies**.

constituency groups—Name given to associations, institutions, or groups—generally of minorities and women—that provide a bridge between **labor unions**, diverse communities, and the community at large. Among such groups are the A. Philip Randolph Institute (APRI), the Asian Pacific American Labor Alliance (APALA), the Coalition of Black Trade Unionists (CBTU), the **Coalition of Labor Union Women (CLUW)**, the Labor Council for Latin American Advancement (LCLAA), Pride At Work (PAW), and **Jobs with Justice (JWJ)**.

contract (labor)—A formal, written, binding agreement between an employer and a **union** (or similar **bargaining agent**) representing employees of that establishment wherein are set the **wages**, hours terms, and conditions of employment plus any **fringe benefits** negotiated, for a specified period of time. Breach of the contract by either side may be cause for a **grievance, arbitration**, or a charge of **unfair labor practice** before the **National Labor Relations Board**. For a contract to become effective, in most cases, it must be ratified by the union **local**'s membership. See **good-** and **bad-faith bargaining; mandatory, permissive**, and **illegal subjects of bargaining; contract violation**.

contracting out—The practice of farming out work or a phase of production, hitherto done by **union** members in a union workplace, to another company, sometimes in another state or country—and almost always at lower, nonunion **wages**. Of sporadic occurrence up to the 1980s, the practice, under the twin rubrics of free trade and competitive advantage, has become widespread and has been the cause of numerous strikes in the industrial **trade unions**, particularly those representing autoworkers and aerospace workers. Employers' tonier synonym for this practice is **outsourcing**.

Contract Labor Act—Legislation enacted in 1864 as a measure to fill the need for a greater labor supply during the Civil War. Its most onerous provision called for the importation of foreign workers, who then would have to pledge a year's **wages** to repay the costs of bringing them to the United States. By the same token, some employers used the law to bring in foreign workers to break **strikes**. The law was repealed in 1868, thanks largely to a relentless campaign by the **National Labor Union**.

contract violation—An action, whether by management or the **union**, that triggers a **grievance** and, if that's unresolved, **arbitration**. Extremely fine hairs often separate a violation from an acceptable or **past practice**, and the ambiguities inherent in any contract, no matter how closely bargained and fine-tuned, can lead to an infinity of interpretations as to meaning and intent. A contract violation allowed to go long enough ungrieved or unreported eventually acquires the status of past practice—and is likely to be held as such by an arbitrator unless found to be in violation of the law as well.

contract worker—Also called independent contractor, a status with a specific Internal Revenue Service definition; not to be confused with **temp**. An employee, usually nonunion, who works under individual or private contract with a company—sometimes for only a specified time, coinciding with the duration of a particular task or job—and for an agreed-upon salary or commission. Such contracts may or may not cover **fringe benefits** and other permanent-employee plans, depending on the acuity of the contractor and/or the generosity of the employer. The employer, at any rate, is not required to withhold federal taxes from or pay a portion of Social Security, Medicare, **workers compensation**, or unemployment insurance for a contract worker, who is not covered by the general provisions of the federal **Fair-Labor Standards Act**. On the other hand, neither can the employer compel the independent to abide by company rules, attend meetings or be otherwise subjected to "company direction," although often the worker does these things voluntarily. In 1997, the 105th Congress attempted to broaden the definition of "independent contractor" so it would include a larger number of employees, a move fought hard by **organized labor** and eventually defeated. See **Industrial Revolution**.

cooling-off period—Usually referring to the **Taft-Hartley**-established 60-day grace period after a contract expires during which no **strike** can be called, ostensibly allowing time for the **union** and management to reach a new agreement. That may be followed by an additional cooling-off period—an 80-day **injunction** against striking if the U.S. president judges such action as endangering the nation's health or safety, or creating a national emergency. It can also mean a required period of delay, fixed by federal or state law, following legal notice of a pending labor dispute, during which there can be neither a strike nor a **lockout**. In either case, **wages** and conditions of work are usually frozen under conditions set by the previous **contract** as long as the cooling-off period lasts. See **national emergency strike, emergency dispute.**

coordinated bargaining—See **pattern bargaining.**

COPE (Committee on Political Education)—The political-action arm of the **AFL-CIO** established shortly after the labor federation merger in 1955 by combining the AFL's Labor's League for Political Education with the CIO's Political Action Committee. It provides support for labor-friendly issues and for federation-endorsed political candidates and is financed by individual members' contributions and fund-raisers rather than union **dues** (which would be illegal under **Taft-Hartley**). Through its vigorous campaigning, COPE is credited with playing a key role in the reelection of a Democratic Congress in 1956—of the 288 candidates endorsed that year for the House of Representatives, 159 were successful; of the 29 for the Senate, 15 won. Since then, COPE has had varying degrees of success—high in the Kennedy-Johnson years, low from 1980 on—but it has never equaled the 1956 ratio, though it came close in the 2006 elections. On occasion, COPE regional and state officials, mindful that Republican lawmakers in the past have sponsored some of labor's more progressive legislation (the **Davis-Bacon Act** is but one), have backed individual GOP candidates as well, based on their sympathy with labor causes.

corporate campaign—A concentrated coordinated effort by a

union or a coalition of unions to leverage different aspects of corporate power against each other, relying strongly on **solidarity** and getting the message through to the public, with a satisfactory **contract**, correction of long-standing abuses, or recognition of a union the ultimate goal. The acknowledged creator and master of this strategy is Ray Rogers, who runs the consulting firm of Corporate Campaign out of New York City. But Rogers's record and that of others in the field has been spotty, leading many in the **labor movement** to question whether such drives are worth the time, money, and effort. Rogers was successful in his long, drawn-out 1970s campaign against textile giant J.P. Stevens; it finally recognized the Amalgamated Clothing and Textile Workers union in 1980. He was stunningly unsuccessful in the campaign behind the 1985–86 **Hormel Strike** of United Food and Commercial Workers Local P-9, which ended in a **sweetheart contract** that cost the strikers their jobs, though that failure has been attributed to factors other than the campaign itself. Other unions have run their own corporate campaigns, some with and some without Rogers's help: the Steelworkers targeted **Phelps Dodge** in 1983, the United Paperworkers International Union battled International Paper Co. in 1988, and the Farm Labor Organizing Committee (FLOC) took on Campbell Soups in the late 1980s. Of these, only the FLOC effort brought success. Not to be confused with a campaign by a corporation to **decertify** a union or keep a union out.

cost-of-living index—See **COLA**.

craft union—A popular early 1920s term for **trade union**, a **labor union** of craftsmen or workers in related crafts, as distinguished from general workers or a union including all workers in an industry. In the 1870s and 1880s, the **Knights of Labor** and, shortly after the turn of the century, the **Industrial Workers of the World** attempted to break out of this limited structure with their "one big union" concept, but until the 1930s and the **CIO**'s hugely successful push for top-to-bottom industrial organization, the craft or trade union constituted virtually the whole of the American labor experience.

cyclical unemployment—Joblessness caused by fluctuations in the economy or downward trends in the business cycle. It's usually of far greater magnitude than **seasonal, frictional**, and **technological unemployment**.

D

Danbury Hatters' Case—First application of the **Sherman Antitrust Act** to **organized labor**, this 1908 U.S. Supreme Court decision made individuals responsible for actions of the **unions** to which they belonged, and called into question the very legality of a union. It arose out of a 1902 United Hatters of America strike and **boycott** against D.H. Loewe & Co. of Danbury, Connecticut, after which the company sued the 250 union hatters involved for $240,000 on grounds they conspired, by their boycott, to interfere with interstate commerce in violation of the Act. Unresolved differences in this decision led directly to the 1914 **Clayton Act** whereby unions were declared legal.

Daughters of St. Crispin—See **Knights of St. Crispin**.

Davis-Bacon Act—Also known as the prevailing-wage law. A federal law authored by Republican legislators—U.S. Rep. James J. Davis (R-Penn.) and U.S. Rep. Robert L. Bacon (R-N.Y.)—and signed by Republican President Herbert Hoover in 1931, stipulating that construction **wages** and benefits paid under federal and service **contracts** must be no lower than locally prevailing—**union** or nonunion—wages and benefits for the same kind of work. The Act, designed to prevent big business and big government from undercutting local wages, has been a major bugbear of the **Business Roundtable** and an ongoing target of GOP congressional budget-cutters far more than a decade and even looms intermittently in the gunsights of big-city mayors, who see repeal as a way of knocking down construction costs. Proponents argue the only things repeal would lower are standards, job safety, productivity, and the local economy, as has happened in Utah and Iowa, two of twelve states that repealed their own prevailing-wage laws. See **Little Davis-Bacon, prevailing wage.**

Debs, Eugene V. (1855–1926)—U.S. labor organizer, impassioned battler for workers' causes, and five-time Socialist candidate for president, including one candidacy while in prison. National secretary of the Brotherhood of Locomotive Fireman (1880–92) and a member of the Indiana Legislature (1886–88), Debs orga-

nized the American Railway Union in 1892 and led a **boycott** of all Pullman cars during the 1894 **Pullman strike**, for which he was jailed six months. A co-founder of the Social Democratic Party in 1897, Debs also helped found the **Industrial Workers of the World** in 1905 but later disavowed the IWW because of its proclivity for violence. In 1918, he was sentenced to ten years in prison for sedition when he spoke out against prosecution under the 1917 Espionage Act, but was pardoned by President Warren G. Harding in 1921. In the 1920 presidential election, Debs, running on the Socialist ticket and still behind bars, won 920,000 votes—his largest tally ever.

Memorable quote: *"Ten thousand times has the **labor movement** stumbled and bruised itself. We have been enjoined by the courts, assaulted by thugs, charged by the militia, traduced by the press, frowned upon in public opinion and deceived by politicians. But notwithstanding all this . . . labor is today the most vital and potential power this planet has ever known, and its historic mission is as certain of ultimate realization as the setting of the sun."* (1894)

Debs Revolution—See **Pullman Strike.**

"Decatur war"—So-called because of the confluence of three major labor disputes over work rules and 12-hour shifts in the central Illinois city of 80,000 during the early 1990s, a conflict that has pitted, as seen by some, the very soul of the U.S. **labor movement** against what political-economist writer William Greider calls the "manic logic of global capitalism." In contention were 1,800 workers at Caterpillar Tractor, represented by the United Auto Workers, who went on **strike** in 1991; 1,250 workers at

Bridgestone/Firestone Corp. represented by the United Rubber-workers **union** (now an **affiliate** of United Steelworkers of America), who struck in 1992, and 760 workers at British-owned A.E. Staley, represented by the United Paperworkers International Union (UPIU), who were hit by a company **lock-out** in June 1993.

The often-bitter disputes, which in the aggregate lasted the better part of seven years—and continue, in one form or another, to simmer to this day—were marked by massive community and national displays of **solidarity**, tear-gassings and clubbings of strikers by police, an infusion of **permanent replacement workers**, and a sense of both foreboding and hope by national labor leaders. Of the three union factions involved, the UPIU at Staley, a major producer of corn syrup ingredients for soft drinks, fared the worst. With a less-than adequate **settlement** in late 1996, the **local** has all but disintegrated. Bridgestone/Firestone came off with a more-or-less satisfactory **contract** about the same time, while Decatur's Caterpillar workers in March 1998 accepted, along with 11,200 of their Midwest UAW brethren, a something-is-better-than-nothing accord. Nonetheless, Decatur labor spokesmen said in late June 1998, labor sentiment remains strong in the community, with 50 to 60 percent of the area workforce unionized (the national average is 12–17 percent).

In the words of labor writers Tom Frank and David Mulcahey, who covered the ongoing American heartland drama extensively, *"The war in Decatur has been as much about conflicting ideologies as it has been about workplace conditions. As such, it strikes at the heart of the new international business order."*

decertification ("decert")—A National Labor Relations Board–sponsored election to vote a **union** out as the **bargaining agent** in a workplace. A majority vote is required to decertify a union, though the names of only 30 percent of the employees in the **bargaining unit** are required as signatories on the petition calling for such an election. Should the decert fail, a year must pass before a similar attempt can be made. It is not uncommon for employers to instigate, finance, and actively campaign for a decert election, as happened in the late 1980s when the West Coast department store chain Nordstrom effectively engineered the ouster of its main Seattle thorn, the United Food & Commercial Workers union, in retribution for the latter's successful suit against it for **off-the-clock** practices.

Department of Labor, U.S.—The department of the federal government charged with improving the welfare, opportunities, and working conditions of **wage** earners. Origins: As early as 1866, National Union of Iron Molders founder **William Sylvis** called for a separate federal department of labor. On June 27, 1884, Congress established a Bureau of Labor within the Department of the Interior, then in 1888 gave this bureau independent status as the Department of Labor. In 1903, it became part of the Department of Commerce and Labor, then in 1913 became the separate Department of Labor again, this time with its head serving as a member of the president's cabinet as the secretary of labor. See **Bureau of Labor Statistics.**

deregulation—The removal of federal controls on an industry or other area of the economy, such as banking, usually by congressional action; an activity begun during the Carter administration, greatly accelerated by the Reagan and George H.W. Bush administrations, and rocketed sky-high in the openly antiunion administration of George W. Bush. Usually this has severe repercussions on the labor market, particularly at unionized workplaces, because deregulation results in a fierce competitiveness in which jobs and **wage** scales are the first to go in the wave of cost-cutting. In the airline industry, for example, deregulation did away with most guidelines that governed fares, schedules, and mergers. Frank Lorenzo, former head of Texas Air, infamously symbolized the dark side of deregulation when first he slashed the wages of pilots, machinists, and flight attendants in his own airline and then, after selling hundreds of millions of dollars worth of "junk bonds" in 1983, bought Continental Airlines and declared it bankrupt in order to break its long-standing union **contracts.** He then offered to rehire the fired Continental employees at half their old pay. When they struck, Lorenzo broke their unions by hiring **permanent replacement workers** from among the tens of thousands of unemployed pilots and machinists idled by the recession of the early 1980s. Lorenzo then moved on to Eastern Airlines in 1986, but employees there balked at his demand for major wage reductions and went on **strike.** But this time, well-paid pilots joined the striking machinists and flight attendants on the **picket line**, and the strike won **solidarity** from the **labor movement**, sympathy from passengers and the public, and even grudging admiration from Wall Street, which had been singing the praises of airline deregulation. The prolonged strike grounded most Eastern planes, threw Eastern itself into bankruptcy, and eventually forced Lorenzo out of the airline business.

Detroit newspaper strike (1995–97)—Labeled by **AFL-CIO** President **John Sweeney** as "the most important strike in America today," the 19-month walkout pitted six **labor unions** against two of the largest newspaper chains in the country. Two years later, it would seem the Goliaths won the battle but lost the war,  though the Davids gained a fragmented, Pyrrhic peace at best. With court appeals and counter-appeals, the issues may take years to be resolved. The strike began in July 1995 against Knight-Ridder's *Detroit Free Press* and Gannett's *Detroit News*, both under joint operation of the Detroit Newspaper Agency. Essentially, it was over **union-security** provisions management wanted to void. In particular, the papers sought to eliminate union **jurisdiction**; to replace full-time employees with part-timers getting less pay and no benefits; to **contract out**, thus eliminating hundreds of jobs; and to effect health care **takebacks**. Some 2,500 union employees, among them The Newspaper Guild, the Teamsters, the Communications Workers of America, and the Graphic Communications International Union, said no. In the course of the sometimes violent strike, during which the papers also imposed a **lockout**, the unions sued the police and the city of Sterling Heights, Michigan (site of the major newsprinting plant), the newspaper agency, and the Vance International security-guard firm for violation of workers' constitutional rights, alleging numerous beatings, intimidation, trucks driven at pickets and unwarranted arrests and searches. The strike ended in February 1997 with no clear gain for the strikers and with many of them now jobless—but with circulation and advertising of the two newspapers considerably reduced. However, an earlier **National Labor Relations Board** ruling that management had incurred an **unfair labor practice** with **bad-faith bargaining** from the very beginning was followed up in June 1997 with a federal judge's ruling that both papers had to rehire their fired strikers, with back pay, even if that meant discharging the **permanent replacement workers** hired since the strike began. The newspapers fought the ruling, and won. All in all, the strike was considered a disaster for both sides. The unions, especially the Teamsters, suffered substantial wage and job cuts and, as usually happens in such cases, the newspapers never regained their readership.

differential pay—Additional pay for time or duties beyond those normally required. For example, an employee starting earlier or working later than a regular daytime **shift** may be paid a night differential of $5 a shift; those temporarily substituting in a supervisory position or higher-paid classification may earn a $10 shift differential. Such distinctions are usually spelled out in the **contract**. See **incentive pay**.

disability insurance plans—Plans, generally negotiated in a union **contract**, to compensate workers for **wage** loss from illnesses and injuries usually incurred while *not* on the job (as opposed to **workers compensation**). Several states—California, New Jersey, New York, and Rhode Island among them—have disability insurance laws whereby payments are limited for a fixed time, usually 10 to 26 weeks. Disability benefits—also called weekly wage-loss benefits or weekly accident and sickness benefits—are widely available to nonunion employees as well on an individual or private basis. See **welfare plans**.

dismissal pay—See **severance pay.**

dispatch—A principal function of the union **hiring hall** in which worker requirements from companies are logged, sorted, and matched with **union** members' skills, availability, and order on the hiring list. The qualifying worker is then dispatched, or sent, to the job. Used mainly in the heavy-construction and longshore trades.

double-breasted—A building and construction-trades term for a unionized contractor who sets up a nonunion company to underbid and compete with his **union** company.

Douglass, Frederick (1817–95)—Former slave, noted abolitionist and writer, and outspoken advocate not only for civil rights but also for labor and **trade-union** rights for African Americans. Born Frederick Augustus Washington Bailey, he was **apprenticed** while still a slave as a caulker at the Baltimore shipyards in the early 1830s but escaped in 1838 and fled to work as an anony-mous laborer in New Bedford, Massachusetts, where he changed his name to Douglass to evade slave hunters. After the Civil War, during which he played a major role in shaping the Lincoln administration's attitude toward slavery and blacks, he took an active part in championing—often in vain—the entry and continued employment of black freedmen in the workplace both North and South. In 1869, he helped form, along with another former Baltimore ship's caulker, **Isaac Myers**, the short-lived **National Colored Labor Union.** On more than one occasion Douglass witnessed firsthand the corrosive influence of workplace bias. In the 1870s, one of his sons, Lewis, was hired as a **journeyman** printer in the Government Printing Office—only to see the other, white printers walk off the job in protest. The younger Douglass eventually had to quit, over which the father wrote a bitter tract on the racial prejudices of the American workingman of his day. Douglass himself held a number of government posts, including, in his later years, that of U.S. minister (ambassador) to Haiti. Memorable quote: *"Power concedes* *nothing without a demand. It never did and never will."* See **blacks in the labor movement.**

downsizing—A euphemism for the **layoffs** occasioned by a company's decision to merge, **outsource**, shift operations to another, usually lower-wage state or country, or reduce its workforce for greater profit. Even more offensive to many in the **labor movement** is the corporate synonym "right-sizing."

Dubinsky, David (1892–1982)—Russian-born U.S. labor leader and activist; head of International Ladies' Garment Workers Union (ILGWU) from 1932 to 1966, during which it became one of the most successful **unions** in the nation. Exiled to Siberia as early as 1911 for union activism, Dubinsky escaped to the United States and joined the ILGWU as a cloak cutter. Later, as president, he led the union back into the American Federation of Labor (**AFL**), and when the AFL merged with the Congress of Industrial Organizations in 1955, he was elected to the organization's executive council and then to its vice-presidency. Active in the then-nascent global labor movement, Dubinsky represented the AFL in the United Nation's **International Labor Organization** and in the UN Economic and Social Council. He also helped found the **American Labor Party** (1936), the Liberal Party (1944), and Americans for Democratic Action (1947).

dues—Monthly fees or charges paid by **union** members to their **locals.** The amount is sometimes set by the **international union**, but more often by the local, with the international receiving **per caps.** Dues money is used to finance the functions of the local and the costs of serving the members—publishing a newsletter, legal fees incurred in arbitrations, etc. Locals in turn pay dues to a **central labor council**, while internationals pay dues to the **AFL-CIO.** See **agency fee payer.**

duty of fair representation—The legal requirement of a **union** to represent fairly all members of a bargaining unit, including **agency fee payers.** Failure to represent can result in sanctions from the **National Labor Relations Board** as well as open the union to a possible lawsuit by the party or parties who feel their complaints were not adequately grieved. Legal action of this kind has been filed frequently in recent years by minorities and women.

E

early buyout—An inducement by employers to workers faced with **technological unemployment**, **downsizing**, or other forms of **layoff** whereby employees within shooting distance of retirement age—usually 10 years or less—can "retire" with full or nearly full **pension benefits**, health coverage, and other fringe emoluments they might have enjoyed under the **contract**. This is often accompanied by a straight cash settlement or **severance pay** as well, likely based on the employees' years of service. Despite its up-front costs, the cash buyout represents considerable savings to the employer in the long run.

Eastern Airlines strike (1989–91)—See deregulation.

EEOC (Equal Employment Opportunity Commission)—A body established by the Civil Rights Act of 1964 to enforce provisions of the Act such as forbidding companies and **labor unions** with more than 25 employees to discriminate on the basis of race, religion, sex, color, or national origin. The EEOC is also frequently called on to secure equal rights for women performing the same job as men, though action on such complaints can often be slow and ponderous—often two or three years or more—while enforcement depends on the administration in power in the White House.

eight-hour day—A goal of the American **labor movement** ever since 1836, when realistically all **union** leaders dared press for was the ten-hour day. It is based on a holistic post-Enlightment ideal that a man's day should be divided into three equal parts: eight hours for work; eight for sleep; and eight for recreation, leisure, and family matters. In 1863, **Ira Steward** of Boston became the acknowledged leader of the eight-hour movement when he persuaded a convention of machinists to adopt that goal as a central plank. In 1865, believing the goal had to be achieved through politics rather than the **trade-union** movement, Steward created the Grand Eight-Hour League of Massachusetts—similar leagues spread as far as California—and even forced the infant Republican Party that year to adopt an eight-hour plank in their campaign platform, though that's as far as it got in GOP politics. In 1868, Democratic President Andrew Johnson established the eight-hour day in the Government Printing Office and later that year extended it to cover mechanics and laborers employed by the federal government. The eight-hour day became a major rallying cry, successively, of the **National Labor Union**, the **Knights of Labor**, and the American Federation of Labor (**AFL**) and even the League of Nations (1919); but while it was written into a number of union contracts over the years and the 1916 **Adamson Act** made it mandatory for railway workers, it did not become a norm in the American workplace until, ironically, it was decreed by antiunion magnate **Henry Ford** for his auto-manufacturing plants in 1926. He was unique in the enterpreneurial world; Ford's confreres a couple of states away, the Employers' Association of Pittsburgh, were posting pamphlets that read, "The 8-hour day is not practical . . . is not economical . . . cannot be put into successful operation in our plants . . . the men themselves want to work more than 8 hours a day . . . [and] it will drive other industries away from Pittsburgh." Labor historian David Montgomery contends that in the 1930s, when some unions were clamoring for a six-hour day and said so in their banners, photographs of those banners were doctored to have the "6" read as an "8" so big business in general and advertisers in particular wouldn't get unduly alarmed. See **Fair Labor Standards Act**.

eight-hour guarantee—A West Coast longshoremen's contractual entitlement to eight hours' pay when they present themselves on a job to which they have been **dispatched** so long as they are not fired during a **shift**. The men are paid for six hours at **straighttime** rates and two hours at **overtime** rates, regardless of how many hours they actually work. Known in the industry also as "six and two," these terms were awarded after the 1934 **strike**. The reasoning is that with the guarantee, longshoremen can be induced to work faster without suffering potential loss of pay.

emergency dispute—A labor-management dispute deemed as endangering public health and safety; a decision on the national level that can be made by the president under the **Taft-Hartley Act**. The "appropriate action" in such cases is a **cooling-off period** and the appointment of a **fact-finding** board. Several states have also passed emergency-dispute legislation, for the most part covering public utilities. States deal with such disputes in various ways ranging from fact-finding to **binding arbitration** to seizure (temporary control of a business shut down by a **strike** or about to be).

Emergency Railroad Transportation Act—A 1933 law that guaranteed railway workers the right of **collective bargaining** and specifically recognized the regular railway **unions** as **bargaining agents**. A precursor of the **National Labor Relations Act**, which broadened the right to workers in other unions. See **Erdman Act** and **Newlands Act**.

Employee Free Choice Act (EFCA)—Thwarted congressional attempt in June 2007 to make it easier for unions to organize workplaces and be certified by demonstrating that a majority of potential members had signed cards—a method long in use in Canada and other countries—rather than their having to endure an employer's antiunion harangues and on-the-job coercion leading up to a **certification** election. The measure passed 241–185 in the House and garnered 51 votes in the Senate, but lacked the 60 needed for passage. Individual states, however, have passed laws similar to EFCA, among them Oregon, New York, New Jersey, and Illinois. Opponents of the national bill had cited a study showing that 18 percent of employees who signed cards don't want the union and argued that, overall, EFCA would be "undemocratic" and "unfair" to employers. See **authorization cards**, **captive-audience meeting**, and **cards (certification)**.

Employers Liability Law—A 1908 act of Congress providing workers compensation on railroads. Though struck down shortly after by the U.S. Supreme Court on the grounds its wording was too vague, it was upheld when Congress rewrote the act.

Equal Pay Act—Federal bill signed into law by President John F. Kennedy in June 1963 that made it illegal for companies with more than 15 employees to discriminate in hiring, pay, promotion, and perquisites; a breakthrough for job applicants in securing hitherto "male only" or "female only" employment (e.g., law-firm partners or flight attendants). However, a study in 1979 revealed that overall pay equality had actually gone down for women in the intervening years, from 63 percent of what men made, on average, to 60 percent. The drop was attributed to large numbers of women joining the labor force in low-paying, entry-level jobs. Currently, women earn 76 cents for every $1 men make.

equal pay for equal work—Just what it says, without any regard to sex, age, or other difference. A concept born of the age-old discrepancies in pay between white male **wage** earners and anybody else, it began to be voiced not long after women entered the **labor movement** in significant numbers in the 1830s and gradually extended, in the latter half of the 20th century, to other minorities in the workplace. In its 1868 congress, the **National Labor Union** became the first labor federation in world history to vote for equal pay for equal work, an action that impressed even Karl Marx half a world away. Though even today, the equal-pay goal has yet to be reached in many areas of the American workplace, particularly nonunionized ones; federal laws and the threat of lawsuits have made more and more employers aware the concept is good, trouble-free policy. Not quite the same as **comparable worth**.

equal pay for women—See Equal Pay Act.

Erdman Act—Embodies the concept that employers should recognize and deal with labor organizations. A direct outgrowth of the bitter and brutal **Pullman Strike** of 1894 and the findings of the resultant United States Strike Commission, the 1898 Act also outlawed the use of **yellow-dog contracts** by the railroads. That part of it, however, was later struck down by the U.S. Supreme

Court on grounds it was an "unwarranted interference with freedom of contract" and was not to resurface until the 1935 **National Labor Relations Act**. Though limited to employees engaged in the operation of interstate trains, the Erdman Act provided the groundwork for future labor legislation. A key clause in the Act imposed criminal penalties for firing or threatening to fire employees for **union** membership, though this part also was nullified by the Supreme Court, in 1908. See **Esch-Cummins Act, Norris–La Guardia Act, Railway Labor Act, Railway Labor Board**.

ergonomics—Human engineering; an applied science that coordinates the design of devices, systems, and physical working conditions with the capacities and requirements of the worker. With the onslaught of **repetitive strain injury (RSI)** in the workplace, ergonomics has played an increasing role in the design of chairs, desks, and other accoutrements of workstations to minimize or alleviate RSI and attendant afflictions such as **carpal tunnel syndrome** and tendinitis.

ERISA—The federal Employee Retirement Income Security Act, a 1974 congressional attempt to attack a multitude of problems affecting employee benefit plans, especially the lack of information and adequate safeguards concerning their operation. Through various statutes and regulations, the Act creates minimum standards to assure the equitable character and financial soundness of those plans.

escalator clause—A contractual clause that ties **wage** rates to the cost of living in order to keep **real wages** reasonably stable. See **COLA**.

escape clauses—See **maintenance of membership, one-in-ten clauses**.

Esch-Cummins Act—A 1920 law passed by Congress providing for the **settlement** of disputes on interstate carriers by **collective bargaining** and for the appointment of a **Railway Labor Board** to act as arbiters if bargaining failed. See **Railway Labor Act**.

ESOP (Employee Stock Option Plan)—An arrangement in which a determined amount of an employee's contractual benefits are diverted to purchase company stock shares and placed in a retirement account. For some companies, this serves as a **pension plan**.

Ethical Practices Committee—A panel established by the **Executive Committee** of the **AFL-CIO** in 1955, when the two giant labor groups merged, charged with keeping the new federation "free from any taint of corruption or communism." The committee was given authority to investigate allegations of abuses such as **collusion** and **sweetheart contracts**, hold hearings, and make recommendations to the Executive Committee. This has resulted in costly sanctions and even ouster of member **unions**, as happened with the Teamsters in 1957.

Everett Massacre—Name given to an incident of November 5, 1916, in which a group of **Industrial Workers of the World (IWW)** members aboard the vessel *Verona* docked at Everett, Washington, to attend a lumber workers' **strike** and rally, only to be met with a hail of fire from sheriff's deputies and gunmen from the local Commercial Club. At least six IWW members were killed along with two deputies. When the *Verona* limped back to Seattle, the 74 IWW men aboard were arrested and subsequently tried on charges of murdering the two deputies, who, evidence subsequently showed, were fatally shot by bullets from their own forces. The defendants were eventually acquitted; the sheriff's deputies and other gunmen were never arrested, let alone tried.

evergreen clause—A **contract** clause assuring that the terms and benefits of the contract will continue from the time the old agreement expires to when a new one is negotiated and approved.

excluded positions—All employees and positions explicitly excluded from a **contract** by mutual consent. While these are mainly management personnel, they also may include those not necessarily **exempt** under **National Labor Relations Act** guidelines. When subsequent disputes arise over who or what jobs should be excluded, a **National Labor Relations Board**–sponsored **unit clarification** can be called to settle the issue. N.B. Those who opt out of the **union** or become **agency fee payers** in a union shop cannot properly be said to be in excluded positions. See **one-in-ten, free riders, Appendix II.**

exclusivity—The right acquired by an employee organization to be the sole representative of a **bargaining unit.** Exclusive representation is usually covered in labor-relations statutes, though some laws governing public-employee labor relations provide for alternatives such as proportional representation, whereby bargaining rights are accorded to one or more organizations in direct proportion to the number of members in the unit who belong to or vote for the organization.

Executive Council, AFL-CIO—A body within the **AFL-CIO** consisting of the president, secretary-treasurer, and 27 vice presidents. The council, which meets three times a year, is the actual governing body of the federation. Many of its actions, however, are subject to approval of the annual AFL-CIO convention, a principle embedded in many unions since the mid-1800s: duly authorized and democratically elected delegates to such conventions are the true and clear voice of the **rank and file.**

Executive Order 10988—A fiat issued by President John F. Kennedy in 1962 establishing the nation's first government Labor Relations Program by extending limited **collective-bargaining** rights to federal employees. These rights were reduced in 1969 by President Richard M. Nixon, no friend of labor, by his Executive Order 11491.

Executive PayWatch—An **AFL-CIO** watchdog group started in 1997 to track chief executive officers' multimillion-dollar **compensation** and compare it to salaried workers and wage earners in their organizations. One 2006 finding: the CEO of a Standard & Poor's 500 company raked in an average $14.7 million—in some cases, despite poor performances and corporate scandals. Another finding: the CEO of pharmaceutical giant Pfizer, who headed the **Business Roundtable,** a major backer of the George W. Bush administration's drive to privatize **Social Security,** retired in 2006 with an annual **pension** of $6.5 million.

exempt employee—Almost the same as an **excluded employee,** but not quite. Exclusions can be negotiated; exemptions are, per se, positions and the employees who occupy them outside the **collective-bargaining** agreement as defined by the **National Labor Relations Act**. Examples are top and middle management, company negotiators, supervisors, **confidential** secretaries, and foremen, although the latter in some industrial and craft unions are allowed to retain their **union** membership. Exempt employees are not subject to the provisions of the **Fair Labor Standards Act** and usually earn compensation expressed in yearly figures rather than hourly wages. See **one-in-ten**, **free riders**, **open shop**.

F

fact-finding—A method of handling labor-management disputes that prohibits **strikes** and **lockouts** until an official agency, usually a fact-finding board, has had opportunity to investigate and report. Changes in the status quo, such as **posting rules**, except when made by mutual consent of the parties, are forbidden during the **cooling-off period** that runs concurrently with the fact-finding. The resultant report may include recommendations that, unlike the findings of an arbitrator, the disputants have a choice of accepting or rejecting. See **mediation/conciliation** and **arbitration**.

Factory Girls Association—One of the earliest incarnations of the American women's labor movement, born in the mid-1830s amid the grim conditions of New England textile mills—14–16 hours a day for $1.56 a week. In 1836, during a **strike**—an extremely daring action in those days—some 1,500 "factory girls" marched through the streets of Lowell, Massachusetts, singing what later became a popular refrain:

> Oh isn't it a pity that such a pretty girl as I
> Should be sent to the factory to pine away and die.
> Oh! I cannot be a slave

For I'm so fond of liberty
That I can not be a slave.

The association also put out two periodicals, *Factory Girl* and the *Factory Girl's Album*, demolishing the myths of bucolic mill life whose onetime farm girls could always "go home to Pa." See **Female Labor Reform Association, working women's movement.**

factory system—The first visible evidence of the **Industrial Revolution** and the biggest overriding influence on work habits, the workplace, and **labor unions** until **automation** in the 1960s and cybernetics in the 1980s. It came into being around the turn of the 19th century, when merchant-capitalists realized the need for four composite ingredients: a large capital outlay, a concentration of labor, use of mechanical power in place of muscle power, and use of machinery in place of skills. A water-powered cotton mill set up in 1791 in Pawtucket, Rhode Island, is generally regarded as the first American factory. By 1840, census figures showed 800,000 men, women, and children employed in U.S. factories, 2.7 million by 1880, and 4.2 million by 1890.

But by the turn of the 20th century, new technology—assembly-line production techniques in particular—and access to a vast and cheap labor pool via massive waves of immigration had given the American factory system a scale and organization undreamed of. In 1870, only a handful of factories, such as the McCormick plant in Chicago, had employed 500 workers. By 1900, 1,500 had reached that size, and some had become gigantic. The Cambria Steel mill in Johnstown, Pennsylvania, employed nearly 20,000 people in 1909; General Electric had 15,000 at its plant in Schenectady, New York, and 11,000 at another plant in Lynn, Massachusetts. The system's geography changed, too. The East, which had produced 58 percent of the nation's manufactured goods in 1890, turned out slightly more than 40 percent by 1929. The slack was taken up by the upper Midwest and, increasingly in the 1930s, 1940s, and 1950s, in the hydropower-abundant far West with its giant aircraft factories and aluminum plants.

Though still very much alive in its mechanized and automated form, the factory system began to decline as the major component of the U.S. economy in the late 1960s and early 1970s as more and more manufacturers, having failed to reinvest capital sufficiently in new equipment and facilities, closed down or sold off increasingly obsolete plants, or moved their production overseas because of cheaper labor costs. The United States' shift from a production to a retail, money-managing, and service economy only hastened the decline. See **immigrants and the labor movement**.

Fair Employment Practices Act—A law passed in 1948 at the behest of President Harry Truman (and the urging of black leaders such as **A. Philip Randolph**) that forbade employment discrimination based on race, color, or creed. In 1941, a Fair Employment Practice Committee had been established under the Roosevelt administration, but a bill to establish it as a permanent agency was defeated by a Dixiecrat filibuster in Congress. See **National War Labor Board**.

Fair Labor Standards Act (FLSA)—Also known as the Wages and Hours Act; a congressional act of 1938 that set federal **minimum wages** and **overtime** rules, established limits on **child labor** and wrote the 40-hour workweek into federal law—a **labor movement** goal since the 1880s. However, the Act left millions out: agricultural workers, service workers, public employees, and anyone employed outside interstate commerce. But it did immediately raise the **wages**—to 25 cents an hour—of some 300,000 workers and shorten the workweek for 1.3 million Americans who were putting in a "regular" 44 hours a week or more at the time. In the early 1990s, however, congressional legislation forced FLSA regulators to relax some of the rules on overtime, making it possible for companies to pay certain nonunion hourly employees, particularly **temps**, straight time for extra hours worked instead of at the usual rate of **time and a half**. Starting in the mid-1990s, Republicans in Congress and state legislatures, as well as some Democrats in **right-to-work** states, have stepped up systematic attempts to further gut the Act or eliminate it entirely. See **Walsh-Healy Act**, **FLECS**, **minimum-wage rates**.

Family Medical Leave Act—Federal law enacted in 1993 decreeing that if a company has a workforce of 50 or more, employees are entitled to 12 weeks of unpaid medical leave when their children are born or when they adopt a child, take in a foster child, or tend to a sick member of the family. Not to be confused with maternity leave.

farmworkers—When originally drafted in early 1935, the **National Labor Relations Act (NLRA)** *did* include the agriculture industry. But that **collective-bargaining** protection disappeared when the bill emerged from committee a few months later, due to not only grower hostility in a still largely agricultural economy but also to a **Red-scare** residue of bloody farm **strikes** in California the year before, in which the communist label was firmly attached to "agrarian reformers." Despite numerous amendments to the NLRA, including the antiunion **Taft-Hartley** (1947) and **Landrum-Griffin** (1959) acts, farmworker lobbyists and sympathetic Congress members have failed to breach this agricultural wall. Paradoxically, this enabled **César Chávez** to launch his successful grape **boycott** in the 1960s, because **secondary boycotts** are largely forbidden by Taft-Hartley provisions to **unions** under the NLRA umbrella. Oddly, racetrack service employees are also excluded from the NLRA in local taxing jurisdictions where the land has been designated "agricultural."

fast-track negotiations—In a **NAFTA**-like international trade context, the power of a U.S. president or his representatives to conclude bi- or multilateral trade agreements with other nations without fear of congressional amendments or codicils. This power, however, must be granted by Congress *beforehand*; that is, it must be agreed before a proposed trade agreement comes up for a vote that it will be passed or defeated as is, without changes or amendments. In mid-1997, **organized labor**, stung by the 1992 congressionally approved NAFTA agreement with Mexico (it took effect in January 1993) and its subsequently unfulfilled side agreements on **wages** and working conditions in Mexico, lobbied hard against it and this time prevailed upon Democrats in Congress. The Democrats, leery of such all-or-nothing betting

anyway, swung enough GOP support to preclude a vote on—
thus blocking—President Bill Clinton's bid for fast-track ability
to negotiate trade pacts with other Latin American countries.
See **maquiladoras**.

featherbedding—The practice of having more workers on the job
than apparently is needed; used derogatorily, in most cases, by
management. The term seems to have no earlier history than
1943, when wartime railroad **unions** were accused of forcing
management to keep firemen employed on locomotives that no
longer ran on wood or coal. However, one man's featherbedding
is another's job safety: many unions, particularly those with
transportation workers, argued with varying success that having extra crew members often spelled the difference between
dangerous fatigue and relief. Congress attempted to outlaw
featherbedding with the 1946 **Lea Act**, but the subsequent **Taft-
Hartley Act** left the practice intact by and large, with the exception that unions could not exact pay from employers for services
not performed (e.g., having to pay for ten musicians when only
six played). In another aspect of alleged featherbedding, the
courts have upheld the right of a union to insist on and receive
work for its members provided some actual work is performed,
even though the work may be neither necessary or desirable to
the employer. See **bogus type, full-crew rule**.

federal labor union—A **local** chartered directly by the **AFL-CIO**,
usually involving employees over whom no **affiliated** national or
international union claims or asserts **jurisdiction**. Historically,
federal labor unions have often been a transitional stage leading
to the formation of a national or **international** union. At one
time, there were numerous federal labor unions in the rubber,
auto, chemical, and cement industries.

Federal Mediation & Conciliation Service (FMCS)—An agency
operated by the government in most large cities in which a
mediator, usually upon agreement by both parties or after an
impasse is reached, attempts to persuade negotiators, by proposals or arguments, to come to voluntary agreement. A mediator, as opposed to an **arbitrator**, cannot make a decision, binding

or otherwise; he or she *can only recommend* a solution. Despite this, many a negotiation has been brought to a successful conclusion by bargainers who might otherwise be at each other's throats—and into a **strike**—without the intercession of a third party. An arbitrator is agreed on by both parties; a mediator is assigned by the local director of the agency. The FMCS, once part of the **Department of Labor**, was made an independent agency by the **Taft-Hartley Act** in 1947.

Female Labor Reform Association—There were several, and they all started in the 1840s in the Northeast, where the **factory system** had set in earliest, and the founding of most was inspired by the publications of the **Factory Girls Association**. They also were the first women's industrial **trade unions** in the United States. Their major objective was the ten-hour day—a vast improvement over 14 and 16 hours—although they also lobbied for the abolition of slavery and **child labor**, and full rights for women. See **working women's movement**.

fiduciary obligation—Obligation of trust imposed by law on **union** officials, particularly with respect to the union's funds and the fair and disinterested representation of union members in **collective bargaining**.

field examiner—An employee of the **National Labor Relations Board** whose primary duties are to conduct **certification** elections and preliminary investigations into **unfair labor practice** charges.

fink—See **rat fink, Pinkertons, goon squads**.

FLECS (Flexible Employment Compensation & Scheduling Coalition)—A lobbying group composed of GOP and business interests formed in 1996 to push two bills, alternately called the "Working Families Flexibilty Act" and the "Family Friendly Workplace Act," through Congress. Either of the measures would effectively gut provisions of the 1938 **Fair Labor Standards Act** that require employers to pay time and a half for **overtime** worked beyond a 40-hour week, by offering employees the option of **compensatory time** instead. When they could take that comp time, however, would be up to management.

flexibility—A management term in use since the 1940s but in vogue since the early 1970s to stress the need for fewer restrictive **job-security** clauses in the contract so companies can operate more "competitively"; that is, at a higher profit at the expense of union **jurisdiction**.

Flint sit-down (1937)—Watershed event in innovative **job actions** in the American **labor movement** by which **Walter Reuther**'s nascent United Auto Workers (UAW) gained the respect—and membership—it had sought to bring the giant General Motors Corp. to the **bargaining table**. It began in the final days of 1936 when workers at a GM Fisher auto-body plant in Flint, Michigan, literally sat down on the job in protest over the disciplining of three co-workers for **union** activity. The protest quickly escalated to demands for, among other things, a 30-hour workweek, a six-hour day, **time and a half** for **overtime**, **seniority** rights and an end to **speedup**. GM, calling the action the work of "outside agitators" in service of a "vast conspiracy to destroy all for which life is worth living" and a blow that struck "at the very heart of the right of the possession of private property," sought an **injunction** against the sit-down, only to have it fizzle when it became publicly known that the judge issuing the injunction held $219,000 in GM stock.

The corporation also tried more direct measures in the month-long impromptu **strike**, including forming a GM-friendly **company union**, the Flint Alliance; shutting off all heat; and having local police storm the occupied plant. Three times in one day the truncheon-wielding, tear-gas-spraying cops, commonly called "bulls" in 1930s parlance, stormed the Fisher gates only to be repulsed by workers raining two-pound car hinges down on their heads and, in a freezing January midnight, dousing them with fire hoses. The ensuing rout was called the "Battle of the Running Bulls," though it was not without gunshot casualties on the workers' side.

Finally, in a ruse to head off what seemed like an inevitable company victory by dint of sheer force and legal power, other UAW militants seized and shut down a nearby Chevrolet plant, crippling a key component in production. GM caved, acknowledging the UAW as the workers' **bargaining agent** and setting the stage, several months and 18 sit-downs later, for the union's first **contract** with the company. By that time UAW membership had climbed to 400,000, up from only 30,000 a year before, which proved effective leverage not too long afterward for a similar contract with another Detroit-area automaking behemoth, the Chrysler Corp. (Contracts with the more militantly antiunion Ford Motor Co. were not to come until the early 1940s after long and bitter struggles.)

The Flint sit-down has been called the "Gettysburg of the **CIO**," **John L. Lewis**'s fledgling labor federation, which at first had taken a wait-and-see stance until the strikers proved their mettle.

floater—Obsolete term for an itinerant lineman, instrumental in early organizing efforts of the International Brotherhood of Electrical Workers. More recently used to mean a lineman who quits in the middle of the job.

flying picket—A highly mobile contingent of picketers that descends on a number of plants, job sites, or outlets of a struck employer, as opposed to pickets who are assigned to one place for an entire picket-duty **shift**.

Flynn, Elizabeth Gurley (1890–1964)—Labor leader, social reformer; known as "Joan of Arc of the IWW," for which she was an organizer; co-founder of American Civil Liberties Union (ACLU); joined Communist Party in 1936; spent two years in prison under Smith Act; died in Moscow.

Ford, Henry (1863–1947)—Bigoted, provincial, and rabidly antiu-

nion, the auto magnate nonetheless deserves credit for two major advances for the American worker: the **eight-hour workday** and decent **wages**—for the 1920s—of $5 a day ("so they can buy my product"), even if he did so to keep unions at bay.

free rider/freeloader—An employee who, in a **union shop**, shares whatever benefits and salary increases are negotiated in the contract but does not pay dues. Used derogatorily. Some contracts, for example, have a **one-in-ten clause** by which that ratio of employees, given a "time window" following their hiring, can choose not to belong to the union. These would be free riders and are not to be confused with **agency fee payers**. See **Appendix II**.

Free Trade Agreement—An agreement between Canada and the United States that was signed by both sides in 1988 and went into effect in January 1989. Among its terms were a phasing-out of all tariffs on U.S. imports within ten years, an end to U.S. quotas on Canadian uranium exports, abolition of all U.S. import taxes on Canadian oil exports, and no more U.S. customs user fees on any Canadian exports. A precursor to the North American Free Trade Agreement, or **NAFTA**, four years later, it continues to be opposed by Canadian **labor unions** for the same reasons—mainly, the flight of industries south, this time to the United States, where Canadian companies have found they can contend with weaker labor unions and operate under much less strigent labor laws.

frictional unemployment—Unemployment due to time lost in changing jobs rather than a lack of job opportunities; joblessness that would not be reduced significantly even if there were an increased demand on the labor market. See **cyclical**, **seasonal**, and **technological unemployment**.

friendly strike—A device occasionally used in the past whereby a manufacturer, in **collusion** with a **union**, would encourage or sanction a strike for the purpose of reducing the market glut and shoring up prices. The obverse side of a **sweetheart contract**.

fringe benefits—Negotiated contract provisions exclusive of **wages** and hours, such as health insurance, **pensions**, maternity leave, paid vacations, leaves of absence, mileage allowances, travel pay, etc. Although fringe benefits predate World War II, their growth was given a great boost in those years because wage rates were either frozen or subject to the limitations of the **Little Steel formula**, and fringes were not immediately inflationary. Therefore, they were given the blessing of the **National War Labor Board**. But over the past couple of decades they've become extremely inflationary—health costs, for example—and account for a greater percentage of labor costs and hence a greater source of friction between employers and **unions**. The business trend now is to drastically reduce fringe benefits, if not eliminate them entirely. See **permissive subjects of bargaining**.

front-loaded contract—A multiyear labor agreement in which the greater increases in **wages** or benefits kick in the first year. For instance, a three-year **contract** that calls for an overall increase of 15 percent might distribute that with 7 percent the first year and 4 percent the following two years. See **back-loaded contract**.

full-crew rule—A regulation stating the minimum number of workers required for a given operation. Originally devised as a safety precaution for both workers and the public, such rules are now the target of employers who allege they're used by **unions** to protect workers in jobs that are no longer essential. Railroad unions have been generally successful in getting the rule enacted into state law; railroad management contends the rule requiring a fireman to ride in the cab of a diesel locomotive, for example, is **featherbedding**.

full employment—Ideally, an employment level at which anyone willing and able to work can find a job. By taking into account the **frictional** and **seasonal unemployment** that always exists, however, an unemployment rate between 5 and 7 percent is about as close to full employment as labor economists can expect in the U.S. economy. (Up to the 1970s, the accepted figure was between 2 and 4 percent.)

Furuseth, Andrew (1854–1938)—Norwegian-born labor leader and sailor known as the "Abraham Lincoln of the Sea" by admirers, he immigrated to the United States in 1880 and served as president of the International Seaman's Union of America from 1908 to 1938. He was instrumental in passage of the progressive **La Follette Seaman's Act** of 1915. When he died at the age of 84, he became the first union leader to lie in state at the **Department of Labor** in the nation's capital. Asked what he would do if served with an **injunction** restraining him from certain union activities, he said: "I would put it in my pocket and the judge would put me in jail, and there my bunk would be no narrower, and my grub no poorer, nor I there more lonely than in the forecastle [of a ship]."

G

gang boss—In stevedoring, an elected position that carries a pay **differential** and is halfway between a **walking boss** and the work gang or crew. Although a member of the same **labor union** and technically not a supervisor, a gang boss can fire a gang member, but usually he simply transmits orders from the walking boss to the crew, keeps the time sheets, informs the gang about work locations, and sometimes suggests how the work might proceed.

Garner v. Teamsters—A U.S. Supreme Court ruling in 1953 that held that states had no right to regulate or interfere with labor conduct in interstate commerce when that conduct was already controlled by federal law (e.g., the **Hobbs Act**). While hardly a counterbalance to Hobbs, Garner did eliminate redundancy in the matter and had the effect of clearing court dockets nationwide of similar charges brought by states against **unions**.

gearmen—In stevedoring, the longshoremen who work in the "gear locker" and who are responsible for keeping in working order all the chains, bridles, hooks, and lifts used in winch work. They build, repair, handle and haul all stevedoring equipment.

General Motors strike (1945–46)—One of the biggest—it involved more than 320,000 workers—of the numerous strikes to hit immediate post–World War II America in an effort to make up for the **wage freezes** and general lack of labor gains imposed by the war and to set the pattern for all U.S. wage earners in the prosperity labor and business leaders felt was sure to come. **Walter Reuther**'s United Auto Workers (UAW) was asking for a 30 percent wage increase, which the **union** believed justified in light of the huge wartime profits GM and other giant corporations had made.In fact, Reuther asked that GM "open the books" to prove this was so, which an outraged management refused to do. The company countered with an offer of 10 percent; that, too, was refused. Striker attitudes were militant; the GM walk-out triggered well-planned albeit brief **general strikes** in Houston; Oakland, California; Rochester, New York; Stamford and Hartford, Connecticut; Camden, New Jersey; and Lancaster, Pennsylvania. But after 113 days, the UAW settled for an 18-cent-an-hour hike—the same as striking steelworkers and other big **industrial unions** agreed to at the time. Months later, Reuther's and other labor leaders' worst fears were realized when the Truman administration reluctantly lifted wartime price controls and overall consumer prices shot up more than 15 percent, wiping out whatever gains were made in the 1945–46 strikes. In 1950, however, Reuther concluded a **settlement** with GM that brought an increase of 20 percent in workers' standard of living over five years—which meant a built-in **cost-of-living allowance** that greatly cushioned the postwar price spiral.

general strike—A **strike** involving not only the workers of a particular employer or of the representative **labor union** and its allies against that employer but also of other, unassociated unions and the community as well; an effort, in effect, to "shut down the city" until grievances are addressed or a situation remedied. Among U.S. cities hit by general strikes in this century, with varying degrees of success, were Springfield, Illinois; Billings, Montana; Waco, Texas; and Kansas City, Missouri (all during the World War I years); Seattle (1919); Boston (1919), and San Francisco (1934). See **Seattle General Strike.**

givebacks—See **takebacks.**

George Meany Center for Labor Studies—Also called the National Labor College, the center—previously called the **AFL-CIO** Labor Studies Center—was founded in 1969 and is situated on a 47-acre campus just outside Washington, D.C., in Silver Spring, Maryland. It was established in 1974 by AFL-CIO chief **George Meany**, who foresaw a need for special training for union leaders who would face new problems in the 1980s. In

February 2007, an additional 72,000-square-foot facility, the **Lane Kirkland** Center, was built nearby to handle the overload from the college. See **Harry takes a seat**, **Organizing Institute**.

Gompers, Samuel (1850–1924)—English-born U.S. labor leader and a founder of the American Federation of Labor (**AFL**), in 1886; its president until his death. A Marxist in early days, he turned against socialists in the AFL, championing a "pure and simple" **trade unionism** hostile to independent political action.

 Instead, the former Cigarmakers Union head believed labor would fare well in the political arena by simply "rewarding its friends and punishing its enemies"—a strategy employed to this day. Gompers was strictly dollars and sense. Whereas the lofty motto of the earlier **Knights of Labor** was "An injury to one is the concern of all," Gompers's was "A fair day's wage for a fair day's work." A highly respected figure in American public life, Gompers served on the Advisory Commission to the Council of National Defense (1917–18) and as a member of the U.S. delegation to the Paris Peace Conference in 1919.

Memorable quote: *"The working people know no country. They are citizens of the world.*

See **Green, William.**

goon squads—Armed groups employed by companies to discourage unionism, break **strikes**, and generally terrorize unsubmissive workers. Although organized goon squads had been unleashed against **unions** and strikers since the post–Civil War days, the term itself didn't come into use until the 1930s, particularly after the **La Follette Committee** revealed large companies' accumulation of "**industrial munitions**," their practice of the **Mohawk Valley formula**, and the violence of the 1937 **Little Steel Strike**. Before then, the term of approbation was **fink**, which became **rat fink** in the late 1960s.

grandfather clause ("grandfathering")—A **contract** provision stipulating that employees hired or working before a specified date shall not be subject to certain terms of a new contract. For instance, a management employee who is assigned to a job within the union's **jurisdiction** may be "grandfathered," meaning he or she doesn't have to belong to the **union**. Likewise, a union member in a newly **excluded position** may be allowed to stay in that position—"grandfathered"—and allowed to be part of the **bargaining unit** until he or she leaves.

graveyard shift—Usually, a midnight-to-8 A.M. work **shift**; so named because of the traditional spookiness of the wee hours. First heard around 1915 in shipyards and munitions plants, which were scheduling round-the-clock work in an effort to supply World War I allies. See **swing shift, lobster shift**.

great textile strike (1934)—A 133-day strike that began in Woonsocket, Rhode Island; spread to half a dozen states in New England and the South; and eventually involved nearly 400,000 strikers. For Rhode Island, whose textile industry sired the **Industrial Revolution** in the United States, the strike was the state's longest and most violent to date, causing two deaths and hundreds of injuries. In all, 16 workers were shot dead in the course of the strike as governors called out militias and the National Guard.

Woonsocket was not exactly a **company town**; it was a textile town, incorporated in 1888 from six mill village complexes that had harnessed the Blackstone River to power their looms. But by the early 1930s no fewer than 14 large mills had closed, victims of the collapse of the cotton market, the Great Depression, and the move to the South for cheaper **wages**.

It was into this economic uncertainty that the Independent Textile Union, later the Industrial Trade Union (ITU) and then the Textile Workers Union of America, was born in 1931. As the 1934 strike went into its third week, the textile industry was shut down. The union took this to mean victory and staged a number of parades. Big mistake. The strike was already falling apart, particularly in the South, where local governments refused to provide any relief assistance to strikers and there were few sympathetic churches or unions to lend support. Thousands of strikers drifted back to work or drifted away.

Though it represented the high point for union hopes of **organizing** in the South, the strike was a total defeat for the ITU and spelled the later failure of **Operation Dixie**. The memory of post-strike **blacklisting** and loss of jobs soured many southern textile workers on unions for decades. Most of the mills of Woonsocket, where it all began, ultimately closed, moved, or went bankrupt. See **industrial union**.

green grows a union—The United Steelworkers (USW) teams with the Sierra Club to form the environmentally conscious Blue-Green Alliance and demonstrate that, according to a press release, "investments in clean energy can create thousands of new manufacturing jobs . . . across the country."

Green, William (1873–1952)—Successor to **Sam Gompers** as head of the American Federation of Labor (**AFL**), where he presided from 1924 until his death. A coal miner by trade, Green had been an Ohio state senator and secretary-treasurer of the United Mine Workers of America (UMWA). He helped shape the **National Industrial Recovery Act** of 1933 and the **National Labor Relations Act** of 1935, although, like most of his higher-up confreres in the AFL, he had no use for **industrial unionism**. When Green was elected to his AFL post, says historian Foster Rhea Dulles, "the business community breathed a sigh of relief."

grievance/grievance procedure—A dispute between a **union** member or the union and management over a workplace situation, potential or actual health hazard, or alleged **contract** violation that is adjudicated through a procedure established in the contract. Either side may take an unresolved grievance to the next step: **arbitration**, whereby a binding decision sets a **precedent** that governs future grievances over the same issue. The word *grievance* has been used in English since at least 1481 to mean a complaint.

Guaranteed Annual Wage (GAW) plan—In the days of greater **labor union** presence in the American workplace, a plan in which an employer agreed to provide employees a minimum of employment or income for a year. Not widely practiced even in its heyday, the GAW nonetheless was an important

bargaining issue in years past. Unions argued that such plans added significantly to income and job stability; management contended they didn't take into account the fluctuating demand for goods and added greatly to the risk of investment since **wages** would have to be paid even if the investment proved unprofitable. A landmark 1955 compromise resulting from the United Auto Workers'' demand of a GAW from the Ford Motor Co. was the nation's first **supplemental unemployment benefit** plan.

Guffey-Snyder Act—A coal industry law enacted by Congress in August 1935 that established a National Bituminous Coal Commission, promulgated a code, established minimum prices, and guaranteed labor the right of **collective bargaining**.

guild—See **associations, brotherhoods, guilds, & unions**.

gypsies—Independent, nonunion truckers who drive longer hours for less pay than Teamster members. In one sense, they are **scabs** or permanent **replacement workers**; in another sense, they are independent businessmen and women who contract on their own.

H

hard hat—A construction worker, because of the metal or hard plastic helmets such workers wear. In the 1880s, however, it meant a man who wore a derby, an Eastern banker or businessman. Nearly a century later, in the 1960s, the term took on, in addition to its construction connotation, that of **blue-collar** political conservative because of the frequent—and well-publicized—clashes between hard hats and anti–Vietnam War protesters. See **white-collar workers**.

Harry takes a seat—Established in 1992, the University of Washington's **Harry Bridges** Endowed Chair and Center for Labor Studies is one of the few joint endeavors of higher education and labor. The center promotes teaching and research in labor politics and engages in community outreach for and about working people and their organizations. The $1 million–plus start-up funds were raised by Washington state unions and their members, both retired and active, and by the International Longshoremen's and Warehousemen's Union (ILWU) nationwide, in just two years.

Haymarket affair—Alternately called the Haymarket Riot or the Haymarket Massacre; a multiphased event that started May 3, 1886, when police fired on a workers' rally in support of the eight-hour day and of a strike organized against the McCormick Harvesting Machine Co. in Chicago, killing four people. The following day at another rally, this time organized by a small group of anarchists in Chicago's Haymarket Square to protest the

 police shootings, a bomb was lobbed into a group of cops, fatally wounding eight. Police then fired wildly into the crowd, killing another eight people and wounding about 100—half of them fellow officers. In retaliation, hundreds of socialists, anarchists, and other radicals were rounded up, and

eight anarchists were indicted and eventually convicted for conspiracy—though none was charged with throwing the bomb (it was never found out who tossed it; speculation abounds that it was the work of an agent provocateur). Of the eight men convicted, four were hanged, one committed suicide, and three were pardoned by Illinois governor **John Peter Altgeld**. The Haymarket affair proved to be a seminal event in U.S. labor history. It effectively, though unjustly, ended the Knights' meteoric rise, poisoned the public's perception of labor for decades, and laid the groundwork for future **Red scares**.

Haywood, William "Big Bill" (1869–1928)—Radical U.S. labor leader and a hard-rock miner from the age of nine, Haywood became secretary-treasurer of the **Western Federation of Miners** in 1900 and in 1905 co-founded the **Industrial Workers of the World**. In 1907 he was charged in the bombing murder of former Idaho Governor Frank Steunenberg but, defended by Clarence Darrow, was acquitted. Although he later led partially successful textile strikes in **Lawrence**, Massachusetts (1912) and  **Paterson**, New Jersey (1913), Haywood's inceasing advocacy of violence prompted his old union, the WFM, to dismiss him and pull out of the IWW (1918). Earlier, the Socialist Party ousted him from its councils for the same reasons. Convicted of violating wartime alien and sedition acts in 1918 and sentenced to 20 years in prison, Haywood jumped bail and fled to the fledgling Soviet Union in 1921. He died there and was buried beneath the Kremlin walls.

Memorable quote: *"We are going down into the gutter to get the mass of workers and bring them up to a decent plane of living."*

health benefits and coverage—The 1,000-pound gorilla sitting on every **bargaining table**. When President Harry S. Truman proposed a national health care program in 1947, **organized labor** was all for it, but Congress wasn't, so nothing happened.

The problem is the negotiated medical package has long since come unwrapped. As treatment, prescription medicines, and hospital-care expenses have soared, more and more employers are balking at the costs, particularly those involving retirees. (**Medicare** handles those over 65, but employees who took **early buyouts** or who were laid off need companies' extra help.)

In Detroit, the major battlefield in this issue, the Big Three auto companies spent $10 billion to cover more than 2 million United Auto Workers active members and retirees in 2006. It is said only half-jokingly that General Motors (GM) is actually a giant health-insurance provider—just one that happens to make cars. U.S. automakers pay their factory workers an average of $73 in wages and benefits an hour, compared to $44 for the three major Japanese automakers operating plants in North America, according to industry data. Medical benefits account for most of the difference.

In 2005, GM spent $5.3 billion on health care for its employees, up nearly 80 percent from 1996. According to the Labor

Research Association, benefits now represent 37.4 percent of total compensation for union members—the highest proportion ever recorded—compared with 27.6 percent for nonunion employees. Even union leaders concede that, absent a now-desired single-payer national health plan similar to the Canadian or European models, there has to be some give. But they also realize that a cut in health care costs with no equivalent increase in wages is tantamount to a wage cut—not a big sell with members.

One possible solution being bandied about in Detroit is to spin the health care problem back to the union, with the automakers each agreeing to pour billions of dollars into a trust fund affiliated with the UAW to help provide for retirees' health insurance. It would certainly be radical—traditionally, labor contracts have meant concessions *to* the UAW, not *by* them.

Helmets to Hardhats—A national program initiated by the Center for Military Recruitment, Assessment and Veterans Employment, facilitating the transition of military veterans—women as well as men—to construction-industry training and jobs. Helmets to Hardhats business and union participants range from boilermakers to the Walt Disney World Company.

Herrin Massacre—A relatively little-known but bloody event of 1922 in southern Illinois that, like **Industrial Workers of the World** actions of a decade before, turned the public against unionism, and one in which mineworkers chief **John L. Lewis** played an indirect part. Early that year, Lewis began negotiations with area coal operators, but when they balked, the miners went on **strike**. Despite harsh suppression of the striking coal diggers, the **walkout** was peaceful—until the mine owners brought in members of a Chicago steamshovel **union** to resume operations and set up a company stockade. Strikers who attempted to confer with the **scabs** were met with machine-gun fire, which killed 17 men; the enraged strikers responded by attacking the stockade. The stockade surrendered, and 19 of the **strikebreakers** were captured and marched back at gunpoint toward the tiny town of Herrin, Illinois. They never got there. Eyewitness recollections are hazy, and no one seems to remember who provoked whom, but the result was that all 19 unarmed captives were shot to death before reaching their destination. Subsequent trials resulted in the imprisonment of most of the men responsible for the massacre, but, as a National Public Radio oral history of the event in 1997 revealed, feelings remain inflamed. "They were taking *our jobs*," wheezed one unrepentant participant 75 years afterward. Because of a backlash against the massacre, Lewis was forced to make concessions and lost western Pennsylvania, Maryland, Virginia, West Virginia, Alabama, Texas, Utah, and Colorado—a mineworkers constituency he was not to regain till many years later.

Hill, Joe (Joel Hägglund or Joseph Hillstrom) (1879–1915)— Swedish-born U.S. labor leader, songwriter (wrote "pie in the sky when you die" lyrics); convicted of murder on dubious evidence and shot by firing squad in Utah; remembered for his parting words to **"Big Bill" Haywood**: "Don't mourn. Organize." Perhaps even more memorable, though, are the 1938 lyrics of songwriter **Earl Robinson**:

> *I dreamed I saw Joe Hill last night*
> *Alive as you and me*
> *Says I, "But Joe, you're 10 years dead."*
> *"I never died," says he,*
> *"I never died," says he.*

Hillman, Sidney (1887–1946)—Lithuanian-born influential U.S. labor leader and, as such, consultant to President Franklin D. Roosevelt, whose "Clear it with Sidney" became a catchphrase in  the 1930s and early 1940s. As immigrant garment worker, Hillman emerged in the 1910 Hart, Schaffner & Marx **strike** in Chicago as a major leader of the United Garment Workers (UGW) and negotiated a **contract** regarded as a model of labor-management relations. In 1914 he went to New York, where he led a split from the UGW that resulted in the new Amalgamated Clothing Workers of America (ACWA), a **union** of which he remained president from then until his death. By 1940, Hillman's ACWA dominated the manufacture of men's clothing and had pioneered such reforms as the 40-hour week and industry-wide **wage** scales. A strong backer of Roosevelt's New Deal, he was appointed as labor adviser to the National Recovery Administration in 1933 and to several **war-production boards** during World War II; as co-founder of the **Congress of Labor Organizations** (CIO), he was the first chairman of the CIO's Political Action Committee, a forerunner of **COPE**, and a vice-chairman of the newly founded World Federation of Trade Unions (1945–46). An advocate of cooperation instead of confrontation between labor and management, Hillman broke ground in such things as his union's lending money to companies and providing research to improve efficiency. By the 1990s, however, U.S. garment workers' unions were ghosts of their former selves and much of Hillman's work was undone as clothing manufacturers either massively **outsourced** or had transferred operations overseas to avoid paying higher wages.

Memorable quote: *"Labor will rule."*

hiring hall—Often called a **dispatch** office; where **labor union** job-seekers go to find what's available and be sent there. In the days of the **closed shop**, hiring halls were run exclusively by unions for the benefit of their members, and one had to be a card-carrying union member even to get in. Since 1947, when the closed shop was outlawed by the **Taft-Hartley Act**, hiring halls have commonly come to be operated jointly by labor and management, often with state assistance or supervision. In fact, most people looking for work today don't go to a "hiring hall," they go to a "state employment office." Union hiring halls, however, continue to function in some of the casual-labor trades—the construction and maritime industries, for example—but must not limit their services to union members only. Often, though, a worker placed in a job is later asked to become a union member.

hit the bricks—To go out on **strike**; a union term going back to the turn of the 19th century, when most streets, where strikers would walk the **picket line**, were paved with bricks or cobblestones.

Hobbs Act—Enacted by Congress in August 1946 amid a postwar spate of antiunion legislation, this law made it a felony to obstruct, delay, or interfere with the movement of goods in interstate commerce. See **Garner v. Teamsters**.

Hoffa, James P. (1941–)—Son of Jimmy Hoffa and a major contender for the presidency of his father's old **union** despite his narrow 1996 defeat by **Ron Carey**. A relatively obscure Teamster lawyer for most of his professional life, the younger Hoffa quit law practice in 1995 to work as a Teamster staff aide to ready himself for a shot at the 1.4 million-member union's leadership the following year. Carey's downfall came in 1997 from alleged campaign finance violations and Hoffa ascended to the post the year after, following federal scrutiny into *his* campaign finances. He was reelected to a new five-year term in 2006.

Hoffa, James Riddle "Jimmy" (1913–1975)—Fiery and feisty leader of the International Brotherhood of Teamsters (IBT) in the 1950s, 1960s, and 1970s. He first came into the public eye with his acidulous and oft-televised feud with U.S. Senator Robert F. Kennedy during Senate racket hearings in the late

1950s, but is best known among **labor union** members for his winning them substantial increases in **benefits** and **wages** in a cutthroat trucking industry. Born in Brazil, Indiana, Hoffa became an IBT organizer in 1934 and rose rapidly through the ranks until, in 1957, he was elected Teamsters president, succeeding the disgraced and soon-to-be imprisoned **Dave Beck**. With Beck disposed of, Hoffa increasingly became the target of Senate and other investigations, mainly because of his association with known Mob figures and dubious Teamster **pension** investments in Mob enterprises. Though Hoffa probably never profited personally from the corruption and racketeering that infiltrated Teamster ranks, and indications are that no Teamster pensioner ever suffered a loss because of the questionable diversion of funds, Hoffa was eventually convicted in 1967 on charges of jury tampering, fraud, and conspiracy. His sentence was commuted in 1971 by President Richard M. Nixon, report-edly in exchange for Teamster support in Nixon's 1972 reelec-tion and a pledge that Hoffa would not regain power. He was rumored to be trying to do just that when, in 1975, he mysteri-ously disappeared; his likely murder still is a cause of specula-tion. Despite Hoffa's dark side, however, even his detractors con-cede that his negotiation of a 1964 **contract** that covered most of the nation's 400,000 road and cartage drivers ranked among the major accomplishments of any union leader in the history of the **labor movement**. A somewhat sympathetic—and somewhat fictionalized—idea of Hoffa the man emerges in actor Jack Nicholson's outstanding portrayal in the 1992 movie *Hoffa*.

Memorable quote (of his early **organizing** days in Detroit): *"Any labor organizer who didn't get in trouble with the police was either buying them off or he wasn't doing his job."*

holdwork—In conventional longshoring, labor done in the hold of a ship; contractually, the most unskilled labor on the waterfront. The work varies from "hand handling" cargo—literally moving cargo by hand—to driving forklifts, from lashing cargoes to decks to humping 500-pound bales containing the hides of dead animals.

Hollywood—A study in labor-relations paradox. For a town with **wall-to-wall** unions in almost every phase of moviemaking, its depiction of labor and **unions** has been almost universally nega-tive and largely inaccurate. With the exception of a handful of movies—*Norma Rae* (1979), *Matewan* (1987), *Silkwood* (1983), *Salt of the Earth* (1953), *Wall Street* (1987), *The Grapes of Wrath* (1940), *Picture Bride* (1994), *El Norte* (1983), *The Killing Floor* (1984), and a few others—organized workers, unions, and their leaders are the objects of jokes or portrayed as corrupt, mobster-ridden, brutal, duplicitous if not dupes, violence-prone (*On the Waterfront* is a classic in virtually all categories so far), or com-pletely irrelevant to the American scene. Scholars of the subject attribute the bias to a decline of 1930s social liberalism and its subsequent equation with don't-touch dangerous radicalism in the Red-baiting and **blacklisting** 1950s, others to the dominance of the multiconglomerate bottom-line mentality of the industry. Neither explanation suffices. But unhappily for those in the **labor movement**, Hollywood influences to a great extent—and always has—how the American public perceives that movement and its players.

Homestead Strike (1892)—Major steel strike that pitted the Carnegie Corp. against the Amalgamated Association of Iron, Steel, and Tin Workers of the fledgling American Federation of Labor (**AFL**) at the Homestead steelworks near Pittsburgh. Andrew Carnegie, corporate owner of the 12-mill, 3,800-employee Homestead works who wanted a cheap and docile labor force, conveniently left for a lengthy vacation in his native Scotland as things heated up, leaving the dirty work of **union-busting** to hardline associate Henry Clay Frick. Frick immediately surrounded the mills with three miles of 12-foot-high steel fence topped with barbed wire, dubbed "Fort Frick" by the workers; he made plans for replacing all **union** labor with **permanent replacement workers**, and arranged for a bargeload of 300 armed **Pinkertons** to protect these **scabs**. The barge was met, however, by a contingent of equally determined, locked-out steelworkers in a July 5 clash that killed a dozen men on each side and injured scores more. Though the Pinkertons surrendered in that battle, Frick's war eventually broke the strike and ended steel unionism in the Pittsburgh area for a generation. It did, however, give impetus to the rise of the **industrial union**.

Hormel Strike (1985–86)—A spirited but doomed **strike** by Local P-9 of the United Food and Commercial Workers union (UFCW) against the George A. Hormel Co. meatpacking plant in Austin,

 Minnesota, which, along with the **PATCO** and **Phelps-Dodge** strikes, ranked among the major setbacks dealt the **labor movement** in the 1980s. Rejecting a proposed cut in **wages** from $10.69 to $8.25 an hour and a 30 percent reduction in **benefits**—in a year following the company's posting of a $29 million profit—workers walked out in

August 1985. Sympathy was high; tens of thousands of people throughout the Midwest rallied behind the strikers, but the strike was done in by a number of factors, not the least of which was intraunion politics. The pragmatic UFCW **international union** leadership, reading the Reaganite handwriting on the wall, wanted P-9 to settle in a battle it felt it could not win; the **local** instead hired a labor public-relations specialist and waged hardball media war. In the meantime, the company hired **permanent replacement workers** at $10.25 an hour, and the governor called out the National Guard to police the **picket lines** in an increasingly bitter confrontation. In the end, the parent UFCW ousted the local's hard-liners and made its own settlement with Hormel that included a wage of $10.25—the same the **scabs** were making—and no provision for a return to work of hundreds who had honored the picket lines. The new terms were ratified by the dispirited membership of a broken P-9 in September 1986. In 1989, Hormel subleased the Austin plant to a company that paid $6.50 an hour. For an in-depth treatment of the strike, see Barbara Kopple's Academy Award–winning documentary film *American Dream*.

hot cargo—Material that has been produced or handled by **scabs** at a struck plant, or goods that have been placed on the **unfair list**. Contract provisions allowing workers to refuse to handle such shipments were outlawed in the **Landrum-Griffin Act** of 1959, except for some construction and garment-industry work. Such provisions are also known variously as struck-work, chain-shop, trade-shop, refusal-to-handle, right-to-terminate, and right-to-reopen clauses.

hot-shop organizing—Site-by-site **organizing**, as opposed to industrywide or craftwide organizing. For example, if the employees of certain outlets in a nationwide retail chain expressed interest in joining a **union**, organizers of that union might target just those outlets—or the outlets in a given area—for a **certification** election and leave the others alone.

house visits, homecalls, housecalls—Terms used to describe visits by **union** staff, volunteers, or organizing-committee members to the homes of employees they are attempting to organize.

Huerta, Dolores (1930–)—Cofounder, with **César Chávez**, of the United Farm Workers union (UFW) and Chávez's right-hand woman. Born Dolores Clara Fernández in New Mexico, she grew up in California's predominantly agricultural San Joaquin Valley, where she founded the Agricultural Workers Association (AWA) in 1960; after becoming the AWA's lobbyist in the state capital of Sacramento, she was instrumental in passage of legislation allowing the right to vote in Spanish. In 1962, she joined Chávez in Delano, California, where they both began the National Farm Workers Association, predecessor to the UFW. In 1966, both also launched the five-year grape strike and consumer **boycott** that, together with the lettuce and Gallo wine boycotts a few years later, changed the nation's eating and drinking habits to some extent. In 1974, she played a key part in securing **unemployment benefits** for farmworkers and in passage of the Immigration Act of 1985 under which an estimated 1.4 million "illegal" farmworkers received amnesty. In the course of these activities, she was arrested 22 times in peaceful pro-union protests. She currently serves as president of the Dolores Huerta Foundation, which is involved in labor and community organizing and in support of *La Causa*.

I

illegal subjects of bargaining—Subjects that, even if an **agreement** were reached on them through, for example, coercion or expediency, would be held illegal under labor law and therefore unenforceable. For example, **contract** provisions for a closed shop, for a **hiring hall** giving sole preference to **union** members, for separation of employees by race, or for the right to fire employees for union activity all would be illegal under **National Labor Relations Board** rules. See **mandatory** and **permissive subjects of bargaining**.

immigrant rights—In contrast with its occasional outright hostility toward immigrants in the past, the **labor movement** now actively champions immigrants' rights and citizenship for undocumented workers. When asked why unions are fighting for "the illegals who have been taking our jobs," **AFL-CIO** president John Sweeney replied, "I remind them of a powerful statement from labor's past: An injury to one is an injury to all. America's broken immigration system has allowed employers to create a low-wage labor pool. . . . When employers [do that] to one group of workers, they harm us all." He added: "Some 12 million undocumented immigrants are here today—that's reality—and they are working and paying taxes and strengthening our economy and our culture." Unions are also not blind to the fact that record numbers of Latinos coming to the United States can, once naturalized, considerably sway political and labor elections. See **immigrants in the U.S. labor movement**.

immigrants in the U.S. labor movement—Almost always exploited, frequently despised, and on occasion banned outright from entering the country, immigrants have always formed the backbone of the U.S. workforce. Immigrants or their sons and daughters stud the leadership rolls of the American **labor movement: Mother Jones, Philip Murray, Harry Bridges, David Dubinsky, Walter Reuther, Joe Hill**, and **Sidney Hillman** are but a few. Enough foreign-born workers have gravitated to particular industries or trades to form historical patterns, if not stereotypes: the Irish in railroads, mines, and the building trades; the Chinese in railroad building; Slavs and Italians in coal mines; Slavs and Hungarians in steel mills; Jews and Russians in the garment industry; Mexicans, Filipinos, and Japanese in farmworking; Filipinos in fish canneries; women of all nationalities in the textile mills. Although in reality immigrants were all over the labor map, just as they are today, this "ethnic specialization" often was by design; 19th-century corporations and their agents abroad actively recruited workers—usually unskilled—for a particular industry, or met them with offers as they came off the boat. This was especially true of the Italian and Slavic coal miners and of Chinese rail workers. Just as often, immigrants who had secured a job in mine or mill encouraged their friends and relatives in the old country to join them. Frequently, importing workers had unintended consequences, at least for employers. Perhaps the first **strike** in recorded U.S. history occurred in 1619 in the Virginia Colony when Polish workers in a glass factory refused to work further until they were granted the same voting privileges as English settlers (they won). Descendants of the first Dutch glassblowers brought to New Jersey in the 1830s formed the first glassblowing union in the United States. The repression that followed the failed 1905 Russian Revolution sent thousands of Eastern Europeans into U.S. exile and, as their influence spread in immigrant communities, workers grew increasingly receptive to collective action and political radicalism—principally in the form of **labor unions**. About half the thousands of immigrants to Colonial America came as indentured servants—a step above slaves—who worked as **apprentices** in a trade to pay off their debts. (The real slaves, the blacks forcibly emigrated here in slave ships, didn't have it so easy. As freedmen before and after the Civil War, they gradually—and begrudgingly—had to work their way into the ranks of paid labor.) But after the **Industrial Revolution**, the maw of the American **factory system** swallowed immigrants by the millions— more than 1 million arrived in each of six different years between 1905 and 1914 to supplement the millions already here. And employers were always quick to exploit the differences between these largely unskilled, non-English-speaking hordes and their skilled, usually Northern European–descended, English-speaking brethren, the Irish excepted. Animosities were sometimes encouraged; it was a good way of undercutting labor unity. At the turn of the century, workers at the American Woolen mill in Lawrence, Massachusetts, walked off the job because the company had put an Irish washerwoman into their cutting room to scrub the floor. Railroad tycoon/robber baron Jay Gould once boasted he could "hire one-half of the working class to kill the other half."

American labor unions, taken as a whole, were always ambivalent about immigrants. The more militant, vertically integrated **industrial unions** and federations such as the **Knights of Labor**, the **Industrial Workers of the World (IWW)**, and the Congress of Industrial Organizations (**CIO**) openly welcomed them; they saw strength in numbers. On the other hand, the **craft** or **trade unions**, in particular the American Federation of Labor (AFL), saw immigrants as a competitive threat to their relatively high wages. The AFL and its affiliates hailed the restrictive Immigration Act of 1921 and its even more restrictive version of 1924 as a "victory for labor." And both the Knights and the AFL actively lobbied for the Chinese Exclusion Act of 1882 and its extension ten years later.

To this day, immigrants continue to pour into the U.S. labor market. How unions can best recruit them and hold their loyalty is a subject of great concern and debate in American labor circles. See **blacks in the labor movement, Lawrence** and **Paterson textile strikes.**

impasse—A legal term used to describe a stage in **contract** negotiations reached when one, the other, or both sides refuse to bargain further or agree that talks cannot proceed without **mediation** or some other action to break the stalemate. Contrary to frequent media reports, a temporary stall or breakdown in talks is not necessarily an impasse.

improper practice—Conduct prohibited by the New York Labor and Management Improper Practices Act of 1959; for example, bribery of **union** officials by employers and labor relations consultants and conflicts of interest among union officials—actions that would be condemned in any case by the **AFL-CIO**'s **Code of Ethical Practices.** The term is also used in public-employee relations as a substitute for **unfair labor practice.**

incentive pay—In its modern guise, it's called **pay for performance**, a system initiated by the auto and aircraft industries in the early 1940s as a war-production measure whereby some workers would be paid a **differential** for more and better work than others. In a certain sense, it was a bonus for **piecework**, an incentive-pay concept the **War Production Board** broadened from an individual to a group basis. **Unions** had long opposed individual piecework pay, believing it set one worker against another and destroyed unity and **solidarity**. However, they accepted the production board's collective interpretation (i.e., a factory's entire workforce could earn more if production rose).

independent contractor—See **contract worker**.

independent union—A union that is not **affiliated** with the **AFL-CIO**. The National Education Association is an example. Several independent unions have reaffiliated in recent years: the United Mine Workers, the International Longshoremen's and Warehousemen's Union, and the Teamsters, for instance. Not to be confused with **company union**. See **Appendix I** for a list of independent unions.

"industrial munitions"—An employer euphemism of the 1930s to mean weapons especially adapted for use in labor disputes— submachine guns, tear gas, nauseous gas, grenades, and shells. The practice came to light in hearings of the **La Follette Committee** and, along with other tools of the trade such as the **Mohawk Valley formula**, led to widespread public support for the newly enacted **National Labor Relations Act** and convinced the public that labor needed not only sympathy but protection as well. See **goon squads, labor spies, union-busting, rat finks**.

Industrial Revolution—A term coined in the 1870s to describe the transformation, beginning in England in the late 1700s, of a small-scale economy based on the production of individually handmade goods to a large-scale one based on machine- and factory-made products, which gave rise to the **factory system**. This in turn produced a new **working class** called labor (about 1830) and a **labor movement** (1830s), which was not called that until, again, the 1870s. Historians have come to divide this profound transformation into two distinct periods, with some arguing for inclusion of a third, extending into our own times:

The First Industrial Revolution (FIR): Beginning in the 1780s in Britain, resulting in the rapid adoption of three new technologies—the steam engine, usually relying on coal for fuel;

machines for spinning cloth and weaving cloth and increasingly driven by steam rather than waterpower; and furnaces (blast, puddling, and rolling) to make iron ore into finished steel by using coal. Symbolic of this first phase, at least in the United States, was the inauguration of George Washington in 1789—the first president wore a suit made by the Hartford Woolen Manufactory, the first domestic textile mill in which waterpower was used. An essential component of the FIR was the standardization of parts, introduced by Eli Whitney with his 1793 invention of the cotton gin, thus giving rise to an entire family of machine tools—machines for making other machines. The early stages of the FIR were in some ways benevolent, freeing thousands of men, women, and children from the drudgery and hardship of the subsistence family farm in return for a familial albeit paternalistic work setting in which they could actually earn money. This changed in the 1830s when merchant capitalists, who had gained control of most of the mills, demanded increased production and profits. This generated not only the first **speedups** when (usually) women, who earlier had to tend just one loom, now had charge of three or four, but also replaced cooperation with exploitation, in turn giving rise to massive discontent—and to the need for collective action. Early harbingers were the Lowell **Female Labor Reform Association** and the **Factory Girls Association**; a later result was the emergence of **trade** or **craft unions** and their increased **bargaining** power.

   The Second Industrial Revolution (SIR): Beginning at the end of the Civil War and centered in the United States and Germany, characterized by in-place communications and transportation networks—the telegraph, steamships, railroads, and cable—that made possible the high-volume distribution of goods and services; the coming of electricity in the 1880s, which provided a more flexible source of power than steam for industrial machinery, a new means of cheap urban transportation—trolleys and subways—and safer illumination in factories, offices, and homes; as well as transforming chemical and metallurgical processes. A third development in the SIR was the beginning of the application of science to industry and to the creation of new and improved consumer and industrial products. The SIR, lasting well into the 20th century, brought tens of millions into the workforce, many of them unskilled and many of them immigrants, a challenge to the **labor movement** that was met in varying degrees of success or failure by such organizations as the **Knights of St. Crispin**, the **Knights of Labor**, and the **Industrial Workers of the World (IWW)** in the latter half of the 19th century and early 20th. It was not until the 1930s and the rise of the Congress of Industrial Organizations (**CIO**), however, that the movement successfully came to grips with **organizing** America's vast mass-production, capital-intensive industries spawned by the SIR.

The cybernetic or computer revolution (CR): A high-tech, some would say inevitable, outgrowth of the SIR, others that it was a revolution in itself; beginning in the U.S. during the 1950s and accelerating exponentially through the 1970s, 1980s, and 1990s. Called in its earlier stages **automation**, i.e., the replacing of human operators with machines, the CR evolved at already-established corporations that had earlier been turning out business machines such as electric calculators and cash registers—IBM, Honeywell, Remington Rand, and National Cash Register—and now turned their production to mainframe and later, joined by a host of innovating companies (Microsoft, Apple, etc.), personal computers. The CR has transformed production, distribution, communications, and management throughout the U.S. economy as much as its predecessor, the Second Industrial Revolution, did a century before, only this time hastening the decline rather than the rise of the **blue-collar worker**, lessening the influence of **unions** in the workplace, and presenting a new, daunting challenge to the labor movement. See **factory system, immigrants in the labor movement, working women's movement.**

industrial union—A union representing all workers, both skilled and unskilled, in a plant or industry. Before the **CIO**—the Congress of Industrial Organizations—in the 1930s, unions in a plant or industry were organized on **craft** or **trade** lines and were the bailiwick of the American Federation of Labor (**AFL**).

Industrial Union Department—A division of the **AFL-CIO**, often in charge of massive **organizing** efforts.

Industrial Workers of the World (IWW)—Alternately called the **Wobblies** and often, erroneously, the "International" Workers of the World; a radical, heavily socialist labor federation that rose and fell between 1905 and the **Red scares** and vigilantism of the immediate post–World War I period, though it continues to exist today, primarily in the West. The IWW in its brief heyday, fired up by the charismatic **"Big Bill" Haywood** (a co-founder of the IWW was **Eugene B. Debs**), attempted to organize everybody from casual laborers to cowboys in "one big industrial **union**," though its major, if temporary, successes were in hard-rock mining, Northwest timber, West Coast docks, East Coast textiles (the Paterson, New Jersey, and Lawrence, Massachusetts, mill strikes of 1912–13 were spectacular, if doomed, IWW efforts), and among migratory agricultural workers as well as with women and blacks—areas shunned by the more elite, **craft**-oriented American Federation of Labor (**AFL**).

Essentially, the IWW believed in confrontation—strikes and even occasional **sabotage**—to build labor **solidarity** and prepare for the mass strike that would topple capitalism: "Get the bosses off our backs" was a theme song. For this they paid dearly. All over the country they faced coordinated government/company attacks. In Bisbee, Arizona, for example, the local sheriff, with the aid of **Phelps-Dodge** mining execs and 2,000 deputized townspeople, rounded up some 1,200 Wobblies and on July 12, 1917, placed them in cattle cars and towed them out to the desert to be abandoned, waterless, in the searing heat for 36 hours.

More than three million members passed through IWW ranks between 1905 and 1920, though the union was probably no more than 150,000 strong at any given time. Yet the Wobblies left an influence far beyond their numbers. Many of their demands—increased **wages**, a shorter workday, semimonthly paydays, better working conditions—became reality a generation later when voiced by more "moderate" labor forces. On the downside, the IWW and the historical memory of it came to personify for many Americans what they disliked or feared about unions—violence, radicalism, and the concept of class warfare. Some of that uneasiness lives on in **Hollywood**'s depiction of labor unions. See **Centralia** and **Everett massacres**.

informational picket—**Picketing** intended solely to inform the public an employer is unfair, nonunion, discriminatory, etc., without attempting to prevent workers from crossing the picket line or otherwise performing their jobs, or consumers from patronizing a business. The key to informational picketing to remain lawful is that *it must constitute an appeal to the public*, rather than to the employer or employees of the establishment being picketed.

initiation fees—One-time-only fees required by **unions** of new members or, sometimes, of employees who have left the **labor union** and wish to return. Such fees, of course, provide additional revenue, but for many unions they're also regarded as an equity payment by new members to compensate for the efforts veteran members have made in building the union. **International unions** set minimum fees, maximum fees or leave them to the discretion of **locals**. Often, the fee is waived entirely, particularly for returning members. See **dues**.

injunctions—The legal weapon of choice for employers, in collaboration with state or federal government, since the early days of unionism. Technically, a judicial remedy awarded for the purpose of requiring a party—namely, a **union**—to refrain from doing or continuing to do a particular act or activity. It is also a preventative measure that guards against future injuries rather than affording a remedy for past injuries. Federal injunctions against unions became especially plentiful following passage of the **Sherman Antitrust** and **Taft-Hartley** acts and at times were broadened to "blanket injunctions" which, in the case of the 1894 **Pullman Strike**, meant *no* union could interfere with the movement of railcars or the U.S. mail they might be carrying *anywhere* in the country.

insecure security workers—For federal government employees, September 11, 2001, brought an attack on their right to unionize. In creating the gigantic Department of Homeland Security (DHS) and its subdivision the Transportation Security Administration (TSA) following the terrorist attacks, the George W. Bush administration replaced what had been a union workplace inhabited by privately employed airport baggage screeners into one subject to the whims of an antiunion Republican Congress. In fact, U.S. Rep. Dick Armey (R-Texas) candidly explained why he had led a post-9/11 move in the House to quash all attempts to convert the estimated 42,000 screeners to federal employment: most federal employees are Democrats, he said. In the GOP's expressed view, **union** membership and national security were incompatible values. In lobbying for the TSA workers' inclusion, the American Federation of Government Employees argued that it would strengthen airline security by improving their professionalism via better pay, improved **benefits**, and training. Federal law states that the TSA administrator has the power to grant workers collective-bargaining rights. All of the George W. Bush–appointed administrators were opposed to such a decision, but President Barack Obama made a campaign promise to secure collective-bargaining rights for TSA workers. However, more than a year into his administration, Obama has yet to secure a new TSA administrator.

internal disputes plan—A method established by the constitution of the **AFL-CIO** for resolving disputes arising between **affiliated unions**. The federation's so-called Massillon Doctrine extended the plan to unions representing government employees.

International Labor Organization (ILO)—Institution set up at the post–World War I Paris Peace Conference and headed by the **AFL**'s **Samuel Gompers**, now affiliated with the United Nations and headquartered in Geneva. Though originally endowed with legislative authority, the ILO has long since functioned as a fact-gathering agency with the power of recommendation only. It has become, however, a valuable source of information on the status of **labor unions** throughout the world. Belonging to the UN does not automatically confer membership in the ILO, but nations may become members by simply filing a declaration accepting the obligations of the ILO constitution. Most nations now belong to it. The United States joined it only in 1934, withdrew in 1977, and rejoined in 1980. In the 1970s, the ILO launched its "World Employment Program" to encourage all countries, especially poorer ones, to adopt strategies likely to provide jobs for most of their workers.

international representative (IR)—A member, usually elected, of the executive board of an **international union** who participates in the policymaking and budgeting of the union as a whole and may represent **locals'** interests in a particular geographical region. In some unions (the Newspaper Guild, for example), IRs serve as nationwide troubleshooters and assist **locals** in negotiations.

international union—The national organization of a **labor union**, so called because many **unions** have **locals** in Canada. The union as a whole in such cases is often called "the international."

J

Jewish Labor Committee (JLC)—Spiritual descendant of the **Jewish Workingman's Association** of the 1880s and the later United Hebrew Trades, the JLC was established in 1934 to mobilize **trade union** opposition to the rise of Nazi Germany, and remains today a significant voice for American Jewry within the **labor movement** and a unique champion of **organized labor** among American Jews, combating anti-Semitism and other forms of discrimination. It also has generated Jewish community opposition to Walmart and other antiworker employers.

Jewish Workingman's Association (JWA)—A union of garment workers established during the 1880s in New York City's solidly Jewish neighborhoods to demand just **wages** and an end to outside contracting ("**outsourcing**," a century later). Able to enlist massive community support, the JWA for a while was successful and even got the **Central Labor Union** to take up its cause in carrying out a successful **strike** against garment makers. The JWA's cause was taken up after the turn of the century by United Hebrew Trades, which became an influential voice in promoting unionization in all occupations.

job action—Any concerted action, usually but not always by a **union** or its on-the-job members, that slows or disrupts the normal course of work. This may range from the obvious, out-and-out **strike, sit-down**, or **walkout** to the more subtle **slowdown, work-to-rule**, or **partial strike**. It may even be a spontaneous gathering of employees or ad-hoc committee determined to confront management over a supervisor's egregious behavior, an unsafe workplace condition, or a long-unaddressed **grievance**. An individual employee acting on his or her own, even in a manner that disrupts work, does not fall into this category.

job control—When used by employers, the control of every facet of the workplace. When used by the **Industrial Workers of the World** after the turn of the century, the **closed shop**. Management often uses **flexibility** as a euphemism for job control.

jobless benefits—See **unemployment insurance**.

job security—All the elements in a **contract** that combine to assure the employee a steady job at fair wages, "safety net" **fringe benefits**, and an adequate retirement income. See **flexibility**.

Jobs with Justice (JWJ)—An interunion, community-oriented grassroots protest group that grew out of a committee formed in the **Industrial Union Department** of the **AFL-CIO** in 1987 in response to the massive **downsizing, layoffs**, wage cuts, and perception of runaway corporate greed occurring in the American workplace. JWJ's initial thrust was against the workplace abuses and **union-busting** of corporate raider Frank Lorenzo and his Florida-based Eastern Airlines; success there spawned more than 60 such protest rallies and campaigns nationwide within a year. JWJ is now composed of a loose network of about thirty local coalitions. But although many **unions** contribute toward it and participate in its activities, the network exists on the fringes of the AFL-CIO itself and its top leadership.

Jones Act—A federal law enacted in 1915 mandating that ships transporting cargo between U.S. ports and through inland waterways be built and repaired in the United States, owned by U.S. companies, and crewed by U.S. citizens. Implicit in the Act—a complement to the 1904 Cargo Preference Act and a forerunner to the 1936 Merchant Marine Act—is that all jobs related to these activities be **union** jobs. Various efforts have been made in recent years to weaken or repeal the Act. See **La Follette Seamen's Act**.

journeyman (journey-level worker)—A worker who has served his or her **apprenticeship** and is thus qualified for top **wages** in the field or to work independently, as in journeyman carpenter. Used almost exclusively in the **trade** or **craft unions**, the term is an English word going back to 1463, from earlier usage of "journey" as a day's work. The **journeymen-apprentice** scale is *not* the same as a **two-tiered wage structure**.

jurisdiction/jurisdictional dispute—1) That part of a plant, business, or office and its personnel that belongs, by **organizing** rights and **National Labor Relations Board (NLRB)** definition, to a particular union—defined, as a rule, in the **contract**. 2) A dispute between two or more unions over the right to represent employees doing similar work within those jurisdictions. Generally, such disputes are settled by **arbitration**, a **bargaining-unit** vote, or a decision by the NLRB—sometimes a combination of all three. Many unions have learned to avoid disputes of this nature by adopting a **no-raiding agreement**, meaning they won't try to organize workers already belonging to another union.

K

kangaroo paw—A derisive, largely management term originating in Australian newspaper publishing circles in the early 1980s to characterize the various afflictions of the arm, wrist, and hand that became known collectively as **repetitive strain injury** or RSI.

Kennedy-Ives Bill—A 1958 attempt by Congress to respond to the issues raised in the **McClellan Committee** racketeering hearings in the Senate. Despite "sweeteners" for certain **unions** in exchange for their support, the bill failed in the House. The **AFL-CIO** ostensibly supported it, but **George Meany**'s comment, "God save us from our friends," reflected labor's true attitude.

King Jr., Martin Luther (1929–68)—Baptist minister, Nobel Peace Prize winner, and noted African American civil rights leader. Most biographical profiles fail to mention that he was also an outspoken advocate of the **labor movement**, particularly as it pertained to black workers achieving their share of the American dream. In fact, King was slain in Memphis, Tennessee, while lending fervid support to a **strike** of city sanitation workers. Just hours before he was struck down by a sniper's bullet on April 4, 1968, he addressed a black gathering with these words: "Nothing would be more tragic than to stop at this point, in Memphis. We have got to see it through. Be concerned about your brother. You may not be on strike. But either we go up together, or we go down together." A few years earlier, he was asked if he thought **union** representation was worth anything. His reply: "Union meant strength, and union recognition meant the employer's acknowledgment of that strength, and the two meant the opportunity to fight for further gains with united and multiplied power. As **contract** followed contract, the **pay envelope** fattened, and **fringe benefits** and job rights grew to the mature work standards of today. All of these started with winning, first, union recognition." See **blacks in the labor movement, right-to-work law.**

Kirkland, (Joseph) Lane (1922–99)—U.S. labor leader; president  of the **AFL-CIO** from late 1979 to mid-1995. A Merchant Marine veteran of World War II, he joined the staff of the old American Federation of Labor as a researcher in the late 1940s and became **George Meany**'s executive assistant in 1961 and secretary-treasurer of the AFL-CIO in 1969. Though he came from a

South Carolina family that helped chart the Confederacy, Kirkland remained a tireless advocate of civil rights both within
unions and nationally. As labor-federation president, the moderate, highly respected Kirkland, more a technocrat than organizer, inherited from Meany the thankless task of keeping viable a
14 million–member federation whose ranks were fast dwindling
from massive plant closings and **downsizing**, the shipping of
U.S. jobs abroad, and increasing hostility from the federal government as well as from corporate **management consultants**
intent on **union-busting.** The last few years of Kirkland's reign
were beset by dissident leaders in the **labor movement** who felt
he didn't meet these challenges, and his resignation in August
1995 was followed by the first contested election in AFL-CIO
history, between "old line" Thomas Donahue and "young Turk"
John Sweeney. Sweeney won, a victory interpreted by many as a
requiem for Kirkland-style passive leadership.

Knights of Labor—A labor organization founded in 1869 by nine
Philadelphia tailors led by **Uriah Stephens** that eventually
encompassed everything from ship carpenters to railway workers and by 1886, under "Grand Master Workman" **Terence Powderly**, had up to one million members. Born in secrecy and fostered in elaborate ritual—a response to employers' traditional
use of **labor spies**, firings, and **blacklistings** to supress
unions—the Knights gradually dropped their cabalism to
become the biggest and most influential force in the **labor
movement** during the Gilded Age. They were the forerunner of
the American Federation of Labor, which eventually displaced
them, and were the first labor group to promote "vertical" (top-
to-bottom) organization or "one big union," a concept embraced
militantly decades later by the **Industrial Workers of the World**.
Much of labor's later achievements were first voiced as goals by
the Knights: abolition of **child labor**, **wage** equality for women,
integration of black workers, the **eight-hour workday**, **equal pay
for equal work**, the graduated income tax, and **Labor Day** as a
national holiday, to name a few. For all their championing of
unskilled immigrant workers (the Irish were the biggest

beneficiaries) though, the Knights' one big blind spot was the Chinese workforce, or "coolies" as they were commonly called. In the early 1880s, the major focus of the federation's political activity, in fact, was to lobby for passage of a congressional bill to prohibit the Chinese from immigrating to the United States. When the Chinese Exclusion Act was passed in 1882, the Knights hailed it as "a great step forward for American [meaning non-Asian] workers." On the other hand, in Texas the Knights represented a united front of whites, blacks, and Hispanics—the first coalition of its kind in state history.

A fight and marching song in the order's heyday went:

Storm the fort, ye
Knights of Labor
Battle for your cause:
Equal rights for
Every neighbor,
Down with tyrant laws.

The Knights' Waterloo came in an abortive 1886 strike against Jay Gould's southwestern railroad system and their part in organizing a **general strike** that began that year in Chicago on May 1—a day the rest of the world has subsequently honored as Labor Day—and ended with the even more disastrous **Haymarket affair**, a catalyst for **Red scares** for decades to come. Ironically, Powderly and the Knights' leadership were philosophically opposed to strikes and, as it turned out, the Knights were unjustly blamed for the Haymarket violence. By 1890, their membership was down to 100,000 and falling, and they had ceased to be a national power. See **blacks in the labor movement**, **working women's movement**, **Pioneer Garfield Assembly**.

Knights of St. Crispin—Trade **union** of shoemakers, named after the third-century patron saint of the craft, founded in Massachusetts in 1867 by men who considered themselves artisans and protested their being thrown into the decisionless anonymity of the **factory system**. After a number of successful **strikes**, the organization grew rapidly, and by 1870 had a membership of nearly 50,000, making it the largest **labor union** in the country and one of the first to **organize** factory workers. Woman shoe-makers also organized during this period, forming the Daughters of St. Crispin to fight the "unjust encroachment upon our rights." Unlike the **Knights of Labor**, also on the rise at this time, the Crispins defied the wave of anti-Asian feeling sweeping the nation and in fact organized a **local** of Chinese workers who had been brought to North Adams, Massachusetts, to break a shoe-makers strike in 1870. See **labor movement, working women's movement**.

L

Labor Day—A day set aside for the celebration of working people; made a national holiday in 1894 by President Grover Cleveland, who decreed it be the first Monday in September in response to those who opposed the popular **May Day** observance because of its association with the notorious **Haymarket** massacre eight years before. The first Labor Day parade, however, was held by the **Central Labor Union** in New York City in September 1882. In 1887 Oregon became the first state to make Labor Day a legal holiday.

Labor Department—See **Department of Labor, U.S.**

labor force—All persons between the ages of 16 and 65 who are either employed, temporarily out of a job, or unemployed. In 1968, that force constituted 82 million; in 1997, it was 137.1 million. The military has been in and out of these figures at various times. Originally counted as separate, they were lumped in during the Reagan administration on the grounds that the post-draft, all-volunteer armed forces represented job opportunities as much as in the private sector. During the George H.W. Bush administration's 1991 Gulf War buildup, however, the practice was discontinued because of the difficulty of getting accurate, then-top-secret military figures. The **Bureau of Labor Statistics** estimates there is currently only one-tenth of 1 percent difference between civilian and military figures in the workforce.

Labor-Management Relations Act—See Taft-Hartley Act.

labor movement—The movement of workers for better treatment
by employers, particularly through the formation of **labor
unions**. A term not widely used until the 1870s, although the
U.S. labor movement, as such, began as early as the 1820s and
1930s, when the advent of the **factory system** prompted skilled
and unskilled workers to **organize** locally to obtain better pay, a
ten-hour workday (12 or more was the norm then), the right to
make liens against a factory owner for unpaid wages and for
such social reforms as **child labor laws**, and advocating free
public education. The labor movement in the United States has
always been in constant ebb and flow—flow in the 1870s and
1980s, when it seemed the **Knights of Labor** and then the American Federation of Labor (**AFL**) were making their organizational voices heard and increased their membership exponentially;
ebb when the **Haymarket affair** cast public suspicion on the
entire movement, and the **Homestead** and **Pullman** strikes set
labor back a generation in the steel and railroad industries. Flow
in the years preceding World War I, when radical labor organizations such as the **Industrial Workers of the World** and the
Western Federation of Miners brought to public consciousness
the inequities of the capitalist wage system; ebb when the postwar **Palmer Raids** and ensuing **Red scares** alarmed the American public as to the very nature of the labor movement. Flow in
the **Lawrence Textile Strike** of 1912; ebb in the **Paterson Textile
Strike** of 1913. Flow in the Depression 1930s, through World
War II and into the immediate postwar period, when a militant
CIO, tired of the bread-and-butter complacency of the **craft
union AFL**, formed **industrial unions** in such numbers and
strength as to bring mega-corporations such as General Motors
and General Electric if not to their knees at least humbly to the
bargaining table. Ebb when a rash of postwar strikes gave corporate employers the lever to pressure Congress into enacting
the union-restrictive **Taft-Hartley Act** and its later brother, the
Landrum-Griffin Act. Flow in the 1960s and 1970s, when
unions made slow but steady gains in **wages** and **cost-of-living**

allowances; ebb when the **PATCO strike** of 1981 signaled a new wave of **union-busting**, corporate takeovers, **outsourcing**, antilabor **management consultants, takebacks** and **givebacks**, and legislation protecting **permanent replacement workers**. In between have been the repressions, **strikebreaking, Mohawk Valley formulas**, and massacres that have left labor historians in constant astonishment that the labor movement has survived at all, given the forces arrayed against it. No accurate figures are available, but the strikers, organizers, and general workers killed and wounded in the interests of unionism in the past century and a half easily number in the tens of thousands.

Not that the labor movement has been pure. The **Molly Maguires**, the **Chicagorillas**, labor racketeers in general, Mob influence, and strong-arm tactics have brought the movement to low repute throughout its history. In 1911, a Chicago "slugger," paid $50 for every **scab** he discouraged, described his job in an interview with a reporter: "Oh, there ain't nothing to it, I gets my fifty, then I goes out and finds the guy they wanna have slugged. I goes up to 'im and says, 'My friend,' by way of meanin' no harm, and then I gives it to 'im—biff! in the mug. Nothin' to it." The late Teamsters leader **Jimmy Hoffa** used to say such tactics simply leveled the playing field, but the public never really bought it.

Yet there is a down-to-earth dichotomy between the labor movement and the forces that have always opposed it. In his unknowingly prophetic 1887 book, *The Labor Movement: The Problem of Today*, labor reformer George McNeill put it succinctly:

> *[E]xtremes of wealth and poverty are threatening the existence of the government. In the light of these facts, we declare that there is an inevitable and irresistible conflict between the wage system of labor and the republican system of government—the wage laborer attempting to save the government, and the capitalist class ignorantly attempting to subvert it.*

One can almost hear the laughter of the labor-management committees of the 1940s **War Production Board** that helped save management from its own inefficiencies.

labor spies—Professional informants hired by corporations in the 1920s and 1930s—usually from agencies, such as **Pinkerton**, Burns, the Railway & Audit Inspection Co., and the Corporations Auxiliary Co.—during times of labor unrest. Their jobs were numerous: to corrupt **union** strength from inside by sowing suspicion and mistrust, to provoke **strikes** prematurely, to report on labor activities, and to reveal the names of "strong" union members so employers could get rid of them. **La Follette Committee** investigations revealed that between 1933 and 1937 industry had hired 3,781 such agents, who became **affiliated** with 93 unions; some had actually become union officials. There was evidence, moreover, that a labor spy or company-paid stool pigeon could be found in every one of organized labor's 41,000 **locals**—at a cost to industry of some $80 million a year. But the most famous—or infamous—labor spy was long before that: James McParlan of the Pinkertons, who went on from breaking the **Molly Maguires** in 1876 to providing perjured witnesses against **"Big Bill" Haywood** of the **IWW** in trumped-up murder charges in 1907 in Idaho. Lest anyone think labor spies are a phenomenon of the past, it was revealed at the conclusion of the 18-month **Detroit newspaper strike** in February 1997 that a company infiltrator faithfully attended union meetings throughout the strike and reported back just as faithfully to the Detroit Newspaper Agency, representing News and Free Press management, everything that transpired at those meetings.

labor temple—See temple.

labor union/organization—The U.S. Code defines it best: "Any organization of any kind, or any agency or employee representation committee or plan in which employees participate and which exists for the purpose, in whole or in part, of dealing with employers concerning **grievances**, labor disputes, **wages**, rates of pay, hours of employment, or conditions of work."

La Follette Committee—Officially, the La Follette Civil Liberties Committee, a Senate investigative panel headed by Senator Robert M. La Follette Jr. (R-Wis.) that held hearings in 1936–37 into labor abuses by corporate management in alliance with police, a collusion that became apparent in the 1937 Memorial Day Massacre during the **Little Steel strike**. The significance of the committee's findings—about "**industrial munitions**," the **Mohawk Valley formula**, the extent of **labor spying**, and a host of other practices—was that their exposure, publicity, and resultant public uproar indirectly influenced deliberations on the U.S. Supreme Court, which rendered a key decision in April 1937 (<u>NLRB v. Jones & Laughlin Steel Co.</u>) validating the **Wagner Act** and freeing the **National Labor Relations Board** to apply the law in full vigor.

La Follette Seamen's Act—Enacted by Congress in 1915, it guaranteed the rights of seamen to seek a limit to working hours, to obtain part of their pay on demand when reaching a loading or discharging port, and other **benefits**. As a sop to the nativist feelings of the time, it also barred Asians from working on U.S. ships and restricted some maritime jobs to U.S. citizens. The Act was the result of years of lobbying by Andrew Furuseth, general secretary and president of the International Seamen's Union of America. Named after U.S. Senator Robert M. La Follette Sr. (R-Wis.), father of the chairman of the **La Follette Committee** of the 1930s.

Landrum-Griffin Act—Officially, the Labor Management Reporting and Disclosure Act; a federal law sponsored by U.S. Representatives Phil Landrum (D-Ga.), and Robert Griffin (R-Mich.), and passed in September 1959, ostensibly to foster internal **union** democracy by imposing regulations on elections of union officers, requiring unions to file annual reports, and restricting **strikes**, **picketing**, and **boycotts**. Although there were a few ameliorating amendments, the effect of the Act, fashioned essentially by Republicans and Dixiecrats riding on the conclusions of the **McClellan Committee**, was to make many **Taft-Hartley** provisions more severe. Among the latter were a tightening of restrictions against **secondary boycotts** and the outlawing of certain types of **picketing**.

However, Landrum-Griffin did drop the draconian I-am-not-a-communist affidavit provisions of Taft-Hartley, substituting in its place a provision that active communists could not hold union office and former communists had to be out of the party at least five years before holding office. It also stipulated that convicted felons be barred from union officership for five years after serving prison time.

It should be emphasized that **AFL-CIO** President **George Meany** and other labor leaders strongly favored the antiracketering and anticorruption provisions of Landrum-Griffin; it was the "jokers contained in the second half of this bill"—the punitive measures against unions—they found objectionable. Meany openly accused Congress of making a deal: that in exchange for Dixiecrat votes to ensure passage, Republicans, heavily backed by the National Association of Manufacturers and the U.S. Chamber of Commerce, promised to block any civil rights legislation that year. As subsequent investigations revealed, Meany's analysis was not far off the mark. See **Red scares**.

Lattimer Massacre—On September 10, 1897, 500 demonstrators, to all accounts peaceful and unarmed, marched down the main street of tiny Lattimer Mines, Pennsylvania, in support of regional anthracite coal miners of the United Mine Workers of America (UMWA) who had gone on strike to protest **wage** cuts; unfair pay discrimination between English-speaking and non-English-speaking, mostly Slavic, workers; an end to the **company store**; and the right to choose their own physician. Apparently without provocation, sheriff's deputies turned on the parade and fired at point-blank range, killing 19 people and wounding 39. The carnage, followed by massive, demonstrative funeral processions, served to hand the UMWA a resounding victory the following year. The Lattimer incident was the biggest single anti-labor massacre in the violent and bloody coal wars of the past two centuries, including that of **Ludlow**, Colorado, 17 years later. See **immigrants and the U.S. labor movement**.

Lawrence Textile Strike (1912)—A landmark 63-day, occasionally violent strike brought on by intolerable conditions for the 30,000 mostly unskilled immigrant men, women, and children employed by the textile mills of Lawrence, Massachusetts. Initiated by a mass walkout at the dominant American Woolen Co. in January over a cut in already paltry **wages** and a **speedup**, the strike, which quickly spread to all the city's mills, was at first leaderless. But its representatives soon enlisted the aid of the **Industrial Workers of the World (IWW)**, which sent in its top **organizers**, among them **Elizabeth Gurley Flynn**. Mill owners retaliated with a massive show of force—militia, police, and **strikebreakers**—and before long a woman striker was shot dead and a "dynamite plot" uncovered. The strikers, the majority of them women, fought back with weapons ranging from words to red pepper to hefty lengths of pipe. More deaths ensued, but IWW tactics and widespread public outrage and sympathy for the strikers eventually forced the mill owners to capitulate with a **settlement** that included pay raises, **overtime** pay, no discrimination, and other improvements. Though two IWW organizers were subsequently indicted for the first strike death, they were found to have been nowhere near and were acquitted. American Woolen's president, William Wood, was himself indicted for his part in the dynamite plot, which turned out to be a company scheme to blame on the strikers. The Lawrence strike was the high-water mark of IWW success. See **Paterson Textile Strike**, **immigrants in the U.S. labor movement**.

layoff—The temporary or permanent removal of a worker from his or her job, usually because of cutbacks in production, the closing down or moving of a plant to another location, or replacement by new technology. Also known as **reduction in force** or RIF.

layoff by attrition—Not a layoff in the strict sense of the term, but rather a reduction in the workforce achieved by simply not replacing employees who die, retire, quit, or are fired.

Lea Act—A 1946 congressional reaction to management accusations of union **featherbedding** in the broadcasting industry; it outlawed the practice of certain **unions** "to hire people who do no work, to pay for people the employers do not hire, and to hire more people than the employers have work for." It was aimed specifically at the American Federation of Musicians; in fact, the law was informally called the "Anti-Petrillo Act," after James C.

Petrillo, the longtime head of the AFM. The Act was subsumed a year later into the **Taft-Hartley Act** and its anti-featherbedding strictures watered down.

Lewis, John L. (1880–1969)—Peppery, autocratic, thundering Iowa-born labor leader; longtime president of the United Mine Workers of America (UMWA), a founder of the Congress of Industrial Organizations (**CIO**), and the bane of not only two U.S. presidents but of scores of fellow labor leaders as well. A coal miner at the age of 16, head of his **union local** at 29, and

 president of the UMWA ten years later in 1920 (a post he held until 1960), Lewis survived the dark and bloody coalfield wars of the 1920s in Kentucky, Indiana, Ohio, West Virginia, and southern Illinois—a war waged almost as much against rival **union** leaders as against coal operators and **union-busters**—to emerge as a major spokesman for the American **labor movement** by the 1930s. In fact, by 1933 he had rebuilt a badly demoralized mineworkers union into probably the single most powerful bloc within the American Federation of Labor (**AFL**). He attempted to parlay that into official AFL recognition of **industrial unionism** at the federation's convention in 1935, and lost, though he did win headlines by punching out William L. "Big Bill" Hutcheson of the Carpenters Union, calmly relighting a cigar as Big Bill went flying over a convention table. Lewis then promptly went out and founded the Committee for Industrial Organization, the direct forerunner of the CIO, a move characterized by fellow up-and-coming labor leader **George Meany** as "Leninistic." Though Meany and other conservative/moderates also accused Lewis of peopling CIO echelons with communists—which he did; communists were known to be the best organizers—Lewis was paradoxically careful to purge his own UMWA ranks of all communists and their sympathizers. A strong backer of Franklin D. Roosevelt's presidential bid in 1936, Lewis nonetheless turned against FDR in 1940 and backed his Republican opponent. When Roosevelt won, Lewis resigned his

CIO presidency and went back to leading his mineworkers union. In 1943, at the height of World War II, Lewis took his members out on a series of **strikes** as a protest of what he saw as coal operators' attempts to use the war effort to weaken the mineworkers' **contract**. But over the outrage of Roosevelt, Congress, and a superpatriotic public, and two convictions for contempt of federal orders, he won for the miners their desired agreement. His fiery obduracy—he delighted newsmen with biting descriptions of his enemies and sonorous quotations from the Bible and Shakespeare—won him similar clashes with President Harry S. Truman, but by the 1950s Lewis had become a champion of cooperation between mine owners and miners. Somehow, though, he could never quite shake the image of the archetypal **union boss**, and when he died in 1969, it was in relative obscurity. As evidence of his unwavering adherence to union principles, his advocates point to his establishment of union hospitals in the coalfields and his denunciation of the **Taft-Hartley Act** in 1947 as "the first ugly, savage thrust of fascism in America." His critics, however, point to his establishment of a wholly owned union bank that profited the union but not union members and a growing alliance, beginning in the late 1940s, with the Bituminous Coal Operators Association that squeezed out independent coal operators—hence a lot of miners.

Memorable quote: *"I have pleaded your case not in the quavering tones of a mendicant asking alms, but in the thundering voice of the captain of a mighty host, demanding the rights to which free men are entitled."* See **Herrin Massacre**.

Little Davis-Bacon—So called because it is a version of the **Davis-Bacon Act** on the state level. In Washington state, where a "Little Davis-Bacon" was enacted in 1945, it is formally known as the Washington State Public Works Act.

Little Steel formula—A wage measure devised under the **National War Labor Board** in early 1942 for unionized heavy industry that established a statistical cost-of-living baseline at January 1, 1941, and put a ceiling accordingly on overall wartime **wage** claims (about 3.5 percent) but also established guidelines that tended toward a leveling-up of incomes across the entire working class. The formula achieved de jure status with the board's "Little Steel" decision of July 1942; so called because **union** wages at Bethlehem, Republic, and other steel plants (other than "big" U.S. Steel) were a major factor in the baseline.

Little Steel strike (1937)—A strike organized by **Philip Murray** and the Steel Workers Organizing Committee of the **CIO** against Youngstown Sheet & Tube and Republic Steel (called, along with Bethlehem and Inland, "little steel"; "big steel" was the giant U.S. Steel Co.); most notable—or notorious—for the companies' use of a uniformed police force of 400 men equipped with revolvers, rifles, shotguns, billy clubs, and tear gas which, in the findings of the **La Follette Committee**, they "loosed . . . to shoot down citizens on the streets and highways" during the strike. When Chicago police bullets at a Republic strike rally in that city killed ten unarmed marchers (some reports say 17) and wounded as many as 80, a coroner's jury pronounced this Memorial Day Massacre "justifiable homicide." The strike was quashed.

lobster shift—A newspaper workplace term for a shift beginning at 4 A.M.; said to have originated at the now-defunct *New York Journal-American*, whose plant was near the East River docks and whose workers noticed they were showing up for that shift about the same time as lobstermen were putting out to sea. See **swing shift, graveyard shift**.

local/local unions—The local or regional branch of a national or **international union** that has its own officers, **business agent**, or administrative officer and bylaws, and generally handles **contract** negotiations and enforcement for the members in its **jurisdiction**. Although enjoying a certain autonomy and having its own budget, a local is subject to the overall authority of the national/international and must set aside regular **per-capita dues** for it. The term was made widespread by the **AFL** in 1888; before that, locals were called branches or lodges, though the latter word has been retained to this day by some unions, such as the International Association of Aerospace Machinists.

lockout—Management's closing of a plant or business or wholesale dismissal of employees because of a labor dispute. Surprisingly, the word doesn't appear in **National Labor Relations Act** legislation, though it dates back to 1854 as a tactic of closing a factory during contract negotiations to force workers to come to terms. Though the **Taft-Hartley Act** law recognizes lockouts as a lawful economic weapon under certain circumstances, it is illegal if used (1) to prevent **union** organizing, (2) to deny recognition to a **bargaining unit**, (3) to force an employer's choice of a rival union upon employees, (4) to interfere with employees' freedom to join or not to join a union, or (5) to preclude bargaining before it can begin. But lockouts are held legal if (1) a threatened strike would cause *unusual* economic losses or operational difficulties, (2) in the case of a multi-employer association, they are in defense of a **whipsaw** or selective strike tactic. In 1965, however, the U.S. Supreme Court considerably broadened the lockout as an *offensive* weapon as well, with the result that today many companies feel justified in effecting a lockout under minimal pretexts. A lockout is not to be confused with a plant shutdown.

lodge—See **local**.

Long Strike (1875)—A watershed event in coal-mine union lore; a strike led by John F. Walsh of the Miners and Laborers Benevolent Association in the Pennsylvania anthracite fields that lasted from January to June 1875, when hunger forced the miners to yield and accept a 20 percent cut in wages. Notable not only because of its duration but because it was a prelude to the **Molly Maguires**.

Luddites—Members of various bands of English workmen in the early days of the **Industrial Revolution** (1811–16) who smashed industrial machinery, mostly textile equipment, in the belief its use diminished employment. Named after Ned Ludd, a legendary late 18th-century Leicestershire worker who originated the idea. The name is often applied to modern-day opponents of technology, the most extreme example of whom might be the notorious Unabomber of the 1980s and 1990s.

Ludlow Massacre—Bloody end, on Easter Monday 1914, of a months-long strike by more than 10,000 miners of the United

Mine Workers of America and their families against the Rockefeller-owned Colorado Fuel & Iron Co. in Ludlow, Colorado, in which the state militia stormed into a strikers' tent city and, firing machine guns and setting fire to the tents, killed 14 people, including 11 children. The massacre set off an armed rebellion that lasted ten days and ended only when President Woodrow Wilson ordered the U.S. Army into the Colorado coalfields. All told, 66 people were killed between September 1913, when the strike began, and April 29, 1914: 18 strikers, 10 guards, 19 **scabs**, 2 militiamen, 3 noncombatants, 2 women, and 12 children.

M

machinists unions—The cutting edge, literally and figuratively, between the **Industrial Revolution** and the organized workplace. Trade descendants of blacksmiths, machinists were among the first in the working-class crafts to be confronted with—and learn how to fight—the drudgery and abuses that came with mass, assembly-line production. The earliest large union in the field was the Machinists' and Blacksmiths' International Union (1857), followed by the International Association of Machinists (1888). A number of labor terms still in use come from a time when the machine shop was the common point of reference—**shop steward**, for instance.

maintenance of membership—A provision in a **contract** stating that no employee shall be forced to join the **union** as a condition of employment, but all workers who voluntarily join must maintain their membership for the duration of the contract. See **one-in-ten clause**.

management/labor consultants—Firms, often legal consortiums, specializing in advising employers how to avoid getting unionized or, if a union is already in-plant, how to get rid of it, often openly directing a **decertification** campaign. The demand for such services was given a quantum boost in the months and years following President Ronald Reagan's busting of the air traffic controllers union (**PATCO**) in 1981. Among the better-known of these firms nationally are Sayforth & Shaw, King & Ballow, and Ogletree, Deakins, Nash, Smoak & Stewart. See **strikebreakers, union-busting**.

management-rights clause—Also called management prerogatives and, by the irreverent, the divine right of management; a provision in many **contracts** that says, in essence, that the employer reserves all rights to act unilaterally except where restricted in the **collective bargaining** agreement. In general, this is taken to mean control of the product and the scheduling of production, though it may extend to in-house rules and other areas not addressed in the contract. The **National Labor Relations Board** has held, however, that even the broadest of management-rights clauses in no way relieves management of the obligation to engage in collective bargaining.

mandatory subjects of bargaining—Subjects that must be on the table if **union** and employer are to engage in **good-faith bargaining**. Those subjects are **wages**, hours, and other conditions and terms of employment. It's important to note, however, that federal labor law imposes no duty on either party either to agree or make concessions on those mandatory subjects, simply that they agree to include them in negotiations. See **illegal** and **permissive subjects of bargaining**.

manning—A **craft union** term for agreements that determine the minimum number of union workers that shall be assigned to a particular task, or step in production. Manning agreements have been particularly crucial in longshore contracts and their violations the cause of many a **strike** or **work stoppage**. Management often views such accords as **featherbedding**; unions see them as safety and **job security** issues.

maquiladoras—Also called maquilas or "bonded in" plants; foreign-owned factories or assembly plants in Mexico, usually near the U.S. border, where foreign-made parts and components are assembled by lower-paid Mexican labor for the purpose of export. A U.S. tariff provision permits the manufacturer to pay duty only on the "value added" part of the final product (i.e., the amount of labor and the value of materials added on the Mexican side).

A sore point with the U.S. **labor movement** even before **NAFTA**, maquiladoras are seen as a device to export or **outsource** jobs, undermine **unions**, and exploit cheap Mexican labor (maquiladoras took off after 1982, when drastic devaluation of the peso made Mexican labor among the world's cheapest). It is not simply a localized border issue; a mid-1980s U.S. Commerce Department study showed that maquiladora plants in one location alone—Ciudad Juárez, Mexico—were supplied by 5,714 companies in 44 U.S. states. Nor is the maquiladora program a creature of the 1980s; it was inaugurated in 1965 under the Mexican presidency of Gustavo Díaz Ordaz and now constitutes Mexico's third-largest source of hard currency, after petroleum and tourism, employing roughly half a million people. Although initial investment in maquiladoras was overwhelmingly from the United States, the 1980s saw a huge influx of Taiwanese and Japanese capital as well and, to a lesser extent, European, so that now the industry is truly international. All is not docile on the Mexican front, however. Following another peso devaluation in 1995 that lowered the average maquiladora salary from the U.S. equivalent of $37 a week to $19, thousands of workers in Ciudad Juárez staged **wildcat strikes** and gained not only significant increases in wage packages but also, in some cases, meaningful reforms in the corrupt Mexican official union structure.

The word *maquila* derives from the Arabic for "measure"; in Spain it came to mean millage, or the portion received by a miller for grinding grain, and in Mexico the place where the grinding is done.

marriage penalties—Until relatively recent times, working women could be fired or not hired simply because they were married, excellent qualifications notwithstanding. This was particularly true of schoolteachers, airline flight attendants (previously called stewardesses), and public utility employees (especially telephone operators). In 1931, five states—Alabama, Idaho, Indiana, Pennsylvania, and Rhode Island—restricted state employment of wives. A National Education Association survey the same year revealed that 77 percent of 1,500 school districts refused to hire married women as teachers, while 63 percent dismissed them. Among vociferous opponents to this policy was the Communist Party of the United States (CPUSA), contending it was part of "the fascist campaign to degrade women to being beasts of burden, tied down to children, cooking and the church." In 1986, 1,700 female flight attendants won an 18-year lawsuit (and $37 million in damages) against United Airlines, which had fired them for getting married. See **working women's movement.**

master agreement—A **union** contract covering a number of companies and one or more unions, often supplemented with local agreements covering individual plants with the overall **bargaining unit.** Some **locals** with a large number of bargaining units in their **jurisdiction,** for instance, will negotiate a contract that covers most if not all of them, then tailor details or exceptions unique to individual units. In recent years, however, the courts and the **National Labor Relations Board** have struck down several of these agreements on grounds some bargaining-unit members lacked fair and adequate representation. See **multi-employer bargaining.**

Matewan, Battle of—Name given to a May 1920 clash between coal miners of Matewan, West Virginia, and Baldwin-Felts detectives hired by the mining company to quash a **labor union** drive. A gunfight erupted when the detectives and company managers tried to evict miners and their families from the Stone Mountain Mine camp, resulting in the deaths of seven detectives, two miners, and the town mayor, C. Testerman, who was sympathetic to the miners' cause. More than a year later, Baldwin-Felts men killed another sympathizer, Matewan police chief and former miner Sid Hatfield, setting off an armed rebellion of 10,000 West Virginia miners at the so-called Battle of Blair Mountain, dubbed by a local newspaper as "the largest insurrection this

country has had since the Civil War." Army troops had to be
called in to put down the uprising. See **Herrin, Latimer,** and **Ludlow massacres.**

maximum work hours for women—See <u>Muller v. Oregon</u>.

May Day—It is one of the great ironies of history that a day originally marked by the American **labor movement** as a labor holiday in the United States should now be celebrated everywhere
but the United States. It happened this way: in the summer of
1884, the fledgling **AFL** (it was then called the Federation of
Organized Trades and Labor Unions of the United States and
Canada), was presented a proposal drafted by AFL Treasurer and
Brotherhood of Carpenters President Gabriel Edmonston that
read, "Eight hours shall constitute a legal day's labor from and
after May 1, 1886." Since the **eight-hour day** was the major aim
of the new federation, the motion carried overwhelmingly, and
massive publicity in the United States and abroad, with two
years to prepare, ensured giant rallies and marches on the
appointed day. The problem was that two days later, May 3, 1886,
came the disastrous **Haymarket affair**—itself a spin-off of May
Day festivities in connection with the McCormick **general
strike**—with its bombing and shootings. "The Haymarket bomb
in Chicago destroyed our eight-hour movement," AFL head
Samuel Gompers was later to lament. Haymarket didn't exactly
destroy the campaign, but it did set it back considerably—and it
fast distanced labor leaders from a day that would, in their view,
"live in infamy." It is doubly ironic that May Day, particularly in
socialist countries, would henceforth be celebrated more as a
reminder of the Haymarket martyrs than of the eight-hour day.
See **Labor Day.**

McClellan Committee—Officially, the Senate Committee on
Improper Activities in Labor-Management Relations; a panel
whose hearings in 1957 on alleged **union** corruption and illegal
practices, coupled with aroused public sentiment over the issue,
led to **Landrum-Griffin** legislation two years later that imposed
restrictions on unions more severe than those already enacted
under the **Taft-Hartley Act** in 1947. The hearings, chaired by

Senator John McClellan (D-Ark.), also resulted in a big Republican push for **right-to-work laws** and did much, via Landrum-Griffin, to weaken labor's power relative to employers.

Meany, George (1894–1980)—Prominent Irish American labor leader who started out in a New York City plumbers union and rose to become secretary-treasurer of the American Federation of Labor in 1939, its president in 1952, and president of the newly merged **AFL-CIO** in 1955, a post he retained until his death. Reviled in his later years by progressive unionists as the

quintessential Cold Warrior and Establishment, cigar-chomping **union boss**, Meany was all of these—but also very much a product of his times and, as such, a powerfully effective leader in the American **labor movement**. Born into a tradition of "bread-and-butter unionism," whose members regarded themselves as descendants of medieval craft **guilds**, Meany would boast late in life that he had never led a **strike**. Yet throughout his career he demanded more progressive legislation; more compassion for the poor, the elderly, and minorities; more regard for human rights at home and abroad; and a national health insurance plan. If he stubbornly clung to U.S. policies in the Vietnam War long after even big-business leaders wavered, he also abhorred fascist regimes such as Francisco Franco's even as the United States was embracing the Spanish dictator for the air bases he would grant it. Dictatorships of any political stripe, he would say repeatedly, are the death of free **unions**. And if he used secret files supplied by the FBI to discredit anti–Vietnam War factions in the union movement, he also decried a rampant U.S. corporatism that "is in a mad race to produce more and more with less and less labor, without any feeling as to what it may mean to the whole national economy." Direct spiritual descendant of AFL founder **Samuel Gompers** and of a craft union tradition that had won high **wages** by adapting to the contours of U.S. capitalism, Meany's credo was expressed succinctly in a speech he once gave before the AFL-

CIO: *"We do not seek to recast American society in any particular doctrinaire or ideological image. We seek an ever-rising standard of living."*

Mechanization and Modernization Agreement (M&M)—A series of accords between West Coast longshore **locals** and management beginning in the early 1960s that allowed shipping companies to introduce radically new technologies on the waterfront. M&M agreements reduced the union's ability to use the **contract** as a weapon and initially allowed employers to determine **manning** scales.

media coverage of organized labor—Labor leaders and the **rank and file** maintain that the mainstream U.S. media constantly distort, minimize, and otherwise traduce **unions** and workplace issues when they don't omit them outright (see **Pittston Coal strike**). Press and electronic-media people insist that labor representatives are notoriously closemouthed, uncommunicative, and seemingly paranoid about divulging information.

Both sides are right, though which attitude came first is a classic chicken-or-egg conundrum. Most reporters and editors are woefully ignorant of labor and labor history—it isn't taught in schools—and that includes even union members within media organizations. Moreover, they tend to reflect, perhaps subconsciously, the corporate biases of bosses, owners, and the overall business community. Most newspapers have abolished their once-popular labor beats.

They also swim in an unnoticed sea of bias: popular TV dramas and comedies, notes Texas **AFL-CIO** communications director Christopher Cook, overwhelmingly focus on conflict while trivializing genuine union concerns. "Union-related car bombings occur with dismaying frequency," says Cook. Feature films (*On the Waterfront, The Garment Jungle, F.I.S.T., Hoffa*) inevitably portray unions as corrupt and their leaders as stereotypical thugs who are in bed with organized crime. In most news reports, management makes *offers*, unions make *demands*.

The news that does get through is routinely negative: **strikes** that will damage the public weal and union agendas that will bleed the employer dry, often made by cigar-chomping **"union bosses."** The latter image is greatly reinforced by editorial cartoons.

What readers, listeners, and viewers won't find, says William Puette in his book *Through Jaundiced Eyes*, are presentations of the various benefits derived from union memberships: higher **wages**, safety regulations, **health coverage**, due-process protections in the workplace, **pensions**, longer vacations, and so on.

Union leaders, who frequently feel they've been burned in past media dealings, tend to clam up when contacted for an opinion or asked "dumb" questions from "unenlightened" types who think a right-to-work state is great because everyone should have a job. Also, chances are that they haven't been sent to public relations and communications classes, unlike their more media-savvy counterparts in management.

It was in order to provide such enlightenment, in fact, that this *Lexicon* was undertaken. See **Prefatory Note** and **proposals or offers vs. demands.**

mediation/conciliation—The two terms are used interchangeably; a procedure, short of **arbitration**, used by the two parties in **contract** negotiations whereby a third party, usually a federal mediator, is brought in to effect a compromise. The mediator/conciliator does not, like an arbitrator, render a decision but rather tries to persuade negotiators to come to voluntary **agreement**. See **fact-finding.**

medical insurance—See **health benefits** and **coverage.**

Medicare—What some have called the United States' answer to a national health plan, at least for the over-65 set. An outgrowth of ongoing **Social Security** legislation, the program was established in 1965. Its Canadian counterpart was set up in 1968.

meet-and-confer negotiations—Bargaining in the public sector in which the ultimate decision as to the terms and conditions of employment of public employees is made by the employer (i.e., some government branch or agency). Meet-and-confer laws generally extend to public employees the right to **organize** and make presentations and recommendations before the appropriate legislative body, which then makes a unilateral decision. Such laws may supersede written agreements and **exclusivity**.

memorandum of understanding—See **side agreements**.

Memorial Day Massacre—See **Little Steel strike**.

merit pay—A regularly received amount of pay above the **contract** minimum an employer chooses to award individual employees in recognition of their talents, services, performance, etc. Some contracts make specific provisions for merit pay, others do not; it is generally at the sole discretion of management. Contrary to popular opinion, **unions** are seldom if ever opposed to merit pay; they simply insist it be *on top of* negotiated salary floors. See **incentive pay** and **pay for performance**.

Mine, Mill & Smelter Workers; International Union of—Formerly the **Western Federation of Miners**, Mine-Mill was chartered in 1917 and inherited much of its militant, progressive character from the WFM–**Industrial Workers of the World** alliance in the early years of the century. Often the target of smears, as was the WFM, because of its radicalism and alleged—and sometimes real—communist influence, Mine-Mill with its 40,000 members, many of them Hispanic, was absorbed into the United Steelworkers of America in 1967.

minimum-wage laws—See **Fair Labor and Standards Act**.

minimum-wage indexing—With a 1998 ballot initiative, Washington became the first state in the union to automatically tie the minimum wage to the rate of inflation. The then-current $4.90-an-hour minimum went to a previously calculated $5.70 the following January, and then to $6.59 in 2000. The inflation-linked hike began in 2001, bringing it to $7.93 in 2007. By comparison, Mississippi, and five other states don't even have minimum-wage laws but instead are guided by the federal minimum wage, which was $5.85 an hour in 2007. See **West Coast Hotel Co. v. Parrish**, **minimum-wage rates**, **Fair Labor Standards Act**.

minimum-wage rates—The minimum wage set for nonfarm workers across the country has been raised 18 times since the **Fair Labor Standards Act** established a floor of 25 cents an hour in

1938. A chronology:

1939	30¢	1968	$1.60	1981	$3.35
1945	40¢	1974	$2.00	1990	$3.80
1950	75¢	1975	$2.10	1991	$4.25
1956	$1.00	1976	$2.30	1996	$5.15
1961	$1.15	1978	$2.65	2007	$5.85
1963	$1.25	1979	$2.90	2008	$6.55
1967	$1.40	1980	$3.10	2009	$7.25

Finally, after a congressional GOP-induced drought of 11 years, a Democratic-majority Congress raised the minimum to $5.85 an hour in 2007.

Minneapolis Teamsters strike (1934)—Noted for its innovative "cruising picket squad" of International Brotherhood of Teamsters (IBT) **Local** 574 and for its leadership of Trotskyists who had been expelled by the Stalinist-led Communist Party USA in 1928, the five-week strike was marked by bloody clashes; National Guard troops; two strikers dead and 55 wounded by gunfire; two company-sponsored "special deputies" killed in street violence; running battles with bricks, stones, and gas canisters; hand-to-hand fighting; and a virtual halt to all wheeled commerce in the city except for milk, ice, and beer trucks. Altogether, there were three strikes that summer, with the IBT **organizing** 3,000 new members in the process and ultimately winning significant concessions from management. One of the reasons employers were emboldened to confront the strikers was the attitude of AFL Teamsters president **Dan Tobin**, who not only denounced Local 574's leaders as "radicals and communists" but also at one point openly sided with the Minneapolis employers. The Red-baiting worked with management and the press but not with the **rank and file**; a parade of some 10,000 AFL members before the strikes and after Tobin's name-calling proclaimed their support of Local 574.

minority strike—A strike conducted by a minority within the **bargaining unit** without the authorization of the majority. Such a strike is unprotected; that is, an employer can legally fire or take disciplinary action against the participants because he has agreed to bargain only with the **union** and the employees have agreed to bargain only through the union. See **partial strike**, **wildcat strike**.

model contract—An initial set of contract proposals, usually drawn up by an **international union** to be put on the table by a **local**, designed to satisfy all the needs and aspirations of that union in achieving a just agreement, including a reflection of **real wages**, a reduced workweek, the latest health and safety regulations, and fringe benefits. Meant more as a guide and statement of goals rather than **strike issues**.

Mohawk Valley formula—A technique widely used by U.S. industry in the 1930s, first developed by the Remington Rand Co. in New York state's Mohawk Valley, that provided for systematic denunciation of all labor **organizers** and leaders as dangerous radicals, use of local police to break up labor meetings, propaganda campaigns to align the local citizenry behind "law and order," organization of vigilante committees to protect plants that hired **strikebreakers**, **back-to-work movements**, and threats to pull up stakes from the community if labor were not "put in its place." The **La Follette Committee**'s publicizing of these practices led to their abolition or at least their toning down.

Molly Maguires—A secret organization of mostly Irish coal miners of the mid-1870s who, in the face of the intimidation tactics of strikebreaking mine owners led by Franklin B. Gowen of the Pennsylvania & Reading Railroad, resorted to arson, assault, rob-

bery, and occasional murder in striking back. The purpose was to terrorize the mining companies into restoring pre–**Long Strike** wages; the result was Gowen's hiring the **Pinkertons**, who, with the aid of undercover informant James McParlan, broke the organization by bringing criminal charges against 24 Mollies and hanging 10 of them. The identity of the Molly Maguires—named after a secret anti-landlord organization led by the widow Molly Maguire during the mid-1840s Irish Famine—has never been proved, however, and there is evidence to the charge that the entire episode was deliberately manufactured by the coal operators with the express purpose of destroying all traces of unionism in the area after the Long Strike, and that the coalfields "crime wave" appeared *after* the Pinkertons. A good movie treatment of the subject is to be found in *The Molly Maguires*, with Richard Harris and Sean Connery. The Pinkertons went on to gain further notoriety as **strike-breakers** in the **Homestead Strike** of 1892.

Mooney-Billings case—A West Coast labor cause célèbre of the 1920s and 1930s; named after Thomas J. Mooney, an International Molders' Union organizer, and Warren K. Billings, a shoe factory worker and friend of Mooney, both of whom were charged with setting off a bomb during a martial parade in San Francisco on July 22, 1916. The blast killed nine people and injured 40, and Mooney, a onetime **Industrial Workers of the World** member, and Billings were arrested as the "anarchists" responsible, though evidence was scanty. Both men were convicted, but the case dragged on for more than two decades as the **labor movement** defended—and financed appeals for—Mooney and Billings as victims of the antiunion, **open-shop** drive being waged in San Francisco at the time. Eventually, convincing evidence was produced to show that Mooney, who was still on death row, had been nowhere near the scene of the bombing. A new round of appeals in 1938 went all the way to the California statehouse, where Mooney testified he was convicted because "Billings and I stood in the way of an open-shop town." In 1939, Mooney, then 57, was finally given an official pardon. Billings, who had drawn a life sentence, gained his freedom shortly thereafter.

moonlighting—Now called "multi-job holding"; the holding of more than one job, thus suggesting the extra work is performed "by the light of the moon." In 1960, the **Bureau of Labor Statistics** estimated that about 3 million workers, or 5 percent of the **labor force**, were moonlighting. By the end of 1997, that number had climbed to 8.1 million, or 6.2 percent.

"Mother Jones" Mary Harris Jones (1830–1930)—Legendary Irish-born hell-raiser in the American **labor movement**. Widowed at 37 when her husband, iron molder George Jones, and all four children died of yellow fever, she moved to Chicago and became a dressmaker. After her house burned down in the Great Chicago Fire of 1871, she moved down the street and became an **organizer** with the **Knights of Labor** and, beginning in the  1890s, after the decline of the Knights, organized coal miners and **strikes** for the United Mine Workers of America in Pennsylvania, Ohio, Virginia, West Virginia, and Colorado and was at the vanguard of a coal strike in Kansas in 1921, when she was 91. A cofounder of the Socialist Democratic Party in 1898—she declared socialism to be "the remedy that would solve the labor problem of the world"—Mother Jones was already well enough known by 1905 that when the so-called "Continental Congress for the working class" convened that year in Chicago and resulted in the founding of the **Industrial Workers of the World (IWW)**, she was a featured speaker along with such labor stalwarts as **Eugene Debs** and **"Big Bill" Haywood**. Known for her bold tactics, Mother Jones fought on for decades with the only two weapons she said she needed, "firm convictions and a voice." She always seemed to be where the danger was greatest—crossing militia lines, spending weeks in dank and rat-infested prisons tending to sick miners in chains; standing up to armed **strikebreakers**, and incurring the wrath of governors, corporate nabobs, coal operators, and congressmen, all of whom were too happy to spread the canard of her alleged "disreputable and criminal career." At the age of 89 she was jailed for her part in a major steelworkers **walkout**. When she died, on December 1, 1930, her body was carried in grand procession from Maryland to Mount Olive, Illinois, where she was buried, in accordance to her wishes, next to the graves of five of her "boys" who had been shot down by strikebreaking gunmen in 1898.

Best-known quote: *"Pray for the dead, and fight like hell for the living."*

Muller v. Oregon—U.S. Supreme Court ruling in 1908 that sustained the right of a state to enact a law capping women's workdays at ten hours in order to protect health. Previously, state laws limiting women's work were under a legal cloud. As a result of Muller, more than 40 states wrote new or improved maximum-hour laws for women between 1909 and 1917. Most of these extended the scope of the statutes to cover both factories and mercantile establishments and limited the working day to nine hours or the workweek to 54. In addition, five states prohibited night work for women. See **working women's movement, equal pay for women.**

multi-employer bargaining—Negotiations involving more than one company in a given industry and resulting in a **master agreement**. Because of the size of the industries they deal with, the steelworkers, Teamsters, mineworkers, and automakers unions are most apt to engage in such bargaining.

Murray, Philip (1886–1952)—Scottish-born United Mine Workers leader; a co-founder of the Congress of Industrial Organizations (**CIO**), with **John L. Lewis**, and later its president. A coal miner from the age of ten, he emigrated to the United States in 1902  and held numerous offices in the UMW until reaching the vice presidency in 1920, a post he retained until 1942. Meanwhile, as head of the Steel Workers Organizing Committee, Murray astonished the labor world in 1937 by securing a **contract** with the **open-shop** diehard Carnegie-Illinois Steel Co., a subsidiary of the giant U.S. Steel, that included a 40-hour week, **wage** increases, and **union** recognition. When other, independent "**Little Steel**" companies held out, Murray called a **strike** and was horrified when it led to the infamous **Memorial Day Massacre** in which from 10 to 17 unarmed demonstrators lost their lives. When Lewis stepped down as CIO president in 1940, Murray took over and remained head of the federation until 1952. His tact and personal skills are credited with keeping the then-militant CIO together during the difficult World War II years when the needs of labor had to be counterbalanced with the demands and sacrifices of a wartime economy.

Myers, Isaac (1835–1891)—Early African American labor leader who, though moderate, became an inspiration for later generations of black labor activists. Though the son of former slaves, Myers was born free in Baltimore and became a ship caulker at an early age. In 1865, when a **strike** by white craftsmen drove Myers and other black workers from the Baltimore shipyards, white merchants helped the blacks form their own cooperative, the Baltimore Colored Caulkers' Union. Myers fast gained recognition as a major spokesman for black tradesmen and in early 1869 led a delegation of nine African American labor associations seeking admission to the **National Labor Union**. After bitter debate following Myers's speech that "slavery, or slave labor, the main cause of the degradation of white labor, is no more," the delegation was seated. But almost insurmountable racial prejudice among the white **trade unions** of the NLU soon nullified that recognition, and Myers and others founded the **National Colored Labor Union** in December 1869. Despite strong backing from co-founder, noted writer, abolitionist and former slave **Frederick Douglass**, the NCLU lasted but a few years, succumbing to hardening attitudes in the post-Reconstruction South. Myers, a believer in black-white cooperation among unions and in the workplace, became discouraged and dropped out of **labor-movement** activism in 1871 and was in turn a detective for the U.S. Postal System, a tax collector, and the head of several black business organizations in Baltimore, though he continued to champion, less conspicuously now, the rights of black workers. In his final 15 years, Myers became active in the Methodist church and wrote a number of religious tracts and poems. See **blacks in the labor movement**.

N

NAFTA (North American Free Trade Agreement)—A U.S.-Mexico trade pact that took effect January 1, 1994, hitching onto the **Free Trade Agreement** that the United States signed with Canada in 1989. But 16 years after its inception, NAFTA's turkeys have come home to roost. By now it is clear, say economists, that the costs to workers far exceed the benefits: jobs have been lost, the U.S. trade deficit has worsened, and the resultant failed agricultural policies in Mexico have hastened the flight of *campesinos* (farmworkers) to the United States, aggravating tensions around undocumented workers. Mexican employment did increase, but much of it was in low-wage **maquiladoras**, which the promoters of NAFTA promised would disappear. But this is no surprise to the initial skeptics of NAFTA. As a former Mexican foreign minister told the Washington, D.C.-based Economic Policy Institute, NAFTA was "an agreement for the rich and powerful . . . effectively excluding ordinary people in all three societies [Canada, Mexico and the United States]." Defenders of the agreement have two main responses: the damage to workers is exaggerated (but NAFTA was supposed to make things a great deal better and not even a little worse); and the problems of inequality are largely the result of domestic policies, not **globalization** (an argument that ignores the enormous economic leverage granted to transnational corporations, which can shift production out of the country and then sell products back to the country at higher prices). In September 2007, the Bush administration began a pilot program to allow some Mexican trucks to carry cargo anywhere in the United States as part of a NAFTA provision. A development unfriendly to U.S. labor in its effort to take advantage of a low-wage pool of Mexican truck drivers, the program was later ended by Congressional legislation signed by President Barack Obama in March 2009. The Teamsters' campaign against the provision has been accused of playing into the racist and anti-immigrant stereotypes that have been used against "foreign" workers for decades.

National Colored Labor Union (NCLU, also called Colored National Labor Union)—Short-lived trade-union organization co-founded (with famed former abolitionist **Frederick Douglass**) by Baltimore ship caulker **Isaac Myers** in 1869. With its slogan, "free land for freed men," it hoped to capitalize on the post–Civil War land rush as well as a slave-free labor market, and looked to the party of Lincoln, the GOP, for its salvation. Myers had hoped earlier that year to **affiliate** with the mostly white **National Labor Union**, but although that federation did seat Myers and other black delegates, the following year the fifth congress of the NLU spurned the bid for formal affiliation and the NCLU was left on its own. Myers then spearheaded an **organizing** drive throughout the South, but that petered out, as did the organization itself a few years later. Racial prejudice had hardened and African American workers were relegated to the fringes of the skilled trades and to what Myers feared: laboring as "the sweepers of shavings, the scrapers of pitch, the carriers of mortar." They were not to rise out of that labor ghetto in significant numbers until the **CIO** organizing drives of the 1930s. See **blacks in the labor movement, Brotherhood of Sleeping Car Porters.**

National Consumers League—Founded in 1899 by a group of socially conscious women, the league fought for safe workplaces, reasonable **minimum wages**, and decent working hours for women and children decades before the New Deal. Its most notable achievement was bringing public attention, and legal help, to several women who were dying of radiation poisoning from applying radium-activated paint to watches, aircraft controls, clocks, and compass faces in factories in four states between 1917 and 1929. The so-called Radium Girls had been encouraged by their supervisors at U.S. Radium to lick their camel's-hair brushes to a fine point, with assurances that this posed no danger. The issue was brought to a head with an out-of-court settlement in 1928, but the Radium Girls set a precedent in case law for the right of individual workers to sue employers for damages caused by on-the-job abuse. In the wake of the legal battle, industrial safety standards were enhanced by the passage of federal laws that made occupational diseases compensable and extended the time during which workers could discover illnesses and make claims.

national emergency strike—Strikes that are not expressly forbidden by the **Taft-Hartley Act** but which may be enjoined for up to 80 days if, in the opinion of the president, they threaten the national health or safety. See **cooling-off period, emergency dispute.**

National Industrial Recovery Act (NIRA)—Created in 1933 by the Roosevelt administration, it gave birth to the National Recovery Administration (NRA). The fledgling NIRA announced as its goal "the assurance of reasonable profit to industry, and **living wages** for labor," as well as workers' right to organize. Congress appropriated $3.3 million for a gigantic public works program to create business for heavy industry in particular and all industry in general, thus stimulating a Depression-racked economy and providing employment for large numbers of men (women didn't figure into such statistics in those days). One result was the Works Progress Administration (WPA). Despite this, many labor leaders saw the act as a triumph for corporatism. Business hostility to the labor provisions and increasing red tape made a number of the codes unenforceable, and in May 1935 the U.S. Supreme Court struck down the NIRA as unconstitutional. The labor protections were shortly picked up by the **National Labor Relations Act (NLRA).**

National Labor Board—Forerunner of the **National Labor Relations Board**, established in 1933 to enforce the collective-bargaining provisions of the **National Industrial Recovery Act,** but had little power and was in any case invalidated when the U.S. Supreme Court struck down the NRA as unconstitutional in 1935.

National Labor Party—See **American Labor Party.**

National Labor Relations Act (NLRA)—Alternately called the

Wagner Act; the basis of current U.S. labor law, embodying the twin principles of unions' right to organize and employers' obligation to bargain collectively with them on hours, **wages**, and other terms and conditions of employment. The NLRA also established the **National Labor Relations Board**, by which the provisions of the Act could be enforced both through "cease and desist" orders and the circuit courts. Although in the past the federal government revealed favorable attitudes toward labor, passage of the NLRA showed for the first time in U.S. history the government's *willingness to form a partnership with labor*. Obviously, this has changed over the years. But for all its restrictive amendments and watering down since becoming law in July 1935, the NLRA remains the constitution of American labor. See **Railway Labor Act**.

National Labor Relations Board (NLRB)—An independent federal agency created by Congress in 1935 in conjunction with the **National Labor Relations Act (NLRA)** to oversee and enforce the provisions of the NLRA; in effect, serving as a court of appeals. Among other things, the Board supervises union **certification** and **decertification** elections, hears and acts on **unfair labor practice** charges, and conducts **fact-finding**. It also has the power to adjudicate claims before it and to enforce its judgments in the federal courts. The Board's five members— increased from three by the **Taft-Hartley Act** of 1947—are appointed to five-year terms by the president, subject to Senate approval. (Subject also to political mood—a Reagan appointee, Donald Dotson, was former chairman of the National Right to Work Committee.) Taft-Hartley also removed the Board's power to prosecute, and whereas the NLRA focused exclusively on restraining unfair practices by employers, the 1947 legislation required the Board to examine such practices by unions as well. The 1959 **Landrum-Griffin Act** added further to the list of prohibited union activities the NLRB must investigate.

National Labor Union (NLU)—The first "permanent" labor organization in the United States on a national scale, it was founded in August 1866 at a convention in Baltimore attended by 75 delegates representing some 60,000 workers in 13 states. Headed by **William Sylvis** of the International Molders' Union, the NLU stated as its main aim the legal **eight-hour day**, but it also espoused rigorous enforcement of **apprenticeship** rules, the abolition of the convict labor system, and a repeal of the **Contract Labor Act** of 1864—a campaign that bore fruit in 1868 when Congress nullified the Act. The organization was somewhat less successful with the eight-hour day, although President Ulysses S. Grant decreed it mandatory in 1872 for certain sectors of the federal government, and by 1873 the shorter workday was well on its way to becoming a national standard, thanks to the NLU. Reflecting its white male constituency, however, the NLU had problems with women and black unionists, though its leadership favored the aims of both movements—indeed, loudly and unprecedentedly in the case of women. But by 1873, the NLU was moribund, torn between rival factions representing, on one hand, the democratic, egalitarian, humanitarian, politically conscious, and reformist movement of postbellum America and, on the other, the self-centered, wage-driven **trade unionism** that was to mark the **labor movement** of the late 19th century. Future labor confederations would, with varying success, constructively harness both tendencies. See **working women's movement**.

National Trades' Union (NTU)—A short-lived (1834–37) organization, forerunner of truly nationwide federations and **unions** that coalesced in the 1860s and 1970s. Formed as an advisory body only, it soon was actively lobbying for a ten-hour day for naval-yard mechanics—partially achieved in 1835 when President Andrew Jackson established that as the standard workday in the Philadelphia federal shipyards. Not unlike other labor groups of the day, however, the NTU denounced the emplyment of women outside the home, despite their ever-growing numbers—and occasional **labor movement militancy**—in the nation's **factory system**. The downside of the NTU's and other trade associations' relative success was the corresponding proliferation of employers' associations whose sole purpose, in their own words, was the destruction of labor organizations, which "fostered oppression, tyranny and misrule" and obstructed "the free course of trade." See **unions as conspiracies.**

National War Labor Board (NWLB)—Board set up by President Franklin D. Roosevelt after the 1941 Pearl Harbor attack and U.S. entry into World War II to arbitrate labor-management disputes and set **wages** for all workers. A similar board had been set up during World War I. Although it made **strikes** virtually impossible, particularly on the production lines, and held down wage increases, the NWLB in many ways set the pace for postwar **union** advances. In 1943, for instance, it ordered an end to wage **differentials** based on race (thanks in no small part to pressure by black labor leader **A. Philip Randolph**) and insisted on **equal pay for equal work**. And to offset labor leaders' fears of declining union membership because of the military draft and disinclination to join because of stagnant wages, the board enacted a **"maintenance of membership"** policy, which meant that any employee at a unionized workplace had to join and pay **dues** to a union. From that point, expansion of war production led almost automatically to an expansion of union membership. On the other hand, the **Smith-Connally Act** and the board's wartime strike and wage restrictions led to such a flood of postwar strikes that conservatives in Congress found a receptive public response with passage of the 1947 **Taft-Hartley Act**. The most publicized instance of war-board action came in April 1944 when Roosevelt ordered the Army to seize the executive offices of Montgomery Ward for attempting to abrogate **union-shop** provisions in its **contract** with the United Retail, Wholesale and Department Store Employees of America. The photo of defiant store-chain CEO Sewell Avery being carried out bodily by soldiers made the front page of almost every newspaper in the country. See **War Production Board**.

negotiations—The sometimes prolonged procedure by which, through talks, meetings and hard **bargaining**, an employer and a **labor union** arrive—one hopes—at a tentative **settlement** of a **contract**, subject to **ratification** by the union's membership.

Such negotiations are usually said to be conducted across or over a **bargaining table.**

Newlands Act—An act of Congress in 1900 that established a United States Board of Mediation and Conciliation, the forerunner of the **Federal Mediation and Conciliation Service.** The primary purpose of the Act, a by-product of open hostility to the **Erdman Act** of a couple of years earlier, was to set up a new mechanism for handling railway disputes.

New York Central Railroad Co. v. White—A 1917 U.S. Supreme Court ruling that established the right of states to institute compulsory **workers' compensation.**

no-raiding agreements—Pacts between **international unions** in which they pledge not to persuade workers to leave one union and join another—"raiding"—when the first union has already set up shop, as it were. **AFL-CIO**-affliliated unions in good standing are signators to a standing no-raiding policy, and several unions have signed bilateral agreements covering the organization of unorganized workers. In fact, mutual raiding was a primary cause of the AFL-CIO merger in 1955. Probably the most aggressive raiders on the American labor scene in the late 1950s, 1960s, and 1970s were the Teamsters, although it could be argued, with considerable justification, that since the **Brotherhood** had been expelled from the AFL-CIO in 1957 (the Teamsters were readmitted 30 years later, in 1987), it was no longer legally bound by the strictures and codes of the federation. See **raiding.**

Norris–La Guardia Act—The last major pro-labor law to be enacted (1932) before the advent of Franklin D. Roosevelt's New Deal, the Act limited the power of federal courts to issue **injunctions** in labor disputes—in fact, it was called the Anti-Injunction Act—and made **yellow-dog contracts** unenforceable by declaring that workers could not be sued by their employers for breaking such **contracts.** Named for its sponsors, Senator George W. Norris of Nebraska and Representative Fiorello H. La Guardia of New York, both Republicans.

no-strike clause—A clause in a labor agreement that prohibits employees from striking at any time during the life of the **contract**. The **National Labor Relations Board** has held it is not an **unfair labor practice** for an employer to **bargain in good faith** for such a clause, though obviously it must have the consent of the **union**. Many employers have in fact found it worthwhile to purchase labor peace by pushing for a no-strike clause in exchange for significant **wage** sweeteners. See **yellow-dog contract**.

North American Aviation strike (1941)—Like the **Allis-Chalmers strike** two months earlier, this initially **wildcat work stoppage** on June 5 by 12,000 members of United Auto Workers–**CIO** Local 683 was marked by Roosevelt administration antipathy—this time to the extent of sending in federal troops to assault **picket lines**. Union spokesmen later called it the first military engagement of World War II on American soil against American workers (Pearl Harbor was six months away). **Minimum wage** at the Inglewood, California, aircraft manufacturer was 40 cents an hour, 10 cents below even that of Depression-era government relief agencies. The union asked for a 75-cent hourly minimum and 10 more cents an hour for all workers; in response, company president J.H. Kindleberger scoffed: "I don't have to pay any more to my workers because most of them are young kids who spend their money on a flivver and a gal." They weren't and they didn't. Faced with overwhelming force, the strikers folded on June 9. Adding insult to injury, the UAW **international**, spooked by reports of communist infiltration of Local 683, suspended its officers.

Occupational Safety and Health Act (OSHA)—A law enacted by Congress in 1970 establishing minimum safety and health regulations in the workplace, requiring inspections and accident/illness reporting, currently under heavy fire in a big-business-fostered climate of **deregulation**. Under OSHA, the

U.S. secretary of labor is empowered to promulgate national health and safety standards and to enforce such standards by seeking civil and criminal penalties against offenders. But broad congressional authority originally granted to OSHA to make spot inspections of business premises without a warrant has since been held unconstitutional, so such inspections can now be made only under certain legal conditions. Like many other federal regulatory agencies, OSHA has been further vitiated by the George W. Bush administration.

off the clock—Extra work, usually **overtime**, performed by employees that isn't reflected in their paychecks. A practice encouraged by some employers, particularly in the customer-services field, to keep labor costs down—and expressly forbidden by the **Fair Labor Standards Act**. A nationally acclaimed success in countering such practices was achieved in 1991 by the United Food and Commercial Workers (UFCW) **union** when it sued the Seattle-based Nordstrom department-store chain for employees' back wages for years of off-the-clock work. But although the UFCW won the battle, it lost the war—Nordstrom orchestrated a successful **decertification** campaign against the union in retaliation.

offshore/offshoring—The practice of transferring a U.S.-owned business or investment property to foreign, tax-free, and labor-law-free countries, particularly in the Caribbean and third world. See **sweatshops**.

one-in-ten—An "escape valve" practice of some **unions**—The Newspaper Guild, for instance—to allow one out of every ten new hires to opt for not joining the union; often negotiated as a compromise between a union-demanded **union shop** and an employer-demanded **open shop**. The decision usually must be made within a specified number of days after being hired and cannot be exercised afterward. Such an employee—often called a **free rider**—does not have to pay **dues** or **agency fees** but is entitled to the same rights and benefits as union members in the **bargaining unit**.

open shop—A device of employers to maintain a workplace where there is a **union** but nobody is required to join it. Alternately, a workplace where no union is recognized by the employer and union membership is discouraged or prohibited. See **American Plan, closed shop, union shop, one-in-ten.**

opening contract (time constraints)—Unions and employers don't suddenly sit down and start talking about a new contract. **Good-faith bargaining** usually starts with a 60-day "window" during which both sides present their proposals in writing, although there is nothing to prevent either from doing so beforehand or, with due notice, from adding proposals afterward. The object is to give both parties time to prepare counterproposals and to avoid surprises that could derail **negotiations** before they begin.

"Operation Dixie"—An ambitious but unsuccessful 1946–48 campaign by the Congress of Industrial Organizations (**CIO**) to organize the South. Hoping to piggyback on the **organizing** successes of the 1930s and World War II years, particularly among black workers, the federation allocated $1 million—a considerable sum in those days—and hired 400 organizers to send to key cities in the largely antiunion South, many of whose states were already starting to enact **right-to-work laws.** Initially, the drive showed promise. By February 1947, the CIO's Southern Organizing Committee was able to report that 324 new local **unions** had been established, mainly in the textile, lumber, and tobacco industries. But the operation quickly unraveled in the face of a basic dilemma: the South was overwhelmingly Democratic; it was also segregationist Jim Crow. To unionize African Americans was to alienate the local power structure, which provided the key link in the Northern-Dixiecrat coalition that had kept the Democrats in the White House the past decade and a half. And **organized labor** depended on the Democrats for national pro-union legislation. In the midst of this came the 1947 **Taft-Hartley Act,** which further hobbled labor. Add to this the open hostility of white workers, the insularity of Southern **company towns** and the atmosphere of threats and physical that civil rights workers were to encounter—with much more publicity—20 years later, and Operation Dixie folded two years

after it was launched, pronounced by even its promoters as a
"thorough failure." In fact, the proportion of Southern workers
organized into unions actually declined in the next few years.
The South remains largely unorganized to this day.

organized labor—Generally, the entire apparatus of the **AFL-CIO**
and its PACs, **affiliated unions** and organizations and their
members, and the policies enunciated therein. Its polar opposite
is the business/industrial bloc represented by the National Association of Manufacturers, the U.S. Chamber of Commerce, and
the **Business Roundtable.**

organizing—The sum total of the time, money, work, activity, planning, mobilization, and whatever other resources a **union** or
labor federation expends in bringing a new **bargaining unit** into
being. Organizing is to the **labor movement** what recruitment,
volunteerism, and the draft are to the military.

Organizing Institute—A branch of the **AFL-CIO** created in 1989 to
train **union** organizers in a nationwide push to revitalize the
union movement. In 1990, it spent $400,000 to train 25 orga-
nizers; in 1996, it spent $4 million to train 320 new organizers.
It has spent millions more and trained hundreds more in each
year since. See **George Meany Center for Labor Studies, Lane
Kirkland** Center.

outsourcing—The subcontracting of a company's work to a nonunion plant where the **wages** are much lower. Nowadays, it's
usually the case of a transnational outsourcing to a Third World
country. In the past, it meant transferring the work to a Southern or **right-to-work state**, although this, too, continues today.
Outsourcing was a major bone of contention in successful
strikes against Boeing and General Motors in the 1990s.

overtime—Time worked beyond regular hours of a **shift** that is paid
at a higher rate, usually time and a half or, by mutual consent,
compensatory time—so-called comp time. Overtime, as a concept of extra pay for extra hours, was first mentioned in a labor
grievance in 1861, when overtime didn't begin until after the
standard ten-hour day or six-day, 60-hour work week. Labor laws
in many states make overtime compensation mandatory even in

workplaces with no **union** contract, a statute that renders **off-the-clock** work illegal per se.

P

Palmer Raids—A series of raids throughout the United States in 1919–20 guided by Attorney General A. Mitchell Palmer, ostensibly to root out "Bolshevism" in general and communists in particular. Their immediate cause, however, was a crippling steel **strike** in 1919 that virtually shut down the industry as more than 300,000 workers walked out. To justify what in many instances was savage repression of the strikers—clubbings, gassings, and shootings by police and federal troops was common in the Pittsburgh area, for example—the steel companies successfully portrayed the conflict not as a labor dispute but as an attempted revolution. And, because many of the strikers were immigrants, it was not hard to shift the focus to "aliens" as well, although, ironically, the companies were trucking in hundreds of Mexican **strikebreakers** at the same time. Even before the strike was broken in January 1920, the residue was a major **Red scare**. In November 1919, Palmer's agents arrested 250 members of the Union of Russian Workers, beating up many though recommending only 39 for deportation. The next month, 249 foreigners were shipped off to the Soviet Union; most had never been charged with a crime and many had lived in the United States for decades. Based largely on "information" supplied by an up-and-coming Palmer aide, J. Edgar Hoover, the Palmer Raids reached their height in January 1920, when federal agents—without warrants in many cases—arrested 6,000 alleged communists in 33 cities, coerced confessions from some, and held others who had no connection whatsoever to radical activities. The excesses of this raid, however, dampened enthusiasm for the operation. The **Labor Department**, in charge of deportations, ended its cooperation with Palmer's Justice Department and allowed only 600 of the January arrestees to be deported; the public tired of the Red scare, and employers began worrying more about alienating their foreign-born employees and less about revolution now that the steel strike had been defeated. See **immigrants in the labor movement**.

paper local—Just that: a union **local** that exists on paper only, without any real members, based on a charter used for illegitimate purposes. The holder of the **charter** thus enters into a **sweetheart contract** with an employer. Not only is such a local denounced by the **AFL-CIO**'s **Code of Ethical Practices**, it is forbidden by U.S. labor law.

parity—The equivalence established between the **wage** schedules of some categories of employees. Although commonly invoked in public-sector **unions** to describe the percentage ratio between the salaries of, for example, police and firefighters, it is also used in the private sector. The Newspaper Guild, for example, has for years fought for—and often achieved—parity between higher-paid newsroom employees and those in the circulation and advertising departments.

partial strike—A concerted attempt by employees while remaining at work to bring economic pressure on their employer to force him/her to accede to their demands. Akin to a **slowdown**, this type of labor action, like the **minority strike**, is not protected by **National Labor Relations Act** law against an employer's retaliation in the form of firing or disciplinary action.

past practice—A custom or modus vivendi in the workplace outside the **contract** that can, over time, acquire contractual force. If, for example, the contract states that employees are allowed no more than a half-hour for lunch but in fact they've taken an hour for lunch over the past several years and management has turned a blind eye, the **union** could argue in **arbitration**, with probable success, that an hour's lunch constitutes past practice and should be upheld as the norm. By the same token, an employer who over a period of time consistently violated or ignored a clause of the contract, without any **grievance** or formal objection by the **union**, could successfully invoke past practice in the same type of arbitration. Needless to say, past practice is accorded great weight by arbitrators provided it is not in violation of state, federal, or labor law. In the everyday world, however, past practice is the standard procedure many companies and their unions tacitly and nonadversarialy use to paper over ambiguous or nonexistent wording in a contract, with the mutual understanding that no contract can possibly cover all contingencies in a workplace.

PATCO strike (1981)—Professional Air Traffic Controllers Organization **strike**, waged in August 1981 by its 13,000 members, was broken by President Ronald Reagan, clearly signaling that the bargaining atmosphere in both public and private sectors had changed and that the federal government's policies would

 henceforth favor business and undermine labor. Reagan's **strikebreaking** action—which broke the **union** as well—also ushered in a prosperous era for **management consultants** specializing in **union-busting**. The PATCO strike, however, had been years in the making, as accumulated problems and **grievances** went unresolved by the Federal Aviation Administration (FAA) from one administration to the next. In fact, while Jimmy Carter was president, this history of negligence grew into an FAA management campaign of harassment and the formation of the Management Strike Contingency Force in the summer of 1980. Thus, the strike a year later simply put into motion an apparatus already set up under a Democratic administration.

Paterson Textile Strike (1913)—An ill-fated 208-day strike led by the **Industrial Workers of the World (IWW)** that was almost the antithesis of the **Lawrence Textile Strike** a year earlier. Much like Lawrence, Paterson, New Jersey, was a one-industry town: in Lawrence's case, textile weaving; in Paterson's case, silk. As far back as 1835, children in Paterson's silk mills had gone on strike for an 11-hour day, six-day week. The same conditions prevailed in 1913 Paterson as at 1912 Lawrence: a largely unskilled and immigrant workforce, the majority of them women and minors, working for low **wages** in the face of **speedups**. The immediate cause of the strike—which ultimately put 25,000 workers on the streets and resulted in five strikers' deaths—was the mills' conversion from a two-loom to a four-loom system, increasing the wear and tear on weavers without any increase in wages. But from the time of the initial **walkout** at the Henry Doherty Co. on February 28, mill owners were able to exploit the differences between these workers and their higher-paid, English-speaking counterparts in the skilled **AFL**-affiliated **craft unions**, which constituted a powerful minority in the more-exacting silk trade. Despite the appearance of such luminaries as radical writer John Reed and IWW leader **"Big Bill" Haywood** (who was arrested) and a spectacular fund-raising pageant in New York's Madison Square Garden, the strike collapsed on September 24 after the skilled workers—who had taken three weeks to **hit the bricks** after the strike began—agreed to go back to their jobs on a shop-by-shop basis, leaving the unskilled immigrants high and dry. If Lawrence was the high point of the IWW, Paterson was close to the nadir and completely exhausted the Wobblies' treasury.

pattern bargaining—The practice of **labor unions** with like interests or in the same industry holding together in coalitions and presenting a united front, with the object of making **wages**, **benefits**, and **contract** expiration dates uniform in that industry. The goal is not to settle individually but as a group, and "nothing is settled until everything is settled." For years, pattern bargaining—also called coalition or coordinated bargaining—set the pace in the automaking, steel, and mining industries, though it was dealt a severe setback in the **Phelps-Dodge copper strike** of 1983.

pay envelope—The form, which must seem archaic to young workers of the 21st century, in which until the late 1960s most wage earners received their weekly pay: cash, including change, in a small brown envelope, accompanied with a receipt itemizing **dues**, **checkoffs**, tax deductions, etc. Today, most **wages** are paid impersonally via check and/or are direct-deposited into the employee's bank or credit-union account without so much as a whiff of cash—or human contact with a payroll secretary.

pay for performance (PFP)—A **white-collar** variation of **incentive pay** in which employees are graded on performance evaluations and awarded a corresponding raise, usually a percentage in excess of the contractual minimum. Pushed as the ideal "objective" equity compensation system by some employers in the early 1980s, PFP was found by **unions** to be anything but equitable because its basis, evaluations, were subjective at best and fraught with favoritism and rancor at worst. Moreover, although contractual minimums stayed static, **wage** gaps increased as the favored saw steady increments in their base salary and the unfavored many fell further behind in percentage gains. Indeed, as PFP evolved in some contracts and replaced contractual "floors," certain employees received no raise at all because of "poor evaluations." By the early 1990s, PFP—the primary objective of which was to reduce overall labor costs—had lost much of its management glamour in the face of growing divisiveness in the workplace and employees' perception of it as a backdoor approach to a **two-tiered wage system**.

pensions/pension plans—In a labor context, a fixed amount, other than **wages**, paid at regular intervals to a retiree or surviving dependents. A mainstay of the **benefits** portion of most labor **contracts** for at least the past half-century, pensions are almost always a negotiated item and administered jointly by **union** and management; their often-esoteric formulas, rates of payment, and terms of eligibility are spelled out in the contract or, in the case of wholly company-administered schemes—such as **Employee Stock Option Plans (ESOPs)**—referred to in the text. The term *pension* dates back to the mid-14th century, meaning a weighing-out or payment. See **portable pensions, private pension plans**.

PERC (Public Employment Relations Commission)—Representative agency—in this case, Washington state—that mediates in and oversees public-employee union relations and disputes, or relations involving an industrial or **trade union** with a public employer, such as, for instance, Teamsters-organized police **guilds** in dealings with city governments. PERC, an independent agency, functions in the public sector much as the **National Labor Relations Board** and **Federal Mediation & Conciliation Service** do in the private sector. Legislated into being in 1976 to assume the role previously played by the state Division of Labor & Industries, PERC serves about 200,000 employees in jurisdictions ranging from city and county governments to port and public-utility districts to community colleges. Similar agencies exist in Wisconsin, New Jersey, New York, and Michigan, to name a few.

per capita dues (per caps)—The amount, generally set by percentage formula, that a **local** regularly remits to its **international** (or national) from the **dues** collected from individual members. Locals chronically delinquent or faulting in their per-cap payments are subject to sanctions by the larger body, which can range from verbal warnings to fines, to the international delegating someone to run the local's business affairs, to revoking the local's **charter**.

permanent replacement workers—Brought in by employers to break a **strike** or bust a **union**, replacement workers, or **scabs**, have always been part of the American labor scene when it came to strikes. But up to the 1980s, such workers generally lasted only as long as the strike. When it ended, the strikers, unless they committed illegal acts during the dispute, went back to their old jobs. It was their right; they were protected by labor law. Or were they? Technically, no—there was a loophole in the **National Labor Relations Act** that allowed employers to replace them permanently. But, fearing repercussions, they seldom invoked it. That is, until the **PATCO strike** and the labor-bashing that accompanied the Reagan years, when employers found they could not only legally replace strikers for good but also enjoy the tacit blessing of the **National Labor Relations Board**, which was by then majority-weighted with pro-business members. Various efforts to change the law since then have failed, although a notable break in the tenor of the times occurred in the aftermath of the 1995–96 **Detroit newspaper strike** when a federal judge ruled that both papers had to hire back the strikers they had fired. See **Workplace Fairness Bill**.

permissive subjects of bargaining—Subjects that either side of the **bargaining table** may propose but are not required to, in contrast to **mandatory subjects of bargaining**. Permissive subjects might include, but are not limited to, internal union matters such as dues **checkoff**, legal-liability clauses, leaves of absence, employee bonuses, auto mileage rates, sick-leave policy, employee insurance, and **union labels**. On the company side, such subjects might include dress code, liquor and firearms policies, a **management-rights clause**, company cafeteria hours, and an outside-activities clause. None of these subjects, of course, can be at odds with state or federal statutes *even if both parties were to reach agreement on it*. See **illegal subjects of bargaining**.

Phelps-Dodge copper strike (1983)—A pivotal Reagan-era strike that was to unionized Arizona copper miners what the **PATCO**  **strike** of two years earlier had been to air-traffic controllers and the **Hormel Strike** would be two years later to organized meatpackers. All three were broken, in large measure, by permanent replacement of strikers. The Phelps-Dodge strike ended in **decertification** of the United Steelworkers at that company as well as at a number of others in the industry and the extinction of the **union**'s chief **local** in the area. See **Workplace Fairness Bill**.

Philadelphia Plan—A type of **affirmative action** plan of the Nixon administration in 1969 whereby all contractors bidding on federally financed construction projects had to make a good-faith effort to meet a "goal" of black employment based on the ratio of black-white population of a city. Philadelphia, where Nixon unveiled the plan, was to be the model for other cities. But the plan was vigorously fought by **AFL-CIO** chief **George Meany** and the six building-trade **unions** it most affected, with Meany arguing it was a quota system in thin disguise and that the best way to get blacks into the construction trades was through **apprenticeship** programs, which would give them the skills they needed to obtain jobs on the vast number of projects that *weren't* federally funded. The hitch was that such programs were usually operated on family lines or some other exclusive basis and did not as a rule admit blacks. The issue became moot soon after, when Nixon softened his insistence on the Philadelphia Plan in exchange for AFL-CIO support for his Vietnam War policies.

picketing/picket lines—Publicizing the existence of a labor dispute by patrolling, usually with signs and placards, the site where the dispute is taking place. Picketing can also be an attempt to persuade other workers—unaffiliated or from other **unions**—to join a **work stoppage** or **strike**, discourage customers from patronizing a business, or both. A sanctioned picket line means the dispute has the backing of the **local** or **central labor council**; crossing such a line is considered support of the employer, or **scabbing**. *Picketing*, in its current union usage, first appeared in 1867, in England, though the noun *picket*, meaning a soldier or troops set out to watch for the enemy, goes back to at least 1761. See **informational, recognition**, and **common-situs picketing**.

pie card—A paid **union** official; once considered derogatory but now used freely by union officials themselves. An old railroad term, said to have originated from the 19th-century railroad practice of giving out tickets or cards to conductors and other trainmen entitling them to a free slice of pie at train station lunchrooms. By 1908 or so, the term had come to mean a meal ticket and in succeeding years often referred to the little red membership cards given out by the **Industrial Workers of the World (IWW)**, used by bearers to show trainmen and housewives they were honest workingmen worthy of a free ride or backdoor handout.

piecework pay—**Wages** paid on the number of units produced rather than for the time spent. Used in the garment and agricultural industries most often, though the practice was entrenched years ago in steelmaking and coal mining as well. In group piecework plans, much pushed by General Motors and others in the World War II years, the pay of all employees rose in partial proportion to the increase in production, regardless of wage ceilings.

pink-collar workers—Of or pertaining to nonproduction work traditionally done by women, especially in routine, lower-paying jobs such as office secretaries, bank tellers, telephone operators, and sales clerks. Cosmetologists hold that the term, which gained wide currency only in the late 1970s, came from the pink frocks worn by hairdressers and beauticians—almost always women—since the turn of the century. Others say it's an ironic though logical extension of the stereotypical pink-for-girls, blue-for-boys tradition. See **blue-** and **white-collar workers**.

Pinkertons—Generally, a derogatory term given to operatives of the Pinkerton National Detective Agency who, although originally hired by railroads to patrol trains and set up security systems, acquired notoriety from the 1870s on for their willingness to  infiltrate unions as **labor spies**, as in the case of the **Molly Maguires**, and to act as **strikebreakers**, sometimes murderously. (The Pinkertons were held responsible for initiating the violence of the 1892 **Homestead Strike**.) By the 1890s, *Pinkertonianism* was a synonym for strikebreaking by violence, and lexicographers trace the modern term *fink* to earlier slang for Pinkertons as *Pinks* and *Pinkies*. The firm was founded in Chicago in 1850 by Allan Pinkerton and gained fame 11 years later for helping thwart an assassination plot against President-elect Abraham Lincoln.

Now called Pinkerton Investigation Agency and Pinkerton Security in various parts of the country, it is largely given over to private detective work and providing security for corporations and their personnel, leaving strikebreaking duties to other, newer outfits such as Wackenhut, Vance International, and Asset Protection Services. A close contemporary rival to the Pinkertons in strikebreaking and spying was the William J. Burns International Detective Agency.

Pioneer Garfield Assembly—Short-lived women's **labor union** founded in the wake of a bitter but successful 1881 **strike** in Philadelphia by so-called lady shoemakers against their bosses. Its significance transcended the strike, however, when the newly affiliated **Knights of Labor** Garfield Assembly (Knights parlance for **local** or **lodge**) sent its delegate, shoemakers leader Mary Stirling, to the all-male Knights' convention that same year. Forced to take a stand on the issue, Knights chief **Terence Powderly** finally declared that "women should be admitted on equality with men," thus opening the doors to women members in large numbers. By the mid-1880s, women constituted one in ten Knights—a far higher ratio than in any other male-dominated labor organization in the United States. See **working women's movement**.

Pittston Coal strike (1989–90)—Deemed by many one of the most important—and longest and bitterest—strikes in the history of American labor, the nine-month action started in April when 1,700 miners and their families blocked roads to Pittston Coal's mines in Virginia, West Virginia, and Kentucky after the company demanded from the United Mine Workers of America (UMWA) cuts in **benefits**, work-rule changes, an end to **overtime** pay, the right to open nonunion mines, and withdrawal of **pensions** and **health benefits** for 130,000 retirees. The strike ended in January 1990 with some gains for the strikers (the company agreed to retain most benefits) and some losses (Pittston was allowed to subcontract, albeit with limits). Thanks to lopsided—and for the most part nonexistent—U.S. **media coverage**, an informal opinion poll in the Twin Cities midway through the strike showed that only 28 percent of the public were aware of the Pittston struggle, whereas 83 percent knew about a coal strike in the Soviet Union during the same time. See **Long Strike (1875)**, **media coverage of organized labor**.

portable pensions—Pension plans that enable employees who move from one place of employment to another in the same business or industry to transfer earned pension credits. Other plans are multi-employer; that is, several companies not necessarily engaged in the same industry establish a common fund to which their employees may subscribe.

portal-to-portal pay—Originally, a form of **differential pay** for the time spent in travel from the entrance to a mine to the actual place of work; since adapted to other industries where travel time from home to the job is a factor. In the construction business, for example, the job site—a remote dam or roadbuilding project—may be 50 miles or more from workers' residences. Generally paid as a set, predetermined sum, as opposed to mileage reimbursement, which can vary.

posted rules—A system of rules and regulations sometimes put into effect by an employer after a **contract** has expired and negotiations are bogged down or have reached an **impasse**. In other words, apart from state or federal law on **wages**, hours, and safety, the protections of the contract no longer apply. Unions' countermeasure to this is **work to rule**.

poverty index—A measurement formulated by the Social Security Administration that establishes a minimum income required to provide adequate food and housing for a typical family. Ranges in the index are determined by such things as the geographical location of the family, whether it is farm or nonfarm, and the number and age of family members.

Powderly, Terence V. (1849–1924)—One of the most influential labor leaders of the 19th century and head of the powerful **Knights of Labor** during the organization's greatest years. Born in Carbondale, Pennsylvania, Powderly went to work for the railroads at age 13 and rose rapidly in its shop **unions**, becoming president of the Machinists' and Blacksmiths' National Union in 1872. He joined the then-secretive Knights in 1874 and five years later was elected the federation's president or "Grand Master Workman," a post he held until 1893, sandwiching in between the mayoralty of Scranton, Pennsylvania (1878–84). An Irish Catholic whereas his predecessor, **Uriah Stephens**, was a staunch Protestant, Powderly implored workers to "throw strong drink aside as you would an ounce of liquid hell" and strongly advocated land reform, public education, and abolition of the **"wages** system." Championing a "union open to all," he gradually weaned the Knights from their Masonic-like ritualism and secrecy and brought new blood, both skilled and unskilled, and large numbers of women and immigrants, into the organization until it had 1 million members in 1886—the same year **Samuel Gompers** co-founded the American Federation of Labor (**AFL**). Aside from the AFL's making immediate inroads into the Knights' **rank and file**, 1886 was a fateful year for the Knights for another reason: the **Haymarket** riot, which Powderly bitterly denounced but for which the Knights were unjustly blamed anyway because some of the convicted Chicago defendants were members. Thereafter, the federation declined, and by the time Powderly stepped down in 1893, membership was at fewer than 100,000. He was admitted to the Pennsylvania bar the following year and served as federal immigration commissioner from 1897 to 1902 and headed a division of the U.S. Bureau of Immigration from 1907 to 1921. At the end, Powderly and Gompers shared another fate: they both died in 1924. See **working women's movement, immigrants in the labor movement, Pioneer Garfield Assembly**.

precedent—In labor-law usage, a finding, ruling, or binding decision, usually reached through **arbitration**, that governs future **grievances** or arbitration over the same issue even though the **contract** itself or its **side agreements** are silent on the matter. Generally, a precedent, or its essence, is incorporated into suceeding contracts or **memorandums of understanding** or, if found distasteful to either side, becomes an issue to be decided in the next round of **bargaining**. See **past practice**.

preferential hiring—See **union security**.

Pregnancy Discrimination Act—Federal law enacted in 1978 that bars employers with 15 or more employees from using pregnancy as an excuse for not giving a woman a job or from otherwise discriminating against expectant mothers.

prevailing wage—The average wage in a given industry or geographical area; used as an index to determine how the **Davis-Bacon Act** is to be applied. See **real wages.**

private pension plans—Non-government plans providing for regular payments to employees after retirement. In 1996, about 38 million people of all those privately employed in the United States were covered by some protection against the hazards of permanent and total disability, usually through disablity pension or early-retirement benefits. In the past 15 years, however, private pension funds increasingly have been the victims of corporate raids, sellouts, "restructuring" and defaults, and hundreds of thousands of pensioners have seen their checks cut in half or worse. In 1991, U.S. Senator Howard Metzenbaum (D-Ohio) then head of the Senate Labor and Human Resources Committee, testified that from 1984 to 1990, large employers milked workers' pension plans of $22 billion in surplus funds. One example cited was that of Davis Murdock, a Los Angeles–area millionaire who purchased the giant Cannon Mills textile plant in Kannapolis, South Carolina. He abruptly sold out, terminated the employees' pension fund, and took $38 million of the fund's surplus with him back to California. Earlier, he had invested $197 million of the funds in high-flying stock ventures and walked away with $60 million in profits. The Cannon workers took the hit; some were left looking forward to as little as $26 a month in retirement benefits. Probably the most egregious example of employee pension-bilking was described by labor lawyer/writer Thomas Geoghegan in his 1991 book *Which Side Are You On?*, in which International Harvester sold Wisconsin Steel to a "dummy buyer" in 1980. The sale absolved Harvester of any responsibility to manage Wisconsin's pension fund, which was already $65 million in the hole by 1977. When the plant closed shortly after the bogus sale, some 2,000 steelworkers lost not only their jobs but their pension benefits, health insurance, and **severance pay** worth $45 million as well. "The deal was so mean, so vile," writes Geoghegan, "that even the investment bankers gagged."

privatization—The handing over to private business services previously performed by public-sector union members—school bus transportation, prison management, and hazardous-waste removal, for example. Hailed by the business sector as a way to save taxpayers huge amounts of money and called by labor leaders a more subtle form of **union-busting**, privatization has one basic drawback: many of the privatized jobs pay minimum wage; have no health insurance, **pension**, vacation, or sick leave; and often pay so little that workers wind up seeking public assistance—hardly a relief to community tax burdens.

production workers—Those directly connected with manufacturing, operations, or extraction in industry, as contrasted with clerical or **white-collar workers**. Examples: assembly-line workers in the auto industry or coal miners. This category of workers tends to be heavily unionized.

productivity—A measurement of the efficiency of production; a ratio of output to input; for example, five units (output) per man hour (input). Although efficiency experts will argue that productivity is less due to worker effort than to increased capitalization and improved technology, **unions** have long argued that workers should share in the benefits of increased productivity, which tripled in the 50-year period between 1909 and 1959. Beginning in 1948 with an agreement between General Motors and the United Auto Workers, an "annual improvement factor" calling for yearly wage increases in recognition of workers' share in increased productivity was incorporated in several **contracts**.

professional negotiations—Term created by the National Education Association, the nationwide teachers union, to distinguish between the methods of determining the conditions of employment of schoolteachers and **collective bargaining** in the private sector. See **associations, brotherhoods, guilds, & labor unions.**

profit-sharing—A form of compensation over and above **wages** and based on the company's profits. Generally, profit-sharing plans are of two kinds: (1) a cash plan, giving employees a share of profits in cash added to their paychecks, either quarterly, semiannually, or annually; or (2) a deferred plan in which a trust fund is set up and payments are made to employees or their beneficiaries at retirement, disability, or death. Such plans are often bargained within a **contract**, often outside it in a **side agreement** or **memorandum of understanding**; some nonunion companies institute attractive profit-sharing plans to stave off unionization.

proposals or offers v. demands—When reported in the media, with rare exceptions, employers make proposals and/or offers and **unions** make demands. At the negotiating table, the terms are interchangeable; one side's proposals or offers are the other's demands. It all depends on what spin is put on them for outside consumption.

Pullman Strike (1894)—A major labor upheaval in U.S. history, both in its breadth and violence and in its consequences: the crippling of a major railway **union** and the beginning of a new wave of blanket antistrike **injunctions** against unions. In the background of the strike was the economic crash and Great

Depression of 1893, resulting in the collapse of many banks and railroads and the bankruptcy of some 15,000 businesses, which in turn generated massive **layoffs** and **wage freezes**. The more immediate cause was a 25 to 40 percent wage slash for workers of the Pullman Palace Car Co. in the **company town** of Pullman, just outside Chicago, *without* a corresponding reduction in their rents. When a committee of workers formed in May 1894 to discuss the matter with landlord/entrepreneur George Pullman, he reacted by firing three of its members on the spot. The workers appealed to **Eugene Debs**'s American Railway Union (ARU) for support; the union responded with a nationwide strike and **boycott** of all trains hauling Pullman sleeping cars. Escalation piled atop retaliation. The General Managers' Association, composed of the 26 railroads in the Chicago area, ordered the discharge of any worker who refused to handle Pullman cars; the ARU brought most of the nation's rail traffic to a halt by the end of June. The Pullman Strike began to be called the "**Debs Revolution**." By then, 260,000 rail workers had joined the **walkout**; as many as 500,000 may have been idled because of the boycott.

But by then, too, railroad owners were able to prevail on the business-friendly Cleveland administration to attach mail cars to trains with Pullman carriages—and charge strikers with interfering with the U.S. mails. They also secured the dispatch of federal troops and state militia in six states. The arrival of the U.S. Army in Chicago on the Fourth of July, followed by Governor **John Peter Altgeld**'s sending in an additional 5,000 state militiamen—ironically, to quell fears raised by the federal soldiers—precipitated violent confrontations in the next few days that left at least 15 strikers and protesters dead, scores injured, and Debs and other ARU leaders in jail. By July 11, the Debs Revolution had spread to 26 states from Maine to California, its toll some 35 bodies on the strikers' side and untold millions in damage on the railroads' ledgers. The final blow was delivered by **Samuel Gompers** and his American Federation of Labor (**AFL**). Rather than back the socialist Debs and the general strike he called for, as many within its ranks urged, the AFL voted a miserly $1,000 toward Debs's legal defense and urged strikers belonging to AFL **affiliates** to return to work. By mid-July, the strike was broken and the ARU routed. The union dissolved five years later.

Quadragesimo Anno—Papal encyclical by Pope Pius XI in 1931 that reaffirmed the notions of social and working-class justice set forth 40 years earlier in **Rerum Novarum**.
quickie strike—See **wildcat strike, walkout**.

R

Racketeer Influenced and Corrupt Organizations Act (RICO)—
A wide-ranging anticrime bill enacted by Congress in 1970
designed as a tool against organized crime, the Mafia, and
Mob-ridden organizations but which has been used against
labor unions as well. The most publicized examples of the latter
were in 1988, when the U.S. government filed a lawsuit under
the RICO statute against the International Brotherhood of
Teamsters, placing its executive board under federal **trusteeship**,
and in 1990, when the government brought a similar suit
against selected New York and New Jersey **locals** of the International Longshoremen's Association, its top officials and several
employers, virtually placing the entire New York–New Jersey
waterfront under court supervision. What makes RICO such an
effective—some say onerous—legal weapon is the all-inclusive
phrase "pattern of racketeering activity" running through its
many provisions, meaning that a particular offense need only
have occurred twice or more over a ten-year period in order for
the offenders to be prosecuted under the statute. Several states
now also have RICO statutes.

radium girls—See **National Consumers League**.

raiding—One **union**'s attempt to enroll or even outright appropriate
the members of another, thereby encroaching on or negating
the other union's **jurisdiction**, a practice not much in vogue anymore following widespread **no-raiding agreements** and a need
for greater **solidarity** in the face of increasing right-wing and
corporate hostility toward unions. Reasons for raiding were usually either because one union genuinely felt the employees of
the other union belonged to it by nature of the work done or
because a union wanted to increase its size to protect its **bargaining** position. Sometimes, what appears to be raiding really
isn't. The members of one union, dissatisfied with a series of
bad **contracts** or the incompetence of their leaders, may **decerti-**

fy in order to **affiliate** with another union they've sought out and which they feel better represents their interests. Other times, an aggressive union may legitimately *persuade* the members of another union they'd be better off joining it—but through legal and democratic means.

Railway Labor Act (RLA)—Act established by Congress in 1926 that abolished the **Railway Labor Board** created by the **Esch-Cummins Act** of 1920 and in its stead set up a permanent Board of Mediation composed of five members (in later years reduced to three) charged with the task of attempting to mediate any dispute not settled by direct negotiation or by adjustment boards. If mediation failed, the board was to urge the parties to submit to mandatory **arbitration**. If one or both parties refused to arbitrate and an interruption in interstate commerce threatened, the president was empowered to name an emergency board to investigate and report recommendations for a **settlement**; during investigation and for 30 days afterward, no change could be made in labor conditions. The Act has, on rare occasions, been invoked by presidents; most notably by Harry Truman in early 1946 to quell a rail strike, by Lyndon Johnson in July 1966 against an airline strike by machinists, and by Bill Clinton in February 1997 to freeze a strike by American Airlines pilots.

Later expanded to cover the airline industry, the RLA replaced **National Labor Relations Act (NLRA)** jurisdiction, which meant that rail and airline workers must organize nationally rather than locally or on a shop-by-shop basis. This distinction became key in the closing days of the 104th Congress in 1996 when Federal Express Corp. lobbyists had an amendment introduced into a Federal Aviation Administration appropriations bill that restored the words "express carrier" to the RLA, thus ensuring that FedEx's more than 65,000 truck drivers and other non-airline employees—some of whom were about to be organized by Teamsters and United Auto Workers in Indiana and Pennsylvania—would most likely remain nonunion. The amendment passed despite a Democratic filibuster and was signed into law by President Clinton.

Railway Labor Board—Panel established by the **Esch-Cummins Act** of 1920 to act as arbitors of disputes if **collective bargaining** failed, but rescinded by the less-compulsory provisions of the 1926 **Railway Labor Act**.

Rand formula—Canadian equivalent of automatic union dues **checkoff** in the United States. Named after Justice Ivan Rand following settlement of a 99-day strike, the formula, which dates to 1946 and forms the basis of **trade unionism** in Canada, is under growing attack from right-wing lawmakers.

Randolph, A. (Asa) Philip (1889–1979)—Influential African American labor and civil-rights leader; founder, in 1925, of **Brotherhood of Sleeping Car Porters**. Born the son of a Methodist minister in Crescent City, Florida, Randolph moved north to New York City's Harlem in 1911 and worked at a variety  of jobs while putting himself through City College. Labor consciousness came early. One summer, while working as a waiter on a coastal steamship, he organized a protest against the living conditions of fellow black workers. During World War I, he tried to organize black shipyard workers in Virginia and elevator operators in New York City, In 1917, he founded the *Messenger* (after 1929, the *Black Worker*), a magazine that not only exhorted African American workers to demand higher **wages** but also called for more positions in the war industry and the armed services for blacks. After the war and a couple of unsuccessful bids for public office on the Socialist Party ticket, he became more convinced than ever that **labor unions** would be the best way for African Americans to improve their lot.

After founding the Brotherhood in 1925, Randolph began organizing that group of black Pullman porters and, at a time when half the **affiliates** of the American Federation of Labor **(AFL)** barred African Americans from membership, took his fledging union into the AFL. Despite opposition—much of it from black leaders who decried unionism as an all-white affair—he built the nation's first successful black **trade union**, thus fulfilling the aspirations of **Isaac Myers** a half-century before. In 1937, the Brotherhood forced the Pullman Co. to the **bargaining table** and won its first major **contract**, including higher wages, shorter hours, and greater **job security** for maids and porters on the nation's trains, much to the amazement and chagrin of the top executives of a company that employed the largest number (35,000) of black workers in America. The following year, after yanking the Brotherhood out of the AFL for its failure to fight discrimination in the ranks and joining the newly formed Congress of Industrial Organizations (**CIO**), Randolph returned to the question of black employment in the federal government and in industries with federal contracts. When the Roosevelt administration balked in early 1941, Randolph warned he would lead a high-publicity protest march on Washington with thousands of black participants. Aware of what a propaganda feast that would be for a Nazi Germany and the rest of the world, President Franklin D. Roosevelt signed an executive order in June of that year barring discrimination in defense industries (the United States was already tooling up for World War II) and in federal bureaus and creating the Fair Employment Practices Committee. Randolph called off the march.

In the same vein, after the war a much-respected—and much-empowered—Randolph founded the League for Nonviolent Civil Disobedience Against Military Segregation, which quickly led to President Harry S. Truman's signing, in July 1948, an executive order banning segregation in the armed forces. When the AFL merged with the CIO in 1955, Randolph was made vice president and member of the Executive Council of the combined federation; a few years later he also was made president of the newly formed Negro American Labor Council to fight discrimination within the AFL-CIO. In this capacity, he often crossed swords with federation chief **George Meany**, who, although not a racist and who indeed promoted many minority programs in the AFL-CIO, was of the old AFL school and didn't believe in societal progress "too fast, too soon." "Who the hell

appointed you the guardian of the Negroes in America?" a cho-
leric Meany once shouted at Randolph across a union convention floor. Such was his prestige in the black community at that
time, the mild-mannered Randolph, had he chosen to, could
have replied: just about every black man and woman in the labor
and civil rights movements. He didn't.

In an echo of his activities in 1941, Randolph was a director
of the August 1963 March on Washington for Jobs and Freedom,
immortalized by **Martin Luther King Jr.**, and two years later
founded the A. Philip Randolph Institute for the study of the
causes of poverty. Suffering from chronic illness, he resigned
his presidency of the Brotherhood of Sleeping Car Porters in
1968, dying 11 years later at the age of 90.

rank and file—The members of a **union**, excluding the leadership.
A term borrowed by labor in the 20th century from an earlier
military context, wherein the ranks comprised the general body
of soldiers, apart from their officers. A rank was also a line of
soldiers standing abreast in close-order formation, as opposed to
a file, or a single line of soldiers standing or marching, one
behind the other. Hence, rank and file would encompass an
entire corps of volunteers and enlisted men no matter how they
were arrayed.

rank and fileism—The term given to a kind of tumultuous **local**
participatory democracy practiced in the early **CIO** unions and
even today by a few unions, most notably in some West Coast
locals of the International Longshore and Warehouse Union.
See **back-to-the-bench rule.**

Rapoport, Bernard (1917-)—Multimillionaire founder, in 1951, of
the American Income Life Insurance Company (AIL), the only
all-union company in the industry and one that puts its labor
money where its mouth is. In the past five years it has donated
more than $2.5 million to labor-supported organizations and
currently provides more than 9 million union members with life
insurance, with total life insurance in force just shy of $26 bil-
lion. Rapoport also set up the AIL Labor Advisory Board, composed of about 50 union presidents and officials who periodical-

ly meet to give advice and guidance to company officers as to how AIL can serve progressive interests as well as its **trade unions**. In addition to publishing a monthly labor newsletter, AIL also supports organizations such as the **Alliance for Retired Americans**, American Rights at Work, and Working for Good Jobs in America. Memorable quote: *"[I] could never understand why people who have a lot aren't willing to share."*

ratification—Formal acceptance of a tentative **contract** by a **union**'s general membership, either by voice or written ballot, usually the latter. Failure to ratify can either leave the union with no contract and its members subject to the company's **posted rules** or, more likely, send its negotiators back to the **bargaining table** in hopes of better terms.

rat/rat fink—In the printing trades, a rat is a **scab**. In the building trades, it's a nonunion contractor. In general union lingo, a rat is a **strikebreaker**, although that usage came about only in the 1930s; rat fink was a coinage of the 1960s. See **Pinkertons**.

real wages—The actual purchasing power of wages; the amount of goods and services wages will buy, compared to what they bought a year ago or ten years ago, often computed by dividing current earnings by the **cost-of-living index**. For example, if wages increased from $4 an hour to $5, but the cost-of-living index also increased 25 percent, real wages will have remained constant. Another illustration: in 1946, the Newspaper Guild determined that, based on prevailing housing, food, medical, and transportation costs, $100 a week was a contractual wage goal (and a few newspapers were actually paying that). This figure, based on the same constants, rose through the years until it reached $1,400 a week in the early 1980s and soared out of sight shortly thereafter. See **model contract**.

recognition picketing—Sometimes called organizational picketing; a **union**'s attempt to force an employer to recognize it as a **bargaining agent** or to persuade unorganized workers to join the union.

Red scares—Recurring—some say ongoing—periods in U.S. history in which organized workers, their **unions**, and the American

labor movement in general have come under concentrated attack for imaginary or real Bolshevism, communism, radicalism, anarchism, nihilism, socialism, or whatever un-American-sounding *ism* of the moment that prevailed; usually with the immediate intent of **strikebreaking** and lowering **wages** and the long-range aim of discrediting labor and weakening it in any further confrontation with industrial interests. Labor historians generally group the Red scares into three eras: (1) 1870s to

 around 1900: characterized, to take just one example, by the invective "communistic" hurled by politicians and the press against workers involved in the 1877 Pennsylvania rail strike; (2) 1919 through the 1930s: an era that began with massive arrests, and sometimes massacres, of **Industrial Workers of the World** activists and with the infamous **Palmer Raids**, one of which, in January 1920, netted 6,000 foreign-born labor "anarchists" for deportation. The **Seattle General Strike** of 1919, which arose directly from a postwar stagnation of wages, was nonetheless said by much of the sensationalist press to be run on direct orders from the Kremlin. In the 1930s, a booklet published by the National Association of Manufacturers but purporting to be a product of the labor press enjoined workers to "Join the **CIO** and Help Build a Soviet America." (3) 1946 through the 1950s, coinciding with the height of the Cold War. Although the public focus may have been political—McCarthyism, Hollywood, the State Department, etc.—the underlying objective was never lost on the drafters of the **Taft-Hartley Act** and industrialists such as General Electric's Charles Wilson, who declared before a congressional committee in 1946 that "the Cold War had two targets—the labor movement at home and the Soviet Union abroad." Two years earlier, the House Un-American Activities Committee reported that "the political views of the Communist Party and of the CIO's Political Action Committee coincide in every detail."

Actual communists, of course, always were in the U.S. labor movement—they were considered the best **organizers**. By 1940, it was no secret they controlled locals in the electrical, radio, woodworking, fur, and leather industries, and the unions of municipal, transport, and maritime workers. The CIO's reply to accusations of harboring Reds was "The bosses hire them; why shouldn't we organize them?" Most if not all communists, along with many of their allies and sympathizers, were purged from union ranks in the post-Taft-Hartley and McCarthy years—a move whose wisdom even conservative labor leaders later had reason to question.

A major theme in Red scares has been the blaming of "alien" or "foreign" influence for strikes or labor unrest; countless legislative and congressional committees subsequently found them to be the result of specific grievances. A major coincidence has been that the more virulent scares immediately followed major wars in which workers made significant gains and competed for "a larger slice of the pie."

reduction in force (RIF)—See **layoff**.

reopening clause—A **contract** provision stating the circumstances under which **wages** and other issues can be reconsidered while the **agreement** is still in force. Thus a reopening clause may have the effect of permitting a **strike** before the contract itself expires.

repetitive strain injury (RSI)—Not a condition itself but rather a term covering a broad range of injuries to the arms, wrists, hands, neck, and shoulders that can result from a number of factors, or combination of factors, in the workplace: repetitive motion, forceful exertions, long periods at a task without a break, improper position, sitting in one position too long, improperly adjusted equipment, and stress. Likewise, RSI can manifest itself in a variety of ways: carpal tunnel syndrome, tendinitis, and thoracic-outlet syndrome are but a few. During the 1980s, RSI struck particularly hard in the newspaper publishing industry, where editors and advertising salespeople were confined to keyboarding video-display terminals for large parts of their **shifts**, and it took the Newspaper Guild considerable effort to get publishers to acknowledge the problem, let alone apply **ergonomics** to alleviate it. Today, many Guild contracts address it, as do those protecting supermarket checkout clerks, meatcutters, and others who labor where RSI is a workplace hazard. A controversial bill to bar further RSI studies was defeated in the U.S. House of Representatives by a bipartisan vote in July 1996. See **kangaroo paw.**

representation election—An election supervised by the **National Labor Relations Board (NLRB)** to vote on what, if any, union will represent employees for **collective bargaining.** A majority vote is required for **certification** by the NLRB. See **decertification.**

Rerum Novarum—Literally, "Of New Things"; an 1891 papal encyclical, or worldwide letter to Roman Catholic bishops, of Pope Leo XIII stating that workers, as people of God, had a moral right to a living **wage** and a voice in the workplace. It was the first time the Vatican had come out on the side of **labor movement** aspirations and had considerable influence on the way U.S. Catholic bishops—a large portion of whose dioceses abounded in Irish, Polish, German, and Italian immigrant workers—addressed the issue from that time on. In effect, *Rerum Novarum* bestowed the official Vatican "blessing" on **labor unions** and marked a rebirth of Catholic labor militancy, which itself helps explain why names like **Meany, Carey, Yablonski,** and **Sweeney** stud the roster of latter-day U.S. labor officialdom.

retroactive pay—A delayed **wage** payment for work previously done at a lower rate, or income due employees when a new **contract** provides for a salary increase, covering the time they worked under the old rate before the new rate kicked in. For instance, the old contract expired January 1 and a new one, calling for an increase of 3.5 percent, is signed April 1. Because under the **evergreen clause** the employees continued working, they would receive three months' retroactive pay; that is, the difference between their old pay and the new for that time. Not to be confused with **back pay.**

Reuther, Walter (1907–70)—A founder of the United Auto Workers

(UAW) and one of the nation's most influential labor leaders of his time. Born the son of an immigrant German ironworker in Wheeling, West Virginia, Reuther started at a Ford Motor Co. assembly plant in 1927, then five years later went to the Soviet Union to work at the Gorki auto plant—an experience that would provide his foes grist for decades. Upon his return to the United States in 1935, he and his brother Victor, who had accompanied him to Russia, set about founding the UAW and then

 persuading General Motors (GM) to recognize the fledgling but militant union through **sit-down strikes** and other innovative tactics. GM finally capitulated, though his old employer, the staunchly antiunion Ford, held out considerably longer and dealt him and other UAW **organizers** a severe company **goon**–administered beating during a 1937 donnybrook. Nonetheless, Reuther entered the World War II years with a solid reputation as a responsible labor leader, as well as a trade unionist at ease with the shop-floor militants of Detroit, and was elected UAW vice president in 1942 and then president in 1946.

Though decidedly left-liberal in his socioeconomic views, former Socialist Reuther became an outspoken postwar opponent of communists in the Congress of Industrial Organizations (**CIO**), which he had helped found and to which the UAW belonged. At the same time, he called on the government to convert taxpayer-financed war plants to the mass production of badly needed housing and railroad equipment under a New Deal–style agency. Moreover, he not only sought a 30 percent wage increase for autoworkers but also challenged Detroit to keep car prices at prewar levels, asking that GM "open the books" to prove that high wartime profits justified the demands. The world's largest corporation naturally refused, claiming it was a ploy by "**union bosses**" to infringe on **management rights** and called Reuther "the most dangerous man in Detroit." Reuther called a 320,000-worker strike against the auto giant but had to call it off almost four months later when it appeared he was headed for a direct confrontation with the Truman administration. However, four years later, in 1950, he cemented a pact with GM hailed by *Fortune* magazine as the "Treaty of Detroit" in which he won acceptance of the **union shop** and a 20 percent increase in workers' standard of living over five years—which meant not only a hefty pay hike but a built-in **cost-of-living allowance**.

In 1948, Reuther joined with other centrist liberals such as Eleanor Roosevelt and Hubert Humphrey to form the Americans for Democratic Action to thwart the Progressive Party candidacy of Henry Wallace against Harry Truman. Many labor leaders, like Reuther, had had their doubts about Truman; many, like Reuther, now saw Wallace as a communist dupe.

In 1952, Reuther was elected president of the CIO and worked for its merger with the American Federation of Labor (**AFL**) in 1955. But he pulled his million-member autoworkers union out of the federation in 1968 over what he called **George Meany**'s "knee-jerk anticommunism" and what he saw as a "lack of social vision" on the part of the AFL-CIO Executive Council. Active throughout the 1960s in the civil rights movement, the restive Reuther—and still UAW head—for a time also entered into an **Alliance for Labor Action** with another outcast union, the Teamsters, but that attempt at revitalizing the U.S. **labor movement** died with Reuther in a May 1970 plane crash.

Memorable quote: *"The fight of the General Motors workers is a fight to save truly free enterprise from death at the hands of its self-appointed champions."*

RICO—See **Racketeer Influenced and Corrupt Organization Act.**

right-to-work law/right-to-work state—A type of statute embraced by more than 25 states, mostly in the South, Southwest, and Midwest, under which the **union shop** is prohibited, as are **maintenance of membership**, preferential hiring, or any other clauses requiring **union** membership. In blunter terms, no one has to join the union, but everyone gets the **contract** benefits. State legislatures were authorized to pass such laws by the **Taft-**

Hartley Act of 1947. Unions have long objected to "right to work" as a deliberately misleading and loaded term and often call it the "right to work for less" law since **wages** are always lower where such laws prevail. Right-to-work laws are perennially championed by the U.S. Chamber of Commerce and other employer groups, and there is a standing National Right to Work Committee in Washington, D.C. Significantly, a national right-to-work bill was beaten back by a bipartisan vote in the Republican-dominated U.S. House in July 1996. **Martin Luther King Jr.** also had something to say on the subject: "In our glorious fight for civil rights, we must guard against being fooled by false slogans, such as right-to-work. It is law to rob us of our civil rights and job rights. . . . Its purpose is to destroy **labor unions** and the freedom of **collective bargaining** by which unions have improved wages and working condition of everyone. Wherever these laws have been passed, wages have been lower, job opportunities are fewer and there are no civil rights." As an example of how language gets usurped, early 1920s legislation in Illinois held that able-bodied men and women had the "right to work," that is, had the right to an **eight-hour day** at fair wages. See **free riders.**

Robinson, Earl (1910–91)—American songwriter, best known in labor circles for "Joe Hill" and "He Built the Road," two of but some 474 songs he wrote on themes ranging from civil rights to love, from McCarthyism to a celebration of Americanism, during a lifetime that weathered the worst of the **Red-scare** years. His last significant public appearance was as a featured performer at the Labor Music Heritage Festival in Port Townsend, Washington, in April 1991.

Rockefeller plan—An outgrowth of the long, bloody **Ludlow Strike** of 1914 at the Rockefeller-owned coal mines, whereby employers actively began encouraging the formation of docile **company unions** and the **open shop**. It became more popular a decade later as the **American plan**. See **blacklist.**

runaway shop—A unionized plant transferred to another location, **unions** say, in order to evade bargaining obligations or to destroy a union. Proponents of such moves, however, argue that the decision to transfer are often due to other factors such as community tax inducements and the need to be nearer sources of raw materials or markets.

S

Sabo-Tabby—Unofficial mascot of the **Industrial Workers of the World (IWW)**, depicted as a black cat. The product of IWW songwriter-cartoonist Ralph Chaplin, it was, he said, a symbol of the **slowdown** as a means of "striking on the job." It often appeared by the slogan "Direct action gets the goods!" See **"cat in the hat."**

sabotage—In the commonly accepted sense, any underhanded interference in production, work, etc., in a plant or workplace by enemy agents in wartime or by employees during a trade dispute. In the specific sense espoused by the **Industrial Workers of the World** through the words of organizer **Elizabeth Gurley Flynn**: "The conscious withdrawal of worker efficiency. . . . Sabotage means either to slacken up and interfere with the quantity, or to botch in your skill and interfere with the quality of capitalist production or to give poor service. Sabotage is not physical violence, sabotage is an internal, industrial process. . . . Sabotage is a means of striking at the employer's profit for the purpose of forcing him into granting certain conditions."

salting—A union **organizing** tactic in which a covert organizer secures employment in an aggressively nonunion establishment, establishes a spotless work record for several months, perhaps as long as a year, and then attempts to organize fellow employees. Inevitably, this person is fired—ostensibly for some other shortcoming, because discharge for trying to organize a union is, per se, an **unfair labor practice (ULP)**. But when the ULP is filed, the employer is hard-put to document the firing of such an ideal employee, thus often losing the case and opening the way for a union **certification drive**. Salting is a variation of **hot-shop organizing**.

sanctions—In National Education Association (NEA) parlance, a range of censures levelled against local or state school systems to denote unsatisfactory working conditions for teachers; public declarations whose purpose is to discourage teachers from seeking or accepting positions in such schools. The NEA may discipline members who accept such positions, relegating them, in effect, to a union category only slightly above that of **scabs**.

scab—Someone who takes a striker's job, works behind a **picket line**, or refuses to go on **strike** with co-workers. Theories abound as to the word's origin. According to Stuart Berg Flexner's *Listening to America*, it's from the Scandinavian *scab* and akin to the Latin *scabies/scabere*, mange, to scratch; and has meant the crust over a wound in English since the 13th century and a despicable person by 1590. In the colonies it meant a shirker as of 1690 and by 1806 acquired its current labor connotation. The phrase "to scab on" a fellow worker seems to have been coined in 1917, says Flexner.

In a piece published posthumously in the *CIO News* of September 13, 1946, American writer Jack London (1876–1916) took the ultimate negative view: "After God had finished the rattlesnake, the toad and the vampire, He had some awful stuff left with which he made a scab. A scab is a two-legged animal with a corkscrew soul, a waterlogged brain, and a combination backbone made of jelly and glue. Where others have hearts, he carries a tumor of rotten principles. . . . Judas Iscariot was a gentleman compared to a scab. For betraying his master he had the character to hang himself—the scab hasn't. . . . There is nothing lower than a scab."

In fairness, it should be pointed out that few scabs are itinerant professionals, though some certainly are and are trained at a special school in Oklahoma City. Most, however, are driven by economic necessity and often are ill-paid or jobless minorities deliberately exploited by **strike-breaking** employers, a point powerfully illustrated in John Sayles's classic 1987 movie *Mate-*

wan. See **permanent replacement worker, Workplace Fairness Bill.**

scissorsbill (sometimes scissors bill)—An old term, no longer in use, meaning a worker who lacks class consciousness; one who will not join a **union,** a nonunion worker. A derogatory term dating from 1871 for law-abiding citizens who settled in Western frontier towns who were determined to clean up the "rowdy" elements; later it came to mean someone whose income was not from **wages**—a "coupon clipper." The **Industrial Workers of the World** gave the term its labor connotation about 1910.

"scissors" school—A mining-management philosophy of the 1980s, during generally declining metals prices, that held that the way to reestablish a rational relationship with the metals market, particularly that of copper, was to terminate **COLA** and connect wages back to metals prices. In fact, **Phelps-Dodge,** the Arizona copper-mining conglomerate, proudly advertised itself at the time as the "un-COLA company."

scrip—Paper chits that substituted for currency, usually redeemable only at **company stores,** that many companies paid their workers in lieu of cash. A 19th-century practice that lasted well into the 20th, it was particularly prevalent in "company towns" where workers had little choice.

seasonal unemployment—Joblessness due to the seasonal nature of the work, usually dictated by weather. Farmworkers, construction workers, and lumberjacks fall into this category, as do resort hotel workers and roofers. See **cyclical, frictional, structural,** and **technological unemployment.**

"sea turtles"—See **World Trade Organization.**

Seattle General Strike (1919)—Though not the nation's first or only **general strike,** certainly the best known of the World War I–era upheavals and one that certified Seattle as a union town for decades. It began when the national Shipbuilding Adjustment Board set a uniform wage scale for shipyard workers on both the Atlantic and Pacific coasts, thereby destroying a traditional wage **differential** favorable to West Coast workers. When metal-trades workers failed in their efforts to restore the differential and they appealed to the Seattle Central Labor Council for help, 60,000 workers from 110 mostly **AFL**-affiliated local unions dropped their tools, bringing every industry in the city to a standstill. From February 6 to 11, 1919, the city was run by a General Strike Committee, which set up 21 community kitchens to feed strikers and other residents, issued special permits to allow milk deliveries for children and laundry service for hospitals, established collective butcher shops and laundries, and even organized 500 uniformed war veterans to patrol the streets and keep the peace. Peace there was (there was not a single arrest)—although that in itself was a sign of how ominous things were, according to Seattle Mayor Ole Hanson, who, at the behest of a business community thoroughly alarmed by **Industrial Workers of the World** participation in the strike and by thousands of leaflets hailing the Russian Revolution, denounced the strikers as Bolsheviks out to overthrow the U.S. industrial system. Stridently denounced by the local press and pressured by the **international**s of the various unions involved, the AFL itself, conservative local labor leaders such as **Dave Bec**k, and by strikers' fears that violence *could* erupt at any time, the strike committee voted to end the strike at noon on Tuesday, February 11, with the shipyard workers' beef still unresolved.

The effect of the Seattle General Strike had a double edge: it taught workers **solidarity**, but it also fanned fears of incipient Bolshevism, thanks to Mayor Hanson's widely disseminated comments, and strengthened a nationwide **Red scare** already in progress.

secondary boycott—Refusal of **union** members to handle or work on a product that has been handled or made by **replacement workers/scabs**. More formally, it's economic pressure by a union upon an employer with whom the union has no dispute but hopes to pressure into not doing business with the target of a primary boycott. For example, the United Farm Workers (UFW) and their supporters conducted a secondary boycott in the 1960s and early 1970s against Safeway Stores to protest the supermarket chain's wholesale purchase of grapes from growers with whom the UFW had not signed contracts. The **Taft-Hartley Act** of 1947 outlawed most types of secondary boycotts, and additional restrictions were placed by the **Landrum-Griffin Act** of 1959, although the scheme of legislation has been to ban only specific types of conduct rather then the secondary boycott itself. (See **common-situs picketing**.) Defining the hairline differences between primary and secondary boycott activities has given full employment to generations of lawyers and jurists. Before they were codified under labor law, secondary boycotts were also outlawed on criminal charges such as rioting or disturbing the peace.

seniority—An employee's standing in the workplace, acquired through length of continuous employment. Seniority is used to determine, among other things, vacation preference and order of **layoff** ("last to be laid off, first to be rehired"), and employees with the most seniority often have the option of **bumping**.

servicing—The day-to-day enforcement of a union **contract**.

settlement—The prelude to a **contract**; when **union** and employer agree, no matter what the compromises, that a successful conclusion to the current round of **bargaining** has been reached and all that remains is **ratification**. A settlement can also be taken to mean the new contract itself.

severance pay—Sometimes called dismissal pay; compensation paid to an employee permanently laid off because of a plant closing or **reduction in force (RIF)**, replaced by technology, or fired for other than what is perceived as gross misconduct or as a self-provoked discharge. Even in such cases, a union may succeed in obtaining severance through **arbitration** or private agreement with the employer. The amount of severance pay is often spelled out in the contract and is normally based on **seniority** (e.g., the equivalent of two weeks' salary for every year with the company).

Shanker, Albert (1928–97)—Hard-charging head of the United Teachers Federation (UFT), which he helped found in 1960, and, later, of its national parent, the American Federation of Teachers; a leader in the nation's education policy and a significant if controversial figure in the tumultuous history of race relations in the 1960s. The son of Russian-Jewish **immigrants**, Shanker didn't speak a word of English when he entered first grade in New York's public school system. Under him, UFT members acquired one of the first collectively bargained teacher contracts in the nation and, thanks to him, a poorly paid profession became a respectable salary competitor with the best of them. Seven years after its founding, the New York–based UFT became the largest **union local** in the entire **AFL-CIO**. By the mid-1980s, Shanker the rabble-rouser had become Shanker the statesman, with the publication of *A Nation at Risk*, a report commissioned by President Ronald Reagan (it was later published as a book) and with the appearance of his weekly labor column in the *New York Times*.

Memorable quote (referring to a proposal that strongly resembled the future No Child Left Behind program): *"We will totally oppose any system that says kids can do nothing and move along and not be held accountable."*

Sherman Antitrust Act—A federal law enacted in 1890 outlawing trusts and conspiracies. Meant as a curb on corporate monopolies and price-fixing, the law was quickly interpreted by many courts, however, as forbidding unionization as well ("interference with free trade"). In fact, the first successful application of the Act was against **Eugene Debs** and other **Pullman Strike** leaders in 1894–95. This unintended consequence triggered an unprecedented number of employer-instigated **injunctions**, and it was not until the **Clayton Act** of 1914 that labor organizations were exempted. It should be noted, though, that for all its early flaws and current dormancy, the Sherman Act remains the most stringent in the world in its attitude toward corporate monopoly power. Named after its sponsor, Ohio Republican U.S. Senator John Sherman (1823–1900), brother of Civil War General William Tecumseh "War Is Hell" Sherman and treasury secretary under President Rutherford B. Hayes.

shift—A scheduled period of a (usually) eight-hour work, called variously day shift, night shift, **swing shift**, **graveyard shift**, and **lobster shift** depending on the time. Generally, shifts other than day shifts are paid a **differential** because of the off-hours and inconvenience to family life. The word *shift* has meant work in English since at least 1572 and a relay of workers and span of working time since around 1810.

shop committee—A duly **union**-empowered delegation of employees whose task it is to represent fellow workers in considering **grievances** and other matters that may arise between management and union.

shop steward—**Union** representative on the job who is authorized to receive, investigate, and attempt to settle complaints before they become formal **grievances** or, if they do, process the necessary paperwork; collect **dues** in the absence of a payroll **checkoff**; solicit new members; and provide information to union members. In short, the steward is the eyes and ears of the union and, today, has most likely attended training sessions with an emphasis on workers' rights and interpersonal diplomacy. Elected by fellow union members or appointed by **local** officers, the steward usually continues to work at his or her regular job and handles union duties on a part-time basis or in off-hours. The term seems to have been coined around 1915.

sick leave/sick pay—Paid absences due to illness. The policy varies from company to company, **contract** to contract. Some contracts contain sick-leave incentive (i.e., the employee is paid a bonus at the end of a certain period for *not* using any sick days, or using less than the "average"). Other contracts contain unlimited sick leave for medically certified illnesses. Others allocate a set number of sick days or "sick periods," beyond which the employee's pay is docked; still others dock only the first day of a period following the maximum "allowed" leave.

sick-out—A form of union protest or **work stoppage** in which large numbers of employees stay home, claiming they are sick. See **blue flu**.

side agreement—An agreement outside the main **contract**; more of an addendum to it but which is as binding as anything in the contract itself. Often more formally called a **memorandum of understanding**, such an agreement usually covers the gaps in the contract or spells out the specifics of a company policy—use of the employer's equipment, for example, or insurance coverage, or mileage-allowance rates. The accord is generally more easily reworded, replaced, modified, or nullified than the main contract; otherwise, it's renewed with the **ratification** of each new contract.

sit-down strike —A form of **job action** in which workers sit down at their machines, desks, or job site and refuse to let other workers take their place until a strike or particular **grievance** is settled. The term was first used in the automotive industry in Detroit around 1935 during **Walter Reuther's** United Auto Workers **organizing** drive, then gained national popularity after January 1936, when more than 1,000 employees sat in at the Firestone Tire and Rubber plant. Sit-down strikes, however, are rarely if ever used anymore as a **bargaining** device and the sporadic few that have been called in recent years have been short-lived, unsanctioned **wildcat strike**–type actions, ended quickly with **injunctions** and/or arrests and the likely firing of the participants. So widespread was the enthusiasm for the new weapon that labor put the new technique into a song:

When they tie the can to the union man, Sit down! Sit down!

When they give him the sack, they'll take him back. Sit down! Sit down!

When the speedup comes, just twiddle your thumbs. Sit down! Sit down!

When the boss won't talk, don't take a walk. Sit down! Sit down!

Not to be confused with sit-ins, used by civil rights and other protest groups in public places during the 1960s as a tool against racial segregation. See **Flint sit-down.**

slowdown—A deliberate reduction in output—whether it be sales slips, phone calls, nails driven, or widgets on an assembly line— on the part of workers in an attempt to gain concessions from an employer. Not to be confused with a **strike** or **work stoppage.** See **speedup.**

Smith-Connally Act—Known better as the War Labor Disputes Act when passed by Congress in June 1943. It outlawed **strikes** for the **closed shop**, gave the U.S. president authority to seize and operate struck plants, made instigating a strike subject to criminal penalties, and required 30 days' notice of any labor dispute that might interrupt production. It also deprived violators, who struck illegally or engaged in **boycotts** or jurisdictional strikes, of the protections afforded by the **Wagner** and **Norris–La Guardia** acts. It was passed over President Franklin D. Roosevelt's veto. Parts of it were abolished in 1946.

snap-back clauses—Clauses written into the Teamsters constitution since 1988, when the Brotherhood was placed under federal restrictions, that were to "snap back" into effect once the federal consent decree was lifted. For example, at the 1991 Teamsters convention, a majority of "old guard" delegates, chafing at a loss of significant power to the reformist faction, wrote into the constitution a section that would have abrogated the right of the **rank and file** to vote for convention delegates in the federal-free future.

Social Security—Basically, a national insurance program covering workers' old age, disability, and survivors' benefits paid into by taxes from both employers and employees. Established by the Franklin D. Roosevelt administration's Social Security Act of 1935 and opposed ever since by powerful conservative lobbies and long-entrenched attitudes toward "handouts" and "big government," the program met a need previously filled only by **pensions** provided to war veterans, government workers, and some companies. Amendments to the act between 1950 and 1972 greatly broadened coverage, sizably increased the real value of benefits, and indexed them against future inflation. **Medicare** and Medicaid were added to the system in 1965. A Supplemental Security Income system was inaugurated in 1972 to provide means-tested assistance for the elderly and disabled poor. Monkeying with the sacred cow that Social Security has become has long been considered the "third rail" of American politics, which may help explain the failure of President George W. Bush's strenuous attempts to **privatize** or eliminate what is arguably the government's most successful program in U.S. history. The term "social security," also called the "social safety net," describes a much broader goal of protecting a nation's citizens against poverty, ill health, incapacitation, and homelessness. See **private pension plans.**

solidarity—"The bedrock idea that workers should join together to fight exploitation by management. In its most basic form, solidarity means winning members and forming a **union** community. . . . In the traditional conception of solidarity . . . workers and their families educated each other about their rights and goals and supported each other as they provided labor to run the American industrial machine. Solidarity meant putting the community above individual interests, although unions held out hope that these interests would converge."—Jonathan D. Rosenblum in *Copper Crucible.* The spirit is best typified in the lyrics of the old song "Solidarity Forever," penned by **Industrial Workers of the World** songwriter and cartoonist Ralph Chaplin, sung at many a strikers' rally:

> *There can be no power greater anywhere beneath the sun*
> *Yet what force on Earth is weaker than the feeble strength of one*
> *But the union makes us strong.*
> *Solidarity forever! Solidarity forever! Solidarity forever!*
> *For the union makes us strong.*

Solidarity Charters—See **Change to Win.**

(South) Korean–U.S. Free Trade Agreement—The latest proposal along the lines of **NAFTA** and **CAFTA.** South Korea's strong **labor unions,** like their counterparts in Western **"free trade"** countries, strongly denounce the proposal. The unions are demanding that any agreement guarantee workers' rights—in particular the right to organize—as well as environmental standards and the protection of public services.

speedup—A condition imposed by an employer in which employees are required to produce more or increase their performance without a compensating increase in pay. However, except in cases where production can be quantitatively measured—as on an assembly line, for example—unions generally have found it difficult to verify cases of true speedup before an **arbitrator.** See **slowdown.**

split shift—A work **shift** that is divided into two or more nonconsecutive parts instead of eight hours straight. An example: an employee is told to work from 8 A.M. till noon and then report back for duty at 6 P.M. for another four hours. The newspaper industry, for one, commonly used this as a way of getting reporters to cover evening meetings without having to pay **overtime**. The majority of Newspaper Guild contracts now contain a no-split-shift clause.

Steelworkers' "open house"—The United Steelworkers' new Associate Member Program opens up the **union**'s rolls to individual workers and activists regardless of workplace or profession—even if they are unemployed or in college. The program involves paying nominal **dues** as well as receiving **benefits** and services.

Stephens, Uriah (1821–82)—Early U.S. labor leader; a founder of the Noble and Holy Order of the **Knights of Labor** in 1869 and its first head. Born in New Jersey, Stephens studied for the ministry before apprenticing as a tailor, and his Protestant background shaped his thinking on the labor question. He denounced long working hours, for instance, as "an artificial and  man-made condition, not God's arrangement and order," and proclaimed that "Knighthood must base its claims for labor on higher ground than participation in profits. . . . The real and ultimate reason must be based upon the more exalted and divine nature of man, his high and noble capacity for good." One of the last labor leaders whose intellectual roots were sunk in the politically conscious and reform atmosphere of the pre–Civil War days, he also called for the creation of a Lincolnesque organization that would bring all workers together regardless of race, nationality, or occupation. Stephens resigned the organization's leadership in 1879, paving the way for the Knights' heyday under his successor, **Terence Powderly**.

Stetler v. O'Hara—1917 U.S. Supreme Court ruling upholding the constitutionality of Oregon's **minimum-wage** laws for women. See **maximum work hours for women**.

stipulation-by-consent agreement (stip)—An agreement between the employer and the **union**, sanctioned by the **National Labor Relations Board**, which establishes the terms of a union-**representation election** and the scope of the future or potential **bargaining unit**.

stretchout—An employer practice in which a worker is asked to perform beyond his or her usual duties, or operate machinery or equipment other than is normally done, without corresponding compensation or **differential pay**. See **speedup**.

strike—To stop work or withhold services collectively for the purpose of gaining concessions from the employer—namely, in most cases, a workable **contract**. Although most strikes are over economic issues (i.e., **wages**, **benefits**, employer **takebacks**, etc.), many are not. In recent years, teachers have struck over class size, aeromachinists over **outsourcing**, and nurses over hours and **job security**. Earliest known use of the word is 1768, when a group of English sailors read a list of **grievances** and refused to work by *striking*—taking down—their sails. The first strike in U.S. labor history was in 1799 by an organized group of Philadelphia cordwainers, or workers in Cordovan leather, against master shoemakers. The cordwainers won a new contract after staying ten weeks off the job. See **sympathy strike**, **wildcat strike**, **strikebreaker**.

strike benefits—**Union** payments to workers during a strike, usually a small proportion of regular **wages**. Because many unions have limited, if any, **strike funds**, the advantage is clearly to the employer, who most likely carries strike insurance. That unions can muster community **solidarity** in the way of food banks, contributions, and extra jobs for strikers is the main reason many strikes endure at all. Often the union's **international** will also levy a special assessment on other **locals** to sustain strike benefits.

strikebreaker—An outsider, commonly called a **scab**, brought in by a struck employer so as to keep doing business while the strike is on, and to lower strikers' morale. Management personnel who continue to work during a strike, however, are not regarded as strikebreakers. In pre-Reagan days, a strikebreaker

 was usually let go once a labor settlement was reached. This is no longer necessarily the case, however, since the **PATCO strike** of 1981 gave a clear message to employers that hiring **permanent replacements**—technically legal since the 1930s but seldom utilized—would meet with little effective action from the **National Labor Relations Board**.

strike fund—Money held by the **local** or **international union**—often both—for use during a **strike** to cover the costs of **strike benefits**, legal fees, publicity, and the like. Some unions assess each member each month to build the fund; other unions use the international's general fund. Strike funds are often designated in union financial statements as "emergency," "reserve," or "special" funds.

strike issue—In **contract** negotiations, both sides come to the **bargaining table** with wish lists, provisions they would like to have and are willing to bargain for in good faith, but ultimately can live without. However, both company and union also have "gut" or strike issues based on proposals they feel they must obtain or maintain and over which, if not resolved, they are willing to take a strike or go on strike. For the employer, it may be a perceived usurpation of vital **management rights**; for the union, it may be a company's unacceptable proposed cutback in **wages** or workers' rights. In either case, it's a strike issue, and as a rule negotiators on both sides proceed very cautiously around it.

strike notice—A formal advisory filed with the **Federal Mediation & Conciliation Service**, **central labor council**, and other appropriate state agencies that a union has rejected the company's latest **offer/demand** and that a strike is very likely.

strike sanction—Official authorization for a strike, usually from a union's **international** and a **central labor council**. This is not only to show that the contemplated strike has gone through the necessary procedures and is not a spur-of-the-moment decision but also to ensure that striking members will receive **strike benefits**.

strike vote—A vote of the membership of the affected **local** whether or not to go on strike. This is usually done at the recommendation of the union **bargaining** team, which feels it can proceed no further without such action. Often, a strike vote is the only way negotiators can convince an employer that the issues are serious and indicative of membership sentiment. Thus, a rejection or very narrow "yes" strike vote considerably weakens a union's hand at the **bargaining table**.

structural unemployment—Joblessness resulting from major changes or shifts in a nation's economy; i.e., workers who are suddenly, in the terminology of British and Irish laborites, "redundant"—made obsolete by **automation**, technological advances, or consumer spending patterns. The term is also used to describe unemployment among those who are not hired because of discrimination because of age, sex, race, or nationality, or among workers who are unable or refuse to relocate where there is a demand for their skills. See **cyclical, frictional,** and **technological unemployment**.

sunshine bargaining—Labor **negotiations** in which the media or public at large is permitted to attend the **bargaining** sessions.

supervisor—See **Kentucky River decisions**.

supplemental unemployment benefits (SUBs)—Private, employer-financed plans providing wage loss to laid-off workers, usually in addition to **unemployment insurance** benefits. SUBs originated in 1955 as a compromise when the United Auto Workers negotiated a guaranteed annual wage from the Ford Motor Co.

sweatshops—A term originating in the early 20th century in the garment industry and needle trades, which were often referred to as the "sweating system." It soon came to mean any small factory, shop, or workplace characterized by extremely low wages, long hours, intolerable conditions, and, often, child labor. Sweatshop conditions caused the 1911 Triangle Shirtwaist fire and led to the organization of the International Ladies' Garment Workers' Union. The practice is still alive and well, as evidenced by periodic raids by U.S. Occupational Safety and Health Act agents on sweatshops exploiting immigrant Asians in the Los

Angeles area. Today, many American sweatshops are located off-shore, particularly in U.S. possessions such as the Mariana Islands, where unscrupulous—and cynical—manufacturers can affix "Made in U.S.A" labels to their products.

Sweeney, John (1934–)—President emeritus of the **AFL-CIO**, elected in a 1995 race with Thomas Donahue, interim federation president after the resignation of **Lane Kirkland** earlier in the year. Born in New York City and graduated from Iona College with a degree in economics, Sweeney first went to work for the  International Ladies Garment Workers Union but was persuaded in 1960 by Donahue, then with Local 32B of the Service Employees International Union (SEIU), to join the **local** as contract director. In 1976, he was elected president of 32B, which merged with another local the following year to become one of the largest in the SEIU. He succeeded to the presidency of the **international** in 1980 and was into his fourth term when he edged out his old mentor for the AFL-CIO leadership. Seen as more activist than his predecessors and surrounding himself with activists—Richard Trumka of the UMW, Linda Chavez-Thompson of AFSCME, and others—Sweeney has reemphasized **organizing** in the AFL-CIO and restored a public visibility to labor and labor issues, and by guaranteeing a multimillion-dollar strike fund was instrumental in helping the Teamsters achieve a favorable settlement in the 1997 **United Parcel Service Strike**. He stepped down in September 2009 after four terms as president, replaced by Richard L. Trumka.

sweetheart contract—An agreement, usually between a racketeer head of a **paper local** (but sometimes a legitimate union) and a corrupt employer, to pay less in **wages** and benefits to keep a legitimate **union** from **organizing** the shop. The employer's advantages are obvious; the union racketeer benefits from the payoff he receives from the grateful employer and the dues he collects from employees, or both. Sweetheart contracts are denounced by the **AFL-CIO** in its **Code of Ethical Practices**.

swing shift—Usually, a 4 P.M.-to-midnight work **shift**; a term first recorded in 1944 to describe a defense-plant work period that swung between a regular day shift and a full night shift. See **lobster shift, graveyard shift.**

Sylvis, William H. (1828–1869)—U.S. labor leader and founder of the **National Labor Union.** Born in Armagh, Pennsylvania, Sylvis helped organize the Iron Molders International Union (also known as National Union of Iron Molders) in 1860 and served as its president from 1863 until his death in 1869. Though he looked to the English cooperative **labor movement** and was opposed to **strikes,** he took an active role in fighting for labor's rights and was one of the first labor leaders to call for—even before the Civil War—a national **department of labor.**

sympathy strike—A strike by workers not directly involved in a labor dispute, in an attempt to show union **solidarity** and further pressure the employer to come to a satisfactory settlement with the employees directly engaged in the dispute.

T

Taft-Hartley Act—Officially known as the Labor-Management Relations Act, it was passed in 1947 by a Republican-controlled Congress over President Harry Truman's veto. Designed to offset the gains of the **National Labor Relations Act (NLRA)** of 12 years earlier, Taft-Hartley—named after U.S. Representative Fred Hartley Jr. (R-N.J.) and U.S. Senator Robert A. Taft (R-Ohio)—was drafted largely by officials, lobbyists, and attorneys of the National Association of Manufacturers (NAM) and U.S. Chamber of Commerce, though its more strident provisions were watered down somewhat by congressional Democrats. Among other things, the Act: (1) outlawed the **closed shop;** (2) increased the **National Labor Relations Board (NLRB)** from three to five members; (3) inaugurated the 80-day **"cooling-off period,"** or **injunction,** as a measure to "protect the welfare of the nation"; (4) removed the **Federal Mediation & Conciliation Service (FMCS)** from a sympathetic **Department of Labor** and made it an independent agency; (5) required unions to file financial reports with the Labor Department; (6) forced labor leaders to swear under oath that they were not communists; (7) declared illegal the **secondary boycott**. In subtler ways, it (1) ended for good the massive organizing drives that characterized the 1930s; (2) held up *any* new organizing at all, even on a quiet, low-key scale; (3) gave employers license to break the **Wagner Act**; and (4) bureaucratized labor. Many—and not just on the left— objected to Taft-Hartley's anticommunist section, saying it reduced union heads to second-class citizens. The **CIO**'s **Philip Murray** said the bill was "conceived in sin," its promoters "diabolical men who, seething with hatred, designed . . . this ugly measure for the purpose of imposing their wrath on the millions of organized and unorganized workers throughout the U.S." "Repeal the Taft-Hartley Slave Law" became the watchword of a subsequent political drive that, although not dislodging the Act, did give Truman an unexpected victory over Thomas E. Dewey in the 1948 elections and swept the Democrats into a House majority that, with the exception of a two-year period (1952–54), they were to hold until 1994. Labor leaders at the time also claimed that Taft-Hartley, by prohibiting **secondary boycotts**, encouraged the **runaway shop**. A 1978 Charlie King song summarized many mineworkers' feelings about the bill:

> *Part of me says we shouldn't be striking*
> *But most of me says we should*
> *'Cause when the owners get together with the U.S. government*
> *You know it ain't gonna do me no good . . .*
> *Mr. Taft can dig it, Mr. Hartley can haul it*
> *'Cause I'm gonna leave it in the ground.*

takebacks—Union benefits or contractual advances, won in previous negotiations, that are ceded to management in subsequent bargaining—for that reason sometimes called givebacks— usually because of economic pressure, decline of union strength or membership, the threat of plant closure, or a combination of all of these. Takebacks, relatively unknown on a large scale until the 1980s, accelerated during the antilabor Reagan administration and emerging globalization of the economy. Particularly hard hit have been **union-security** provisions and **fringe benefits.**

take-home pay—What's left over in a worker's paycheck after the usual deductibles—federal and, sometimes, state income taxes; Social Security withholding; health-insurance premiums; and, of course, union **dues,** in the case of payroll **checkoff.**

Taylorism—A system of production pioneered late in the 19th century by efficiency engineer Frederick Winslow Taylor (1856–1915) and publicized in his book *The Principles of Scientific Management,* whereby management would control the planning of each worker function to increase efficiency and allow machines to complete that sequence. That, he argued, would ultimately improve **productivity** and remove more strenuous tasks from workers' hands. Taylor advocated studying each job by breaking it down into small components, timing them, and setting standards. As a result, productivity was often raised enormously. But some critics, particularly **labor unions,** contended that Taylorism was frequently corrupted, that management fragmented jobs to take control away from individual workers, and set increasingly higher production standards—often making jobs simultaneously harder and less meaningful. A basic tenet of Taylorism was that the turn-of-the-century American workforce, largely unskilled, uneducated, and often immigrant, needed close supervision as much for their own protection and for the machinery they operated as to increase efficiency. However, the onset of technology and **automation,** coupled with the increased education of the average worker has rendered such supervision largely obsolete or moot. Yet, observers note, this has not stopped many less-progressive industries from continuing the legacy of Taylorism with an extra-heavy overlay of middle management.

TEAM Act—An acronym for Teamwork for Employees and Managers; a bill the Republican-dominated U.S. House and Senate passed in the 104th Congress that would have made the **company union** legal again by amending the **Wagner** and **Taft-Hartley** acts. Describing the bill as a "revolutionary approach to employment policy," its proponents said it would "enable employers to give power directly to employees," something opponents and labor leaders point out the Wagner or **National Labor Relations Act** already does. President Clinton vetoed the bill.

Teamsters for a Democratic Union (TDU)—Grassroots reform group within the Teamsters **international**, founded in 1976, as an offset to the big unionism of the **Jimmy Hoffa–Dave Beck** legacy. The TDU's sister organization, the Teamster Rank and File Education and Legal Defense Foundation (TRF), provides members with the help they need to fight for justice on the job and handle potential grievances against the international.

technological unemployment—Joblessness that results from the introduction of labor-saving machinery, **automation**, or other high-tech equipment. In the 1970s and '80s, for instance, printers and typesetters in newspapers throughout the country were rendered technologically unemployed, though much of the shock was mitigated by **early buyouts**, when newsroom video display terminals, electronic typesetting and electronic pagination replaced these workers' functions. See **cyclical**, **frictional**, and **seasonal unemployment**.

Teller Act—Commonly called the Welfare and Pensions Plan Disclosure Act; a federal statute passed in 1958 covering all non-governmental welfare and **pension** plans affecting more than 25 employees. Administrators of the funds must make annual reports to the U.S. **Department of Labor**, describing the plans and submitting periodic financial statements. Several states have enacted similar statutes.

temple—As in labor temple; generally a building serving as headquarters for a regional or **central labor council** that may house the offices of union **locals** as well. The etymology of this use is uncertain. It appears to derive from the earliest days of the **Knights of Labor**, which was originally called in 1869 the Holy Order of the Knights of Labor, modeled after medieval religious-military orders such as the Knights Templars, who would meet in secret (labor organizations in the United States were for the most part outlawed until the landmark **Clayton Act** of 1914) in a place they would designate as a sanctuary or temple. The place name stuck long after the fervor of labor "knighthood" died down.

temps, or temporary workers—Full- or part-time employees hired for a specified time, usually to fill in for vacationing or ill permanent employees, or to augment the workforce for a particular task or job. In a **union** workplace, temps sometimes enjoy at least some of the **fringe benefits** of the **contract**; other times they do not—and almost never are benefits provided in a nonunion environment. In fact, U.S. companies have been increasingly hiring temps in the past decade to avoid paying the extras—a major factor in the **United Parcel Service Strike** in 1997. Unlike **contract workers**, however, temps are covered by the general provisions of the **Fair Labor Standards Act**. See **Industrial Revolution**.

time and a half—The rate at which **overtime** is usually paid; for example, if an employee's hourly wage is $10, he or she would make $15 an hour for any time worked beyond an eight-hour day or 40-hour week, depending on the state, the **contract**, or company work rules. The term came into general use with the **Fair Labor Standards Act** of 1938.

Tobin, Daniel J. (1875–1955)—Irish-born longtime rough-and-tumble head of the International Brotherhood of Teamsters (1907–52), noted for his anticommunism, advocacy of **business unionism**, and contempt for **industrial unions**. In his publicly stated opinion, the men who worked in the mass-production industries were "rubbish" and "riffraff." An outspoken champion of President Franklin D. Roosevelt, he was named to head the National Labor Committee of the Democratic Party in 1936 and kept the post in four presidential elections. FDR asked him to be his secretary of labor, but he declined. Also a longtime member of the Executive Committee of the craft-union-oriented American Federation of Labor (**AFL**). In October 1953, the 85-year-old

Tobin turned over his Teamsters union presidency to **Dave Beck**. Years before, Tobin had seen promise in a young up-and-coming **Jimmy Hoffa** and served as his mentor.

Memorable quote: *"We have to use force in our organizations. If we didn't use force and enforce decisions, we would not have an international union of 135,000 members [Teamsters membership at the time]."*

trade union—See **craft union**.

Triangle Shirtwaist fire—One of the nation's worst industrial disasters, and one that had a profound effect on women's unionism. Occurring on March 25, 1911, at the Triangle Shirtwaist Co., a **sweatshop** in New York City's Greenwich Village, the fire  killed 146 workers, most of them women trapped by the lack of fire escapes and management's practice of locking all the exits to keep employees from stepping out during breaks. The factory's owners were indicted, but a jury acquitted them, fanning public outrage over the tragedy and leading to stepped-up efforts by the Ladies Garment Workers Union, which, ironically, had been founded in 1900 to **organize** Triangle workers and improve conditions in sweatshops. It also led to more stringent factory inspections and to sweeping changes in New York building codes and in garment workers' job conditions.

trusteeship—The status of a union when a third party—sometimes the federal or state government, sometimes a private, independent fiduciary agency—assumes or oversees its financial and legal affairs either for a predetermined period or until a time when certain conditions are met. The occasion is generally alleged misfeasance, corruption, or other form of incompetence. The most recent, best-known case of this happening is in 1988, when the federal government filed a giant civil **RICO** suit against the Teamsters **international** and, as part of the overall settlement, some **locals** were subsequently placed in trusteeship by Teamster President **Ron Carey**.

turnaround time—The time when ships, planes, trucks, etc. are loaded and unloaded at points of embarcation or destination; obviously a factor in the contracts of Teamsters, stevedores, air-cargo handlers and the like, because shippers believe profit margins to be especially sensitive to the length of turnaround time.

turnover—Rates at which workers move into and out of employment, usually expressed as the number of accessions and separations during a given period per 100 employees. Monthly turnover rates, by selected states and regions, are computed monthly by the **Bureau of Labor Statistics**.

two-tiered wage structure—An employers' practice, increasingly widespread since the early 1980s and usually invoking **flexibility**, of **grandfathering** current **union** employees at previous, higher **wage** rates and subjecting all new hires to a lower rate. The general result is growing tension between veteran workers and younger employees in the union because the latter are doing essentially the same work for lesser pay. Although some unions have been forced to accept the two-tiered system under threat of plant closings and no work at all, labor leaders have denounced the system as a subtle form of **union-busting**.

U

unachieved demand—An effort to secure through **grievance** or **arbitration** a provision or condition that either party failed to achieve through previous **contract** negotiations. If the issue is successfully identified as such by the opposing party, arbitrators will usually reject it, saying it has to be resolved at the **bargaining table**.

unemployment insurance (jobless benefits)—A joint federal-state program created by the New Deal Social Security Act of 1935 in which those out of a job through no fault of their own (**layoff**, **downsizing**) can collect cash benefits for a specified time. Such benefits are paid out of funds derived from an employer-financed payroll tax, and their amount, duration, and eligibility rules vary from state to state.

unfair/unfair list—A list circulated by a **labor union** or **central labor council** of employers and products to be **boycotted** and avoided by union members, usually because of a refusal to bargain, antiunion policies, or a long-standing **unfair labor practice** of the targeted company.

unfair labor practice (ULP)—Conduct by an employer—or a union—that violates state or federal labor laws, including failure to engage in **good-faith bargaining**. A ULP complaint must be filed with the **National Labor Relations Board (NLRB)**, which takes the matter under investigation and issues a finding, which must be posted visibly on company premises. If the finding is that a ULP exists, sanctions or fines usually apply. However, a finding may or may not have the desired results, particularly in recent years, as many companies subject the NLRB decision to continuous appeal while continuing the unfair practice until either the union drops it or the issue becomes moot.

unión, sindicato—Both Spanish for "union."

"union bosses"—A cliché the media can't seem to shed, conjuring up in the popular mind the image of cigar-chomping, diamond-stickpinned dons presiding over a Tammany-like den of union goons with brass-knuckled henchmen standing by to bully a cowered membership, hapless entrepreneurs, and the public at large. Though negative portraits of labor leaders have been stock-in-trade for political cartoonists since the antiunion 1920s and before, much of the current caricature stems from the 1957 **McClellan Committee** hearings and the resultant "corrupt union" aura backlighted by conservative Republican and Dixiecrat lawmakers, the Hearst press, and well-funded PR campaigns by big business. The media prominence given the alleged racketeering by the Teamsters' **Jimmy Hoffa**, and any photo of **George Meany**—a true cigar chomper—only limned the verbal and pictorial caricature further. Used alternately with "labor bosses," a term that seems to have been coined in 1903.

union "bug" or label—See **bug**.

union-busting—The planned course of action by an employer to destroy a union already in the workplace or stop one from **organizing** in the first place. The latter is a fairly simple science, according to labor lawyer/writer Tom Geoghegan in *Which Side Are You On?*: "You go out and fire people. And keep firing until the organizing stops. Because at some point it always will. It is like sending people straight into a machine gun, and when the bodies pile up high enough, the drive is over and the employer has won." See **management/labor consultants**.

union dues—See **dues**.

union hypnotists—You are getting drowsy. Now you are asleep. Repeat after us: In 1994, the National Federation of Hypnotists was chartered as **Local** 104 of the Office and Professional Employees International Union (OPEIU), the **union** that, among other professions, represents physicians, chiropractors, podiatrists, acupuncturists, midwives, and other health care workers. The federation is affiliated with the National **Guild** of Hypnotists, which was formed in 1951 and is the oldest organization of its kind in the field. The OPEIU tie has allowed "our hypnotists to provide group sessions in smoking cessation, stress, and weight management for union members as [the local's] well-being programs," says Dr. Dwight Damon, president of both the federation and the guild. . . . When you awaken you will remember all of this.

union security—Provisions or clauses in **collective-bargaining** agreements designed to protect the institutional life of the **union** (i.e., defining conditions under which employees may or may not be required to become and remain members of the union). The ultimate in union security, of course, was the **closed shop**, outlawed these many years by the 1947 **Taft-Hartley Act**. Still in existence, though, are **preferential hiring**, whereby an employer hiring new workers agrees to give preference to union members, and the **union shop**, in which a company may hire anyone it wants but, with exceptions, all new hires must join the union within a specified time and retain membership as a condition of continuing employment. See **agency shop, maintenance of membership, open shop, one-in–ten.**

union shop—An agreement that the employer may hire anyone he/she wants, but all workers must join the union within a specified time after being hired and retain membership as a condition of continuing employment. Some employers are successful in mitigating this kind of arrangement by securing escape clauses such as a **one-in-ten** agreement that gives some new employees the option of *not* joining the union. See **open shop, closed shop, maintenance of membership.**

unions—See **labor unions.**

unions as conspiracies—In England, where **labor unions** first arose, they were indictable as criminal conspiracies as part of the Tudor Industrial Code. When statutes were enacted freeing them from this criminal liability, they were still condemned by the courts as being organizations in restraint of trade and therefore not deserving legal enforcement of their rights—an attitude persisting in the United States for some time after it was abandoned in England. Although the U.S. Supreme Court's landmark **Commonwealth v. Hunt** ruling of 1842 juridically removed this taint, in practice it was business as usual for decades afterward as employers successfully obtained **injunctions** on criminal charges from friendly courts to thwart union **strikes** or **organizing** efforts. Indeed, it was not until the **Clayton Act** of 1914 that unions fully achieved their conspiracy-free status. Not entirely, though. Today, as a coalition of Steelworkers and environmentalists found out in Louisiana when they presented a united front to combat both the pollution and labor practices of a local mill, the employer fought back with charges under the **Racketeer Influenced and Corrupt Organizations Act**, enacted by Congress in 1970 mainly to fight the Mob.

unit clarification—A **National Labor Board Relations (NLRB)** procedure by which either employer or **union** can add to, amend, or decrease a **bargaining unit**. If, for example, the company believes some members of a unit are rightfully management rather than union, it files a petition with the NLRB to "clarify"

that unit. Likewise, a union may do so if it feels certain employees deemed "management" really don't qualify as such, and
merit union protection. Hearings are then held by a **field examiner** who notes the duties and responsibilities involved in the
positions in question and subsequently—weeks or months
later—makes a determination. The clarification sought, of
course, must not have been precluded by a previous NLRB
determination.

United Parcel Service Strike (1997)—Victorious 16-day Teamsters
strike against the nationwide package carrier, the company's
first in its 90 years of existence, that defied the odds by gaining
widespread public sympathy for the 185,000 strikers' major
issues—the curtailment on hiring part-time workers and an

extension of benefits for them. In the **settle-
ment**, UPS agreed to convert 10,000 part-time
jobs to full-time in the five-year life of the **contract** (it had originally offered to convert only
1,000 jobs); to replace subcontractors with
UPS drivers; and to drop plans to pull out of a
multi-employer **pension plan** jointly run by
the union and their members' employers. The
strikers also won pension increases and a 15 percent **wage** boost
over the five years. The August strike was greatly aided by **AFL-
CIO** President **John Sweeney**'s guarantee of a $10 million week-
ly loan to the Teamsters' **strike fund**. The UPS win, **organized
labor**'s first on such a grand scale in more than a decade, was
the apogee of Teamster President (and former UPS driver) **Ron
Carey**'s five-year administration; later in the year his 1996
union reelection was overturned by federal officials and he was
barred from seeking another term.

Uprising of the 20,000—Name given to a short, abortive November
1909 **strike** by women garment workers in New York City in
which many were arrested. When the arrestees appeared before
a judge, they were told, "You are on strike against God."

vesting—The acquisition of **pension** rights that permits employees to end employment with a company without forfeiting employer-contributed pension benefits; usually after five years, though some companies require as many as ten years before an employee is vested.

Volunteer Organizing Committee (VOC)—Term used to describe **union** members who volunteer for the union during **organizing** campaigns. Volunteers may donate their time and/or be compensated for lost wages from their regular jobs while they assist the campaign by **house visits**, leafleting and attending meetings. VOCs were in high profile during the **AFL-CIO**'s "Union Summer" of 1996.

wage/wages—Agreed-upon compensation for work performed; in a **labor union** context, a pay scale spelled out specifically in the **contract**. There is little real difference between a wage and a salary (from the Latin *salarium*, a ration of salt alotted to Roman legionaries)—pay is pay, after all—except for a subtle class distinction: wages are generally paid to **blue-collar**, unionized workers or manual laborers and are computed on an hourly basis. Salaries are generally earned by **white-collar** professionals and are expressed in weekly, monthly, or yearly sums. See **minimum wage**.

Wages and Hours Act—See **Fair Labor Standards Act**.

wage freeze—An act by an employer and sometimes the federal government whereby the **wages** and salaries of workers are frozen at their current levels despite promised or even scheduled contractual raises. The cause may be a national emergency, such as wartime or economic panic, such as those accompanying the crashes and depressions of 1893 and 1929. Or it may be an overheated economy; that's the reason President Richard M. Nixon gave for his 1971 wage and price freeze. At times, a freeze may simply be an employer's decision to effect cost-cutting or break a **union**.

Wagner Act—The **National Labor Relations Act**; named after U.S. Senator Robert F. Wagner (D-N.Y.).

walking boss—In longshore work, a foreman assigned by the company to walk the length of ships and docks to supervise the work. Though management representatives, walking bosses have their own local **union** within the International Longshoremen's and Warehousemen's Union (ILWU).

walkout—Often a synonym for a **strike**, but there is a subtle difference despite the media's labeling of virtually every strike or **job action** as a "walkout." A walkout in the strictest sense of the term means just that—a (usually) unsanctioned, spontaneous get-up-and-leave act on the part of **union** employees fed up with an intolerable or unfair workplace situation created by the employer or in protest of unsafe job conditions; generally reversed upon quick resolution of the issue. The reality of these union-unfriendly times, however, is that workers staging such a walkout usually don't get to walk back in. See **wildcat strike**.

wall-to-wall organizing—Organizing, by a single **union**, all the employees of a company rather than just certain departments or **crafts** within a department.

Wal-Mart Watch—Formed in 2005 with seed money from Service Employees International Union (SEIU) and Five Stones. The Watch, a 501(c)(3) organization composed of members ranging from *Sojourners* magazine to the Sierra Club, challenges the world's largest retailer to live up to its "moral responsibilities" in consonance with the wishes of founder Sam Walton; to observe **family medical-leave** laws; and to stop forced **off-the-clock** work, hiring undocumented workers, allowing supervisors to skip employees' work breaks, and employing teens in unsafe conditions—all violations that the chain has been fined for or charged with by state and federal regulators. Walmart has acknowledged providing such poor **health benefits** that employees are forced to rely on taxpayer-supported public assistance. A November 2005 audit by the U.S. Office of Inspector General found that Walmart engaged in **sweetheart deals** with the **U.S. Department of Labor**'s Wage and Hour Division. Some labor progressives believed that SEIU president Andy Stern's dealings with then–Walmart CEO Lee Scott were too chummy; they accused Stern of **business unionism** and of being a sellout. Stern, who spearheaded **Change to Win**, and his supporters refute this, saying that he's dealing with "real-life choices" and that he's willing to try new things and harbors a profound contempt for **AFL-CIO**-style "stagnant bureaucracy."

Walsh-Healy Act—A 1935 law that established a 40-hour week for contractors manufacturing supplies for the government, directed the secretary of labor to determine **minimum-wage rates** to be paid by manufacturers of such commodities, and forbade the employment of children by manufacturers on government contract. It anticipated the much broader **Fair Labor Standards Act** by three years.

WARN (Workers Adjustment and Retraining Notification Act)— A law passed by Congress in 1988 requiring that any company with more than 100 employees give at least 60 days' notice of a plant closing or **layoff** if 50 or more employees are affected. If less notice is given, the employer must give those workers lump-sum payments for any time under 60 days. A federal audit of the program after its first five years, however, revealed that more than half of those who should have received a WARN notice had not.

War Production Board—One of many boards and agencies authorized under the War Powers Act of late 1941 to coordinate the domestic economy while fighting World War II. The board contained manpower-requirement and labor-production divisions headed by a labor representative and assisted by labor advisory boards, giving labor an opportunity to contribute to the country's overall production drive and to set up labor-management teams in defense plants. Such teams' plans for improving techniques and saving time were denounced by industry as "socialism" and a "foolish experiment," but by the end of the war some 5,000 plants were using labor-management committees and showing marked improvements in efficiency. A similar board was set up in World War I. See **National War Labor Board.**

Weingarten rights—Owing to a 1975 U.S. Supreme Court decision, an employee is entitled to have a **union** representative or **shop steward** present in any interview with management if the employee has reason to believe a disciplinary action or firing may result. However, failure to insist on union representation could mean a waiver of those rights. The union rep may ask questions and take notes, but may not plead for the employee or argue with the supervisor.

welfare funds (union welfare funds)—Trust funds providing benefits for employees covered under **multi-employer bargaining**, usually administered by trustees representing both employers and **labor unions**. Typically, such funds provide health and death benefits and **pensions**, sometimes from separate pension funds.

welfare plans—Benefit plans for employees of a single employer, providing for **disability insurance**, hospital, medical and surgical protection, and life insurance. Such plans used to be financed almost entirely by joint employer-employee contributions; the trend in the 1960s and 1970s was toward employer-financed plans. In the 1980s and 1990s, this was in many cases reversed by employer **takebacks**.

West Coast Hotel Co. v. Parrish—A landmark 1937 U.S. Supreme Court decision recognizing a Washington state **minimum-wage law**, thus prompting a bill in Congress calling for minimum wages, maximum hours, and the abolition of **child labor**. Surprisingly, some of **organized labor**'s big guns—**William Green** and **John L. Lewis** among them—came out against the measure, arguing in essence that "minimum wages become maximum wages." Different winds blew for the ultraconservative National Association of Manufacturers. It saw the measure as "a step in the direction of communism." Nonetheless, a year later the bill, with minor revisions, became the **Fair Labor Standards Act**. It's enough to justify that bumper sticker: "Organized labor—the folks who brought you the weekend." See **minimum-wage indexing**.

West Coast Waterfront Strike (1934)—Also known as the West Coast Longshoremen's Strike, an 83-day struggle that triggered a four-day **general strike** in San Francisco, led to the unionization of all U.S. West Coast ports, established the reputation of longshore **union** leader **Harry Bridges**, and was a key catalyst for the rise of **industrial unionism** in the 1930s. Before this, dockworkers and stevedores on the West Coast either had been unorganized or were represented by **company unions**, with workers required to go through **hiring halls** run by such unions. It was known as the "blue book system" after the color of the membership booklet. Militants rebelled and began organizing, demanding better working conditions, hiring hall reform, and an industrywide waterfront federation. The strike began May 9 in San Francisco and soon spread to Oakland; Portland, Oregon; Seattle; and other ports. Teamsters and other unions joined the fray. The boiling point came July 5, when two strikers were shot dead by private shipping company guards, an event known thereafter as "Bloody Thursday." The eventual settlement was ratified in every port except Everett, Washington. The industrywide federation wanted by the dockers, who were accused of trying to "sovietize" the waterfront, later became the International Longshoremen's and Warehousemen's Union (ILWU), with Bridges as president. It later changed its name, in recognition of women members, to the International Longshore and Warehouse Union.

Western Federation of Miners (WFM)—A metal-miners federation founded in the Rocky Mountain states in 1893, the WFM was, after the socialists, a major rival of the fledgling American Federation of Labor (**AFL**) for the allegiance of workingmen. Its founding tenets: organize all miners, mill men, smelter men and engineers in the industry; secure for miners "an earning compatible with the dangers of the employment"; payment in lawful money instead of company **scrip**; laws establishing safety regulations in the mines; and prohibition of company guards. On the political scene, the WFM also fought for an **eight-hour day**. The WFM's first president was "**Big Bill" Haywood**, and it's no coincidence that it formed the nucleus of initial **Industrial Workers of the World (IWW)** membership, though it later broke away. The WFM was involved in a number of bitter and often bloody **strikes** in the 1890s and early 1900s—at Cripple Creek, Leadville, and Coeur d'Alene, to name a few—but it won more conflicts than it lost, and by 1902 was able to boast a membership of 250,000. Aside from winning victories in mining regulations, pay, and conditions that hard-rock miners today take for granted, the WFM was unique in its day, along with Western chapters of the United Mine Workers of America, for freely admitting Mexican Americans into its ranks. In 1917, the WFM became the International Union of Mine, Mill & Smelter Workers, which in turn was absorbed into the United Steelworkers of America in 1967.

whipsaw bargaining/strike—A strategy of bargaining with or striking against a succession of individual employers, using each gain as leverage to win further gains and to set a pattern for other employers. See **pattern bargaining**.

white-collar workers—A term popularized, beginning in the 1920s, to mean anyone who performs nonmanual labor. It especially indicates salaried office workers, professionals, clerks, and lesser, middle-level management personnel who haven't been unionized (i.e., someone—almost invariably a man until fairly recently—who wore a white shirt, as opposed to the more **working-class** blue shirt). Interestingly, a white-collar worker in Britain is called a *black coat*. In 1956, for the first time in U.S. history, white-collar workers outnumbered **blue-collar workers**, and the gap has widened ever since. See **pink-collar workers**, **hard hat**.

wildcat strike—Sometimes called a quickie or outlaw strike (since 1920); a **work stoppage**, usually of short duration, without

union authorization. Especially numerous in the **CIO**'s early organizing days during the 1930s and Eastern coal mines up until the 1970s, the wildcat strike is largely obsolete today because of its unacceptable job-suicide rate. See **Boys Markets Case.**

Wobblies—See **Industrial Workers of the World (IWW).**

women in the labor movement—See **working women's movement.**

Woonsocket mill villages—See **great textile strike (1934).**

work by the book/work-to-rule—A type of **job action** in which employees deliberately perform only the minimum tasks required by official rules, policies, or job descriptions, with no "extra effort." Often, the reaction to a company's **posted rules.** See **slowdown, work rules.**

workers' compensation—State-mandated industrial insurance programs requiring payment to workers injured on the job or suffering occupational diseases. It is financed in some states by premiums paid by both employers and employees. In exchange for no-fault coverage, employees are not allowed to sue their employers for such injuries or illnesses. Though all 50 states have some form of workers' compensation programs, the amount and duration of payment varies considerably.

workie—A term going back to the 1830s but now obsolete, referring to a member of any political party with a strong labor following or an overt connection with **labor unions.**

working class—A term that came into use in the early 1800s and which today describes those who work for **wages** or with their hands, as opposed to salaried professionals or managerial personnel. As used in the United States over the past 75 years or so, the term has carried a decidedly **blue-collar, labor-union**, industrial, lower-middle-class, almost proletarian connotation, as in "working-class neighborhood" or "working-class bar." It's one of the oddities of the purportedly egalitarian American social system that many if not most **white-collar workers**, though often earning far less than their blue-collar colleagues, resist being lumped in with them in the "working class" category.

Working Trade Union League (WTUL)—Organization formed in

New York City in 1903 by feminist reformers and settlement-house workers to promote the unionization of working women, particularly among garment workers in New York and Chicago. The WTUL's **working-class** constituency proved a catalyst for the older, upper-class National American Women's Suffrage Association, also headquartered in New York, so that by 1915 Jewish and Italian men in the city's garment shops were openly advocating women's right to vote in statewide referendums. The league retained an influential voice through the World War II years but began to fade in the mid-1970s as its functions and aims were assumed by the new, more activist **Coalition of Labor Union Women (CLUW)**. See **working women's movement**.

working women's movement—From the time of their relatively late entry into men's working world with the introduction of the **factory system** in the 1820s, through "Rosie the Riveter" of the 1940s, down to our own times, women have always been a mainstay of the U.S. **labor movement**—and often at its forefront. The earliest recorded instance of women taking collective action to better their working conditions is in 1821 in Waltham, Massachusetts, when several dozen female employees of the Boston Manufacturing Corp. walked off the job for two days in protest of an arbitrary pay cut. They didn't win, nor did they in most **job actions** of the kind in that period: 1824, women weavers in Pawtucket, Rhode Island; 1831, "tailoresses" in New York City; 1834 and 1836, women textile workers in Lowell, Massachusetts. And often, they got little help from men, who either saw women in the workforce as a temporary phenomenon or thought them part of an employer strategy to lower wages—which it sometimes was. In 1859, up to 600 women staged a **walkout**, again in Lowell, but this time with a difference. This time, most of them were Irish, and it signaled a new voice in immigrants' working rights.

However unfruitful these early protests might have been, they served to knot working women into a common-cause **solidarity**. Organizations such as the **Factory Girls Association**, the **Female Labor Reform Association**, and the New York Tailoresses' Society sprang up in the 1830s and 1840s to give women not only a say in their working conditions but also an effective lever to pry out of the body politic reform legislation that might someday abolish slavery and **child labor** and bestow equal rights. The immediate target, however, was the **pay envelope**. A banner held in the vanguard of 800 marching women shoe factory workers on **strike** in Lynn, Massachusetts, in 1860 said it all: "American ladies will not be slaves: Give us fair compensation and we will labor cheerfully!" But it was not *just* wages, either, as another banner, this time held by pregnant women and mothers with infants in the **Lawrence Textile Strike** of 1912, proclaimed with poetic intensity: "Give us bread and roses, too."

The bread, if not the roses, came more plentifully to women in wartime, when they replaced large numbers of men who were off fighting. When the men returned, of course they wanted their jobs back—and usually got them. It was no different after the Civil War than it was after World War II, and in the late 1860s women sought, if not help against this form of discrimination, at least recognition from the newly formed **National Labor Union (NLU)**. They achieved this at least at the national leadership level when in 1867 it pledged support to all working women—the first labor federation in the United States to do so—and adopted a progressive women workers platform. In its 1868 congress, the NLU even came out for **equal pay for equal work**, an action unprecedented in world labor circles. Such progressive attitudes didn't translate well, however, at **local** levels, where **craft unions** continued to bar women. By 1870, only two national labor organizations—the Cigar Makers International Union and the Typographical Union (printers)—allowed women into their ranks. The doors opened considerably more in the next two decades with the advent of the NLU's successor federation, the **Knights of Labor**, which, forced to take a stand on the issue in 1881, declared that "women should be admitted on equality with men." And they were. By the mid-1880s, women constituted one in ten Knights—a far higher ratio than in any other male-dominated labor organization in the United States.

But the doors started closing again at the end of the decade when the craft-union-oriented American Federation of Labor (**AFL**) had succeeded the Knights as the national workingmen's representative. AFL chief **Samuel Gompers**, in fact, derided equal pay for equal work since, he argued, many women had been hired precisely because they could be paid lower wages than men—and why hire women at all if they had to be paid the same as men? He was not entirely wrong.

If they were barred from craft-union membership, women could, however, **affiliate**—as separate unions—with the AFL, and many did. In 1888, the newly founded Chicago-based Ladies Federal Labor Union received a **charter** from the federation and by 1892 its energetic leader, Elizabeth Chambers Morgan, had brought 24 women's labor groups, ranging from bookbinders to watchmakers, under its umbrella. That same year Gompers, under pressure, appointed Mary E. Kenney as the AFL's first woman general **organizer**—an appointment rescinded the following year, under pressure this time from an Executive Council which didn't think it "worked out." There were internal pressures, too, from working women's frustration and desperation. The most visible venting came in November 1909 with the **"Uprising of the 20,000,"** when that many women, mostly Jewish and Italian immigrants, took to the streets of New York in strike against the conditions they were forced to labor under in the garment industry. Such unsafe conditions became all too publicly apparent a year and a half later in that city with the **Triangle Shirtwaist fire**, which killed 146 workers, most of them women.

The radical, **industrial-union**-oriented **Industrial Workers of the World (IWW)**, on the other hand, saw women as a major force in the labor movement and their eligibility for membership equal to men's. When the Wobblies were accused by the AFL during the Lawrence strike of deliberately risking women's lives by placing them on the front lines, IWW strike spokeswoman **Elizabeth Gurley Flynn** pointedly replied, "The truth is, the IWW does not keep women in the back, and they go to the front." It was no secret that women, many if not most of them immigrants, carried the day in that landmark strike. Women were not to see such universal labor acceptance again until the rise of another industrial-union vehicle, the Congress of Industrial Organizations (**CIO**), in the mid-1930s. By 1940, female membership in CIO unions had tripled to 800,000, though by that time the AFL—through its newer affiliates, not its conservative, old-line crafts and building trades locals—had made remarkable progress. By 1943, at the height of World War II, out of a women's workforce of 18.6 million, 3.5 million were organized—1.5 million in the CIO, 1.3 million in the AFL, the rest in **independent unions**. By 1945, women constituted 38 percent of the labor force, up from 25 percent before the war. That dropped precipitously in the immediate postwar period as the men in uniform returned and reclaimed their old jobs. Equally discouraging during those years, and after, was that, despite its reputation as a female-friendly federation, the CIO had few if any women in its leadership; it was as white male–dominated as the AFL, an imbalance that changed little when the two merged in 1955.

The vicissitudes of the working women's movement since then have been many. New federal laws such as the 1963 **Equal Pay Act** have brought, at least on paper, a modicum of fairness to the workplace, as have federal agencies like the **Equal Employment Opportunity Commission (EEOC)**. And a woman, Linda Chavez-Thompson, was elected at the right hand of AFL-CIO chief **John Sweeney**. Yet the discrepancies remain. Equal to men in the voting booth, women, in mid-1998, were only 76 percent as equal to men in the paycheck. Independent women's groups such as the **Coalition of Labor Union Women (CLUW)** have hammered away at those discrepancies with some result, though the **takeback** 1990s have not boded well. Perhaps the message expressed in CLUW's founding convention in 1974 remains as premonitory and full of meaning today as it did then: "We did not come here to swap recipes." See **immigrants in the labor movement, child labor laws**.

Workmen's Benevolent Association (WBA)—Coal miners' **trade union**, an early predecessor of the United Mine Workers, founded in 1868 by Irish-born miner John Siney, who the year before had led a successful **strike** of 400 Pennsylvania miners in protest of a **wage** cut. By 1869, the WBA had more than 30,000 members, thanks largely to its system of **organizing** mine workers literally from top to bottom instead of along **craft** lines, thereby heralding the latter-day **industrial union**. The WBA also successfully lobbied the Pennsylvania legislature for a mining-inspection law that greatly increased coal-mine safety, which to that point had been virtually nil. In 1873, Siney went on to found the Miners' National Association and was its first president. See **Molly Maguires**.

Workplace Fairness Bill—A congressional bill, inspired largely by the failed **Phelps-Dodge copper strike** of 1983, that would prohibit the **permanent replacement** of strikers. Since its introduction in the early 1990s, it has twice passed the U.S. House only to fail in the Senate. Opponents, spearheaded by the **Business Roundtable**, argue that passage would "change the level of the playing field." Proponents say that the field is so uneven now that **union** workers are tumbling down the slopes.

work rules—Rules governing on-the-job conditions, usually spelled out in the **contract** but sometimes extra-contractual. Examples are limiting supervisors' roles in production or what is commonly regarded as **union** work; limiting the assignment of work outside an employee's classification; requiring a minimum number of workers on a job; and limiting or stipulating the introduction of new equipment, **automation**, or mechanization. The counterpart to this is **management rights**, whereby the employer imposes rules to eliminate perceived waste and **featherbedding**. See **Mechanization and Modernization Agreement**.

work stoppage—An action, usually **union**-inspired, ranging from a formal, fully sanctioned **strike** to an impromptu **walkout** or unsanctioned **wildcat strike**, that interrupts, curtails, or halts normal operations in the workplace. See **job action**.

World Trade Organization (WTO)—An entity established in January 1995 by the Uruguay round of multilateral trade negotiations in what would be the successor to the World War II–era

General Agreement on Trade and Tariffs (GATT). It aroused worldwide public attention for five days in late 1999 during a ministerial meeting in Seattle when tens of thousands of environmentalists, members of **organized labor**, animal-rights and community groups, and activists from all over the planet joined to protest the WTO's harmful effects on natural resources and labor rights and incurred a violent reaction from law enforcement. Environmental activists, costumed in green-and-yellow body-length cardboard carapaces, marched as **"sea turtles"** alongside Teamsters, carpenters, longshore workers, and others to highlight an April 1998 ruling by a panel of corporate attorneys of the WTO against the United States and other nations that had required oceangoing shrimp trawlers to provide turtle-excluder devices (TEDS), which prevent sea turtles from drowning in shrimp nets. In fact, no shrimp could be imported into the United States or the European Union from nations failing to use TEDs. The WTO, heeding challenges from India, Malaysia, Pakistan, and Thailand, had held that this was an infringement on free trade. (The organization reversed that ruling in October 2001, its appellate body finding that the U.S. sea turtle protection law complied with recommendations and now was consistent with WTO rules.)

Y

Yablonski, Joseph A. "Jock" (1910–1970)—United Mine Workers  reform candidate who, in his bid to unseat the corrupt Anthony "Tough Tony" Boyle as president of the UMW, was murdered in January 1970 along with his wife and daughter in their Clarkesville, Pennsylvania, home on Boyle's orders. Paradoxically, Yablonski dead may have had a greater impact on the union than Yablonski alive: Boyle was eventually tried and convicted for the killings, paving the way for a cleanup of the UMW and the seating of another reformer, Arnold Miller, as president.

yankee face—West Coast longshore jargon for the last tier of cargo stowed perfectly in a ship's hold to hide the other tiers that are handled sloppily and loaded in slam-bang fashion. On the Los Angeles–San Pedro docks, such a tier is called a Frisco Face.

yellow-dog contract—An illegal agreement forced on newly hired workers in which they state they are not members of a **labor union**, and promise not to join a union for as long as they're with the company. The **Norris–La Guardia Act** of 1932 nullified the yellow-dog contract by declaring it unenforceable in court. The turn-of-the-century term "yellow dog" meant an inferior or worthless person or thing. See **no-strike clause**.

Z

zipper clause—A standard clause in a union **contract** that precludes any discussion of employment conditions during the life of the **agreement**, usually by stating that the contract is the sole and complete instrument between the parties.

Appendix I
Affiliate Unions of the AFL-CIO and Independent Unions

All information as of December 2009

UNIONS OF THE AFL-CIO

Air Line Pilots Association (ALPA):
Founded 1931. www.alpa.org

Amalgamated Transit Union (ATU):
Founded 1892. www.atu.org

American Federation of Government
Employees (AFGE): Founded 1932.
www.afge.org

American Federation of Musicians of the
United States and Canada (AFM):
Founded 1896. www.afm.org

American Federation of School Administrators (AFSA): Founded 1976.
web.admin.org

American Federation of State, County
and Municipal Employees (AFSCME):
Founded 1936. www.afscmc.org

American Federation of Teachers (AFT):
Founded 1916. www.aft.org

American Federation of Television and
Radio Artists (AFTRA): Founded 1937.
www.aftra.org

American Postal Workers Union (APWU):
Founded 1971. www.apwu.org

American Radio Association (ARA):
Founded 1948.
www.americanradioassoc.org/joomla/

American Train Dispatchers Association
(ATDA): Founded 1917.
atdd.homestead.com/atddpg1.html

Associated Actors and Artistes of Ameri-
ca (4As):
- Actors' Equity Association (AEA):
  Founded 1913.
  www.actorsequity.org
- American Guild of Musical Artists

(AGMA): Founded 1936.
www.musicalartists.org
- American Guild of Variety Artists
  (AGVA): Founded 1939.
  www.agvausa.com
- Screen Actors Guild (SAG): Found-
  ed 1933. www.sag.org
- The Guild of Italian American
  Actors (GIAA): Founded 1937.
  www.giaa.us

Bakery, Confectionery, Tobacco Workers
and Grain Millers International Union
(BCTGM): Founded 1999, following
merger. www.bctgm.org

Brotherhood of Railroad Signalmen
(BRS): Founded 1901. www.brs.org

California School Employees Association (CSEA): Founded 1927.
pub.csea.com/cseahome/

Communications Workers of America
(CWA): Founded 1938.
www.cwa-union.org
- Association of Flight Attendants
  (AFA-CWA): Founded 1945.
  www.afanet.org

Farm Labor Organizing Committee
(FLOC): Founded 1967. www.floc.com

Federation of Professional Athletes (Professional Athletes): Founded 1956.
www.nflplayers.com

Glass, Molders, Pottery, Plastics and
Allied Workers International Union
(GMP): Founded 1842.
www.gmpiu.org

International Alliance of Theatrical

Stage Employes, Moving Picture Technicians, Artists and Allied Crafts of the United States, Its Territories and Canada (IATSE): Founded 1893. www.iatse-intl.org

International Association of Bridge, Structural, Ornamental and Reinforcing Iron Workers (Iron Workers): Founded 1896. www.ironworkers.org

International Association of Fire Fighters (IAFF): Founded 1918. www.iaff.org

International Association of Heat and Frost Insulators and Allied Workers (AWIU): Founded 1903. www.insulators.org

International Association of Machinists and Aerospace Workers (IAM): Founded 1888. www.goiam.org

International Brotherhood of Boilermakers, Iron Ship Builders, Blacksmiths, Forgers and Helpers (IBB): Founded 1881. www.boilermakers.org

International Brotherhood of Electrical Workers (IBEW): Founded 1891. www.ibew.org

International Federation of Professional and Technical Engineers (IFPTE): Founded 1918. www.ifpte.org

International Longshore and Warehouse Union (ILWU): Founded 1934. www.ilwu.org

International Longshoremen's Association (ILA): Founded 1892. www.ilaunion.org

International Plate Printers, Die Stampers and Engravers Union of North America

International Union of Allied Novelty and Production Workers (Novelty and Production Workers)

International Union of Bricklayers and Allied Craftworkers (BAC): Founded

1865. www.bacweb.org

International Union of Elevator Constructors (IUEC): Founded 1901. www.iuec.org

International Union of Operating Engineers (IUOE): Founded 1896. www.iuoe.org

International Union of Painters and Allied Trades of the United States and Canada (IUPAT): Founded 1887. www.iupat.org

International Union of Police Associations (IUPA): Founded 1954. www.iupa.org

Marine Engineers' Beneficial Association (MEBA):
• Professional Aviation Safety Specialists (PASS): Founded 1977. www.passnational.org

National Air Traffic Controllers Association (NATCA): Founded 1987. www.natca.org

National Association of Letter Carriers (NALC): Founded 1889. www.nalc.org

National Nurses United (NNU): Founded 2009. www.nationalnursesunited.org
• California Nurses Association/National Nurses Organizing Committee (CNA/NNOC): Founded 1977. www.calnurses.org
• Massachusetts Nurses Association (MNA): Founded 1903. www.massnurses.org
• United American Nurses (UAN): Founded 1999.

National Postal Mail Handlers Union (NPMHU): www.npmhu.org

Office and Professional Employees International Union (OPEIU): Founded 1945. www.opeiu.org

Operative Plasterers' and Cement Masons' International Association of the United States and Canada

(OPCMIA): Founded 1864. www.opcmia.org

Seafarers International Union of North America (SIU): Founded 1938. www.seafarers.org

Sheet Metal Workers International Association (SMWIA): Founded 1888. www.smwia.org

Transport Workers Union of America (TWU): Founded 1934. www.twu.org

Transportation Communications International Union/IAM (TCU/IAM): Founded 1899. www.tcunion.org

Unite Here!: Founded 2004, following merger. www.unitehere.org

United Association of Journeymen and Apprentices of the Plumbing and Pipe Fitting Industry of the United States and Canada (UA): Founded 1889. www.ua.org

United Automobile, Aerospace & Agricultural Implement Workers of America International Union (UAW): Founded 1935. www.uaw.org

United Mine Workers of America (UMWA): Founded 1890. www.umwa.org

United Steel, Paper and Forestry, Rubber, Manufacturing, Energy, Allied Industrial & Service Workers International Union (USW): Founded 1936. www.usw.org

United Union of Roofers, Waterproofers and Allied Workers (Roofers and Waterproofers): Founded 1903. www.unionroofers.com

Utility Workers Union of America (UWUA): Founded 1925. www.uwua.net

Writers Guild of America, East Inc. (WGAE): Founded 1954. www.wgaeast.org

CHANGE TO WIN

International Brotherhood of Teamsters (IBT): Founded 1903. www.teamster.org

Laborers' International Union of North America (LIUNA): Founded 1903. www.liuna.org

Service Employees International Union (SEIU): Founded 1921. www.seiu.org

United Farm Workers of America (UFW): Founded 1966. www.ufw.org

United Food and Commercial Workers International Union (UFCW): Founded 1979, following merger. www.ufcw.org

INDEPENDENT UNIONS

American Association of University Professors–Collective Bargaining Congress (AAUP-CBC): Founded 2008, following restructuring. www.aaup.org/AAUP/about/cbc/

Aircraft Mechanics Fraternal Association (AMFA): Founded 1962. amfanational.org

Coalition of Graduate Employee Unions (CGEU): Founded 1992. cgeu.org

Directors Guild of America (DGA):
Founded 1960, following merger.
www.dga.org

Fraternal Order of Police (FOP): Founded
1915. www.fop.net

Independent Pilots Association (IPA):
Founded 1989. www.ipapilot.org

International Union of Journeymen and
Allied Trades (IUJHAT): Founded 1874.
www.iujat.org

International Union, Security, Police and
Fire Professionals of America (SPFPA):
Founded 1948. www.spfpa.org

Jockeys' Guild: Founded 1940.
www.jockeysguild.com

Major League Baseball Players Association (MLBPA): Founded 1953.
mlbplayers.mlb.com

National Basketball Players Association
(NBPA): Founded 1954.
www.nbpa.com

National Education Association (NEA):
Founded 1957. www.nea.org

National Emergency Medical Services
Association (NEMSA): Founded 2004.
www.nemsausa.org

National Hockey League Players' Association (NHLPA): Founded 1967.
www.nhlpa.com

National Rural Letter Carriers' Association (NRLCA): Founded 1903.
www.nrlca.org

National Treasury Employees Union
(NTEU): Founded 1939. www.nteu.org

National Weather Service Employees
Organization (NWSEO): Founded
1976. nwseo.org

Patrolmen's Benevolent Association
(PBA):
• New Jersey State Policemen's
Benevolent Association, Inc. (NJSP-
BA): njspba.com
• Patrolmen's Benevolent Association
of the City of New York, Inc. (PBA):
nycpba.org

Professional Lacrosse Players' Association (PLPA): Founded 1991.
www.plpa.com

Programmers Guild: Founded 1998.
www.programmersguild.org

Stage Directors and Choreographers
Society (SDC): Founded 1959.
www.sdcweb.org

United Brotherhood of Carpenters and
Joiners of America (UBC): Founded
1881. www.carpenters.org

United Electrical, Radio and Machine
Workers of America (UE): Founded
1936. www.ueunion.org

World Umpires Association (WUA):
Founded 2000.
develop.worldumpires.com

Writers Guild of America, West (WGAW):
Founded 1954. www.wga.org

Appendix II

FREE RIDER'S CARD

I am opposed to all unions. Therefore, I am opposed to all benefits that unions have won through the years: paid vacations, holidays, sick leave, seniority rights, wage increases, pension and insurance plans, safety laws, workmen's compensation laws, Social Security, time and a half for hours in excess of eight in one day or 40 in any one work week, unemployment benefits, and job security.

I refuse to accept any benefits that will be won by union negotiators with this union shop, and I hereby authorize and direct the company to withhold the amount of the union-won benefits from my paycheck each week and to donate it to charity.

_____

Signature   *Date*

—*Origin unknown, author anonymous;*
distributed at a CLUW meeting, Seattle, August 1997

Appendix III
A Select Labor Bibliography

The following works were consulted, extracted from or used to verify information, or simply provided a background understanding in the writing and editing of this *Lexicon*.

The Almanac of American Politics, compiled by **Michael Barone and Grant Ujifusa** (Published yearly by *National Journal*, Washington, D.C.). Useful for cross-checking voting records, congressional legislation and facts and figures on members of Congress.

Alone in a Crowd, ed. **Jean Reith Schroedel** (Temple University Press, 1985). Twenty-five women in nontraditional blue-collar work tell their own stories, ranging from steel hauling to shipscaling to long-distance trucking to organizing unions. Sometimes funny, often not so funny; always lively.

American Labor Struggles by **Samuel Yellen** (Pathfinder, 1995). From a radical viewpoint, the story of ten historic confrontations pitting union men and woman against the owners of mines, mills and railroads, from the rail strike of 1877 to the West Coast longshoremen's strike of 1934. Fact-packed but readable.

Blood in the Water by **John McCann** (District Lodge 751, Seattle, 1989). One-sided but useful history of the trials and tribulations—and occasional victories—of District Lodge 751 of the International Association of Machin-

ists and Aerospace Workers, one of the largest lodges in the union, composed mostly of Boeing workers in the Seattle area.

The Brothers Reuther by **Victor G. Reuther** (Houghton Mifflin, 1976). War tales engagingly told by the surviving, proudly unrepentant, social-activist brother of one of America's foremost and influential labor leaders. Reuther's recounting of the years in Gorky, USSR, and on the front lines of the CIO's all-out strife in the 1930s are especially valuable to anyone who would glean an understanding of labor politics in the United States from post–World War I days to the 1970s.

Building Bridges, ed. **Jeremy Brecher and Tim Costello** (Monthly Review Press, 1990). Useful and thought-provoking essays by progressives on the successes, shortcomings and strategies of grassroots coalitions between local communities and the labor movement in the 1970s and 1980s. Lack of an index, however, severely hampers cross-checking.

César Chávez: A Triumph of Spirit by **Richard Griswold del Castillo and Richard A. Garcia** (University of Oklahoma Press, 1995). Informative, solid, well-researched book on the lifework of Chávez, the United Farm Workers movement and the chief personalities surrounding both, but not as readable and gripping as Matthiessen's earlier *Sal Si Puedes* (see p. 229).

Copper Crucible: How the Arizona Miners Strike of 1983 Recast Labor-Management Relations in America by Jonathan D. Rosenblum (ILR Press, Cornell University, 1995). An excellent backgrounder on the labor and Chicano movements in the Southwest as well as on the anatomy of a major industry and the take-no-prisoners mind-set of its management.

The Developing Labor Law: The Board, the Courts and the National Labor Relations Act by Charles J. Morris (Bureau of National Affairs, 1971; subsequent editions). Dry, often legalistic reading but extremely helpful to anyone interested in learning the byzantine intricacies of labor law and its practical application in arbitration hearings and in the judicial system.

Dictionary of American Biography, ed. John S. Bowman (Cambridge University Press, 1995). Contains good capsule biographies of leading labor leaders, even some of the more obscure ones.

Dictionary of American Slang, 2nd supplemented ed., compiled by Harold Wentworth and Stuart Berg Flexner (Thomas Y. Crowell Co., 1975). Useful in tracking down the etymology of labor terms and jargon.

The Dictionary of Cultural Literacy, 2nd ed., by E.D. Hirsch Jr., Joseph F. Kett and James Trefil (Houghton Mifflin, 1993). Overall, an extremely useful reference work; specifically, its section on business and economics offers concise, succinct definitions of labor terms and usage.

The Eastern Airlines Strike by Ernie Mailhot, Judy Stranahan, and Jack Barnes (Pathfinder Press, 1991). An account of the 1989 strike that eventually drove strikebusting wheeler-dealer Frank Lorenzo, as well as Eastern itself, out of the airline business, told by the people who waged it. Unabashedly partisan and banner-waving Machinists union in its presentation, this small, 91-page book nonetheless contains facts and background that were never available in the national media.

Encyclopedia of Word and Phrase Origins by Robert Hendrickson (Facts on File, 1988). Good for hunting down the origins of such oddities as "lobster shift" and others you think you know but don't, such as "Pullman car."

The Fall of the House of Labor: 1865-1925 by David Montgomery (Cambridge University Press, 1987). Well-written, exhaustive compendium of labor feats and failures, unfortunately leaving off before the reascent of the house of labor in the 1930s. Indispensable for the amateur, not to mention the professional labor historian.

George Meany and His Times by Archie Robinson (Simon & Schuster, 1981). An admiring though not uncritical portrait of a Bronx journeyman plumber's rise to the most powerful figure on the 1950s–60s U.S. labor scene. Those who take Meany to task for his perceived cultural and pro-

THE LEXICON OF LABOR

THE LEXICON OF LABOR

gressive shortcomings and his focus on "bread-and-butter unionism" would do well to read labor reporter Robinson's biography for a better understanding of the man.

The Guns of Lattimer by **Michael Novak** (Basic Books, 1978). Well-written, deep-felt narrative of one of the lesser-known tragedies in labor history, the 1897 massacre of peaceful immigrant marchers in a small Pennsylvania town. Made all the more compelling from being told by a conservative voice, a position not ordinarily given to labor sympathies.

Hard-Pressed in the Heartland by **Peter Rachleff** (South End Press, 1993). The 1985–86 Hormel Strike as suspensefully told by a partisan of United Food and Commercial Workers Local P-9's fight not only against the giant meat packer but also the union's International and much of the AFL-CIO.

A History of American Labor by **Joseph G. Rayback** (The Free Press, 1966). An authoritative, dense, comprehensive, fact-filled, at times engrossing account of the U.S. labor movement and all its diverse personalities through 1964 that unfortunately suffers from a skimpy and incomplete index.

Hoffa by **Arthur A. Sloane** (MIT Press, 1992). Balanced view of one of the more controversial figures of the U.S. labor movement. Sloane makes no effort to hide the seamier, Mob-ridden aspects of Hoffa's life but at the same time is quick to credit his achievements.

How Arbitration Works, **3rd ed.**, by **Frank Elkouri and Edna Asper Elkouri**

(Bureau of National Affairs, 1976; subsequent editions). Case-by-case presentation and analysis of rulings that have altered or strengthened union causes in the workplace. Dry reading, but vital for an understanding of how labor law works—and doesn't work.

An Injury to All: The Decline of American Unionism by **Kim Moody** (Verso, 1989). A well-informed if pessimistic view of the labor movement from Truman to Reagan, particularly in the 1980s, from the viewpoint of an activist who deplores the "business unionism" of the AFL-CIO under George Meany and Lane Kirkland.

In Search of the Working Class by **Leon Fink** (University of Illinois Press, 1994). Scholarly approach in the form of essays on American labor history and political culture. Dry reading and dense going at times, but worthwhile for its many insights.

The I.W.W.: Its First Seventy Years by **Fred W. Thompson and Patrick Murfin** (Industrial Workers of the World Press, 1976). An openly white-hat-black-hat partisan, impassioned, but nonetheless absorbing chronicle of America's oldest surviving radical union from its founding in 1905 to 1975.

Labor's Giant Step by **Art Preis** (Pathfinder Press, 1964). Fact-crammed, well-documented account of the first 20 years of the Congress of Industrial Organizations (CIO), from 1936 to 1955, and how the militant federation transformed the U.S. labor movement—and, in a way, U.S. society.

Labor's Untold Story by **Richard O. Boyer**

and Herbert M. Morais (United Electrical, Radio & Machine Workers of America, 1955). In the authors' words, "not a history of labor at all but a history of the American people from labor's view." In the authors' view, the machinations of financier-mogul J.P. Morgan, merging banking and industrial capital as he threw together ever-larger combinations of corporate power controlled by fewer and fewer men, "may have governed the course of American labor more than the plans of Samuel Gompers."

Labor's War at Home: The CIO in World War II by Nelson Lichtenstein (Cambridge University Press, 1982). Comprehensive and critical examination of a critical period in U.S. history, beginning with the outbreak of war in Europe in 1939 through the wave of major industrial strikes that followed the war and accompanied the reconversion to a peacetime/Cold War economy.

Labor Will Rule by Steven Fraser (The Free Press, 1991). A timely and lively supplement to Montgomery's *Fall of the House of Labor* in which the ascendancy of Sidney Hillman, a cutter in the "rag trade," to the inner sanctum of the U.S. government parallels the coming of age of the labor movement and an albeit short-lived industrial democracy.

Law Dictionary, 3rd ed., ed. Steven H. Gifis (Barron's, 1991). Among general legalisms, want an exact, concise and definitive summary of labor-law terms and their origin? This is it.

Listening to America by Stuart Berg Flexner (Simon & Schuster, 1982). Subtitled, justly, *An Illustrated History of Words and Phrases from Our Lively and Splendid Past.* Flexner's first volume on the subject, *I Hear America Talking,* was woefully deficient in labor language; he made up for it in *Listening,* which has a whole fascinating section on labor and union terms and their sometimes medieval origins.

The Most Dangerous Man in Detroit by Nelson Lichtenstein (Basic Books, 1995). The author of *Labor's War at Home* (see left) tells in minute detail the enthralling story of Walter Reuther, super-influential labor organizer–statesman–politician and, in passing, four of the most tumultuous decades of American labor. Exhaustive; perhaps the definitive biography of the legendary United Auto Workers chief.

Mother Jones Speaks, ed. Philip S. Foner (Pathfinder Press, 1983). Speeches, letters, interviews, and congressional testimony from the legendary Mary Harris in her 60-year fight against the "mine bosses" and anyone else who she thought repressed the American worker. Feisty, up-front, and personal—and entertaining throughout.

No Retreat, No Surrender: Labor's War at Hormel by Dave Hage and Paul Klauda (William Morrow, 1989). A more thorough and balanced treatment of the epic 1985–86 strike in Minnesota than *Hard-Pressed in the Heartland* (see above), which tends to see the struggle as symbolic of the decline of the U.S. labor movement. It is so balanced, in fact, that the reader is left wondering, how do you tell the good guys from the bad?

A Pictorial History of American Labor by

William Cahn (Crown, 1972). Superb compilation of engravings, photos, and text covering from the earliest Colonial struggles through the 1960s. Probably the best work of its kind and highly recommended to anyone approaching labor history for the first time—or the 99th time, for that matter.

The Reader's Companion to American History, ed. Eric Foner and John A. Garraty (Houghton Mifflin, 1991). Pleasingly comprehensive in its entries on specific labor issues and personalities; even more so in its summaries of abstractions such as the Industrial Revolution and the labor movement.

Red Scare: Memories of the American Inquisition by Griffin Fariello (Avon Books, 1995). Indispensable oral history of a vital but fast-fading and shameful era of Americana in which to be a militant unionist was tantamount to practicing 17th-century witchcraft. Of particular interest: the stories of Bill Bailey, Jack O'Dell, Clinton Jencks, Joe Sachs, Claire Hartford, Dave Jenkins, and Herbert Aptheker.

Rise Up Singing, ed. Peter Blood-Patterson (Sing Out, 1988). A comprehensive songbook for all those on picket lines, marches, and rallies who remember the tunes but not the words of their favorite labor songs.

Sal Si Puedes by Peter Matthiessen (Dell, 1969). Literally, "get out if you can," and subtitled *Cesar Chavez and the New American Revolution,* this is still the best book ever written on Chávez and the early days of *La Causa,* indelibly re-creating the atmosphere of 1960s agricultural California and the passions and dreams of those on both sides of the unionized farmworker movement.

Strike! by Jeremy Brecher (South End Press, 1983; rev. ed., 1997). A detailed, well-researched, and compelling history of major strikes, including general strikes, in the United States from 1877 through the early 1970s.

Talking Union by Judith Stepan-Norris and Maurice Zeitlin (University of Illinois Press, 1996). Excellent oral history of 1930s–40s leaders and rank-and-file organizers—radicals, militants and even Communists, many of them of Local 600, the largest in the United Auto Workers union, in their decades-long struggle to "tame" the Ford Motor Co.

The Thesaurus of Slang by Esther Lewin and Albert E. Lewin (Facts on File, 1988). Useful supplement to similar compendiums by Flexner and Hendrickson in ferreting out the origins of labor terms.

Through Jaundiced Eyes: How the Media View Organized Labor by William J. Puette (Cornell University Press, 1992). Valuable primer on the built-in bias of most of the U.S. print and electronic media vis-à-vis labor leaders and labor issues which, the author contends, tends to come from a reliance on employers' perceptions and employer sources rather than from any conscious conspiracy.

The Transformation of American Industrial Relations by Thomas A. Kochan, Harry C. Katz, and Robert B. McKersie (ILR Press, Cornell University, 1994). Dry, chart-ridden, and somewhat pedantic overview of industrial relations, labor history, labor economics and "human resources management," it can nonetheless be profitably culled for useful workplace facts and trends.

Transforming Women's Work **by Thomas Dublin** (ILR Press, Cornell University, 1994). Again (see entry above), the dry and heavily footnoted scholarly approach to a labor issue; this time, more interestingly, women's factory lives in New England from the 1830s to 1900, the cutting edge and culmination of the Industrial Revolution in America. If you want to know exactly what such women earned and how they spent it, this is the book.

The Union Makes Us Strong **by David Wellman** (Cambridge University Press, 1995). True stories and history of radical unionism on the San Francisco waterfront as told by someone who spent three years on the docks for research. Wellman traces in fascinating detail a major longshoreman's local that did not follow the traditional AFL-CIO trajectory of craft to "business union" but chose rather to systematically challenge management's rule on the shop floor—and prevail. Along the way, the reader gets acquainted with some unusual terms: "Yankee face," "back-to-the-bench rule" and "good beef," to name but a few.

The War on Labor and the American Left **by Patricia Cayo Sexton** (Westview Press, 1991). Intriguing look into why the United States has been more conservative in its domestic policies than other Western democracies and why it is almost alone among them in

lacking a mass labor or democratic socialist party to further labor's causes.

We Shall Not Be Moved **by Joan Dash** (Scholastic, 1996). True-to-life descriptions of immigrant life on New York's Lower East Side as a background to the women's factory strike of 1909.

Where the Sun Never Shines **by Priscilla Long** (Paragon House, 1989). Subtitled *A History of America's Bloody Coal Industry*, an often graphic and grisly account of historically one of the most violence-plagued industries in the country. A readable, well-informed look into the whole subculture of miners and their families as well as that of an industry that has begrudged their every step of progress.

Which Side Are You On? **by Thomas Geoghegan** (Farrar, Straus and Giroux, 1991; rev. ed., The New Press, 2004). The subtitle of this engaging, often witty, often bittersweet work by a labor lawyer who has witnessed more defeats than victories is *Trying to Be for Labor When It's Flat on its Back*. The answer to the question asked in the main title: the side of working people, and not that of the unions that have used and abused them.

Who Built America? Working People & the Nation's Economy, Politics, Culture & Society **by the American Social History Project of the City University of New York under the direction of Herbert G. Gutman** (Pantheon Books, 1989, 1992). Without doubt the most thorough, coherent, comprehensive, best-presented work on the subject so far; its two sizable, picture-laden volumes covering every phase of working America from the earliest Colonial times through 1991 should be on the required-reading list of every high school and college in the country. *WBA*'s extensive index and bibliography alone put most other books of this kind to shame.

Women and the American Labor Movement by **Philip S. Foner** (The Free Press, 1982). Necessary supplement to a labor literature that largely neglects or underplays women's role, covering from the first Colonial trade unions to the struggle for a voice in the 20th century. Particularly informative in the sections dealing with the factory women of the early 1800s, the garment workers of the early 1900s, and women's entry to the CIO unions of the 1930s and 1940s.

BROCHURES, PAMPHLETS, PERIODICALS, AND WEB SITES

American Rights at Work—Web site of the nonprofit educational, outreach, and advocacy organization dedicated to promoting the freedom of workers to form unions and bargain collectively. www.americanrightsatwork.org

Extra!—Monthly publication of Fairness & Accuracy in Reporting (FAIR) dedicated to exposing the inaccuracies, bias, and omissions of the mainstream media, it has consistently given a fair shake to labor and occasionally devotes an entire issue or major part thereof to labor coverage—or, better, the news that wasn't fit to print in the regular press. www.fair.org

"Industrial and Labor Relations Terms" by Robert E. Doherty—booklet published by New York State School of Industrial and Labor Relations at Cornell University, 1966. An outdated but still useful compendium.

Labor Notes—Monthly progressive-labor newsmagazine and Web site published by the Labor Information and Research Project, Detroit. Good on coverage of labor reform movements; hard-hitting in uncovering various aspects of "business unionism."

National Catholic Reporter—Informative, well-written independent Catholic newsweekly that isn't afraid to tackle bishops and cardinals, if it comes to that, on labor issues and the treatment of workers. ncronline.org

Northwest Labor Press—Lively and newsy semimonthly put out by the Oregon Labor Press Publishing Co. of Portland, Oregon. Does a good job of covering national as well as regional and local labor issues.

PNW Newspaper Guild Blog—Web site of the Pacific Northwest Newspaper Guild Local 82.

About the Author

Robert Emmett Murray (1939–2008), named after the doomed Irish patriot Robert Emmet of the early nineteenth century, was born in Brooklyn, New York, in 1939 and brought up in New York City, Claremont, New Hampshire, and Montclair, New Jersey. He attended Seton Hall University in South Orange, New Jersey, and the National Autonomous University of Mexico in Mexico City. His introduction to unions came in 1957–1961, when he worked off and on as an oiler in the International Union of Operating Engineers in Connecticut, Alaska, and Seattle, Washington.

After living and working for seven years in Mexico, where he was (among other things) a newspaper city editor, a language teacher, and a translator for the Mexican Olympics Organizing Committee, Murray migrated north and was a reporter and editor with the *Newark News*, *Fire Island News*, and the *Newark Star-Ledger*, before coming to Seattle in 1970. He started with the *Seattle Times* in 1971 as a copy editor, and went on to be a travel writer, assistant city editor, feature writer, book reviewer, Central American correspondent, and editor of one of the *Times*'s suburban editions.

A Newspaper Guild activist since almost the day he walked through the *Times*'s door, Murray was president of the Pacific Northwest Newspaper Guild, Local 82, from 1988 through 1994. Until his death, he lived with his wife, Nancy Rising, a labor and Democratic activist in her own right in suburban Kirkland, Washington.